WORLD GREAT BUSINESSMEN

World Great Businessmen

Anupam Shah

ANMOL PUBLICATIONS PVT. LTD.
NEW DELHI - 110 002 (INDIA)

ANMOL PUBLICATIONS PVT. LTD.

H.O.: 4374/4B, Ansari Road, Darya Ganj,
New Delhi-110 002 (India)
Ph.: 23278000, 23261597

B.O.: No. 1015, Ist Main Road, BSK IIIrd Stage
IIIrd Phase, IIIrd Block,
Bangalore - 560 085 (India)
Visit us at: www.anmolpublications.com

World Great Businessmen

First Published, 2007

ISBN 81-261-3057-1

PRINTED IN INDIA

Printed at Mehra Offset Press, Delhi.

Contents

Preface

World Great Businessmen provides a summary of the lives and legacies of men and women from the areas of business who have "changed the world." The personalities profiled in this volume are different in many ways. They are economically, ethnically, racially, physically, and generationally diverse; they cross cultural and social classes; and they represent different organizational entities in all regions of this country and some that reach out into other lands. These personalities also are similar in many ways. They faced obstacles. They were people of courage, stamina, and tenacity; they were talented jugglers of the demands from multiple social roles; and they achieved against the odds. This work is a celebration of these personalities.

These individuals have developed, extended, or exemplified ideas fundamental to the way human beings perceive the meaning and purpose of their own lives and of their societies. Some have challenged prevailing convictions and worked for immediate change during their lifetimes; others have proposed new modes of thinking that have flourished only after their passing.

It was not easy to decide whom to include in our volume. We have tried to span the breadth of civilizations to identify men and women from various cultures and perspectives who influenced the shape of our present world. We have left out some individuals, but we hope the reader will forgive such omissions. We have tried to be as accurate as possible, but some mistakes are sure to come in.

In preparation of this book, the author has freely consulted large number of books and journals so no authenticity is claimed. Author is especially thankful to Anmol Publications Pvt. Ltd., New Delhi for shaping this book in its final form. Suggestions for further improvement of this book are not only welcome but also greatly appreciated.

Author

Alvar Aalto

As we approach the end of the twentieth century, it is easy to forget that modern architecture was born in the aftermath of the First World War. Grounded in reason, it was intended to transcend national divisions by capturing the spirit of the 'Machine Age'. A related, but different, impulse was apparent in the Nordic countries in the early 1920s, where architects also turned to supposedly timeless values: clarity of form, elegant proportions, minimal ornament. On the Continent the urge was towards innovation, to exploit new building materials and match the industrial achievements of the day - cars, aeroplanes, ocean liners. In Scandinavia it was to reconnect with the mainstream of Western culture - to 'bring grapes to the rowan peoples' as a favourite saying of the time had it - and the style, inevitably, was Classical.

Great artists have a happy knack of timing their arrival, and Alvar Aalto was able to assimilate both the Continental and Nordic influences. Born in 1898, he was young enough to miss the aftermath of the ponderous National Romanticism which gripped Finland at the turn of the century, and just old enough to master the short-lived but liberating episode of Nordic Classicism before confronting the new ideas emanating from Berlin, Weimar and Paris. They reached Finland via Sweden in 1927, entering through the former capital of Turku where, as if in anticipation, Aalto had moved to build a large competition-winning project.

Aalto quickly proved himself a master of the burgeoning International Style: the offices for the Turku newspaper, the Turun Sanomat, provided instant proof, and on its completion in 1933 the Paimio Sanatorium was acclaimed internationally as a major achievement: Sigfried Giedion, self-appointed promoter and critic-in-chief of modern architecture, soon ranked it with Walter Gropius's Bauhaus and Le Corbusier's League of Nations project. Aalto's attention to what Giedion called 'the human side' was evident throughout the buildings. The patients' rooms, with their specially designed heating, lighting and furniture, remain models of what would now be called 'integrated environmental design', and the classic Paimio chair was intended both to assist the patients' breathing and to feel more welcoming than orthodox modern furniture. The Danish critic Poul Henningsen had observed that bent-metal chairs were 'apt to give the modernly dressed woman a cramp in the thigh', and Aalto responded by developing innovative techniques to bend wood, enabling him to design furniture which was simultaneously modern, 'human' and Finnish in its craft-like use of the major national resource.

The Paimio chair and other furniture were rapturously received in London in 1933, when they were exhibited at the Fortnum and Mason store, the *Architectural Review* acclaiming them 'cheap and seemly furniture, light and easy to move . . . For England it may at last spell death to fake Queen Anne'. Following the formation of Artek two years later, Aalto's furniture began to be distributed worldwide, finding its way into numerous design-conscious homes. It did not spell death to fake Queen Anne, however, and it is ironic that over sixty years later the Swedish company Ikea - whose products reflect Aalto's pioneering example - began an advertising campaign to 'modernise' English taste!s

With the benefit of hindsight we can see hints at Paimio of many of the key features of Aalto's mature manner: compositions assembled from deliberately varied forms and materials; the juxtaposition of rectilinear and free, 'organic' geometries, epitomised by his love of counterpointing a straight and undulating line; a fastidious attention to detail; and a conspicuous concern with the building as a complete environment to be experienced by its occupants through all their senses, not just their eyes.

Ideas which were embryonic at Paimio became fully-fledged in other projects completed during the 1930s. The undulating line rippled into a wooden acoustic ceiling running the length of the Viipuri Library's auditorium it did little to improve the sound distribution, but looked stunning - and blossomed in miniature in the exquisite Savoy Vase, designed for a restaurant in Helsinki's central Esplanade and inspired, according to Aalto, by 'a young Eskimo girl's leather breeches' - but suggesting to most people the undulating profile of a Finnish lake. The Aalto wave assumed magisterial form in the three-storey suspended wall billowing through 1939 the Finnish Pavilion at the New York World's Fair, where its relationship to the native landscape was made abundantly clear by large aerial views of lake-and-island scenery.

Widely acclaimed as the finest interior at the Fair, the Finnish Pavilion secured Aalto's reputation in America and led to the commission for what would prove to be his biggest wave of all, the serpentine Baker House dormitory beside the Charles River for the Massachusetts Institute of Technology. Other invitations to build abroad - in Oregon, and in Germany, Denmark, Italy and France - followed in the 1950s and '60s, but as Giedion sagely observed, 'Finland is with Aalto wherever he goes' and, Baker House excepted, his best work was done on Finnish soil.

The idea of treating the interior as a metaphoric landscape had its roots in Nordic Classicism, but what was there a playful conceit - the 'night sky' of Gunnar Asplund's Skandia Cinema in Stockholm springs to mind - became central to Aalto's conception of architecture. The sweeping foyers of his auditoria - such as Finlandia Hall in Helsinki finished five years before his death in 1976, or the Essen Opera House, completed almost twenty years after it - are landscape-like in flow and scale, and almost all his later work is characterised by a contrast between broad horizontal masses and vertically striated surfaces which can readily be read as an abstraction of the Finnish landscape. Sometimes the analogy with nature is obvious, as in the 'forest fragments' evoked by the double-layered windows of his last unmistakable masterpiece, the Church of the Three Crosses in Imatra; often it is highly abstracted, as in the marvellous 'forest foyer' of the Festival Hall of Jyväskylä University, or the craggy council chamber rising out of the Seinäjoki Town Hall.

None of Aalto's later buildings presents as rich a collage as the Villa Mairea - the 'experimental' brick walls of the tiny summer-house on Muuratsalo island come closest - but the additive mode of composition it required proved perhaps the single most influential aspect of his work. Aalto's later plans, for example, are generally hybrid, combining two or more geometric systems. In the libraries and auditoria, orthogonal and fan-shaped elements are juxtaposed, and his own studio in Helsinki features a long inward-curving wall generated by the desire to define an external space - the idea would have been familiar to any Baroque architect, but appeared decidedly racy to more rationally inclined Modernists.

Collage also enabled Aalto to adopt a richly varied palette of materials, combining 'traditional' and 'modern'. Wood was quickly assimilated - first in furniture, then in interiors such as the Viipuri library, finally as external cladding on his own house in Helsinki and the Finnish Pavilion in Paris in 1937. Aalto also turned his attention to brick, a material generally confined to utilitarian buildings in Finland. At Baker House and then in his masterpiece, the tiny Town Hall on Säynätsalo, he showed how this most traditional of materials could be used as part of an unmistakably modern architecture. For architects seeking a less doctrinaire style Säynätsalo was a godsend. It felt at once modern and timeless, and its influence can be traced in schools, parish centres, churches and similarly scaled buildings across northern Europe and Britain, and may even lurk beneath the tougher forms of Stirling and Gowan's seminal Engineering Building at Leicester University. The alternating brick and glass bands of the National Pensions Institute in Helsinki proved no less influential, notably in Britain where Aalto became a hero of the influential Cambridge School led by Sir Leslie Martin.

Any architect of Aalto's stature and originality will have his imitators, and his influence was largely benign - whereas in lesser hands, the post-war style of Le Corbusier readily descended into farce, that of Mies van der Rohe into utter banality. But more interesting historically is the inspiration Aalto provided - and will surely continue to provide - for other innovators. As the homogenising effects of a weak internationalism became apparent, Aalto's Finnish version of modernity provided a model to emulate in other contexts. As the rhetoric of 'place and occasion' began to challenge that of 'space-time' in the 1950s, Aalto's buildings were available as models of inventive place-making. And when Kenneth Frampton sought to articulate a philosophy of 'critical regionalism' to challenge the eclectic Post Modernism of the 1980s, it was to Aalto, and in particular to Säynätsalo Town Hall, that he turned for an exemplar.

To Robert Venturi, whose book *Complexity and Contradiction in Architecture* of 1966 challenged many of the central tenets of Modernism, Aalto's 'responsive' plans were models for a more inclusive, less doctrinaire approach to architecture. Their influence can be traced throughout Venturi's early projects, whose plans were amongst the most elegant being drawn anywhere.

The reasons are not hard to find. Architecture cannot flourish in consumer cultures where image takes precedence over substance, instant appeal over lasting value. The authenticity of everything Aalto designed - difficult to define, but nonetheless unmistakable - offers a compelling critique of many of today's designer-buildings, whose fragile perfection is often shattered by use. For architects bewildered by the heady climate of competing styles, that 'wholesome Nordic sanity' which was so greatly admired during Aalto's lifetime still provides a welcome reminder of the fundamentals of their art.

Believing that 'great ideas arise from the small details of life', Aalto created poetic places out of an intense concern for the needs of what he called 'the little man', and from a deep love of his native landscape. He did not dwell on abstract theory, but immersed himself in the particularities of a site, the texture of materials, the quality of light: wherever architecture is called upon to help define local identities within an increasingly globalised world, Aalto's work will remain a compelling example. His work achieved universal significance not, as the pioneer Modernists hoped, by achieving an 'international style' but by defining a way of being simultaneously modern and Finnish. Aalto's reputation as one of the great architects of the twentieth century is secure, and his legacy for the twenty-first could hardly be more pertinent.

Andrew Carnegie

Andrew Carnegie (November 25, 1835 – August 11, 1919) was a Scottish businessman, a major philanthropist, and the founder of the Carnegie Steel Company which later became U.S. Steel. He is known for having, later in his life, given away most of his riches to fund the establishment of many libraries, schools, and universities in Scotland, America and worldwide.

Andrew Carnegie was born on November 25, 1835, in Dunfermline, Fife, Scotland. He was the son of a hand loom weaver, William Carnegie. His mother was Margaret, daughter of one Thomas Morrison, a tanner and shoemaker. Although his family was impoverished, he grew up in a cultured, political home.

Many of Carnegie's closest relatives were self-educated tradesmen and class activists. William Carnegie, although poor, had educated himself and, as far as his resources would permit, ensured that his children received an education. William Carnegie was moreover a militant political activist and was involved with those organising demonstrations against the Corn laws. He was also a Chartist. He wrote frequently to newspapers and contributed articles in the radical pamphlet, Cobbett's Register edited by William Cobbett. Amongst other things, he argued for abolition of the Rotten Boroughs and reform of the British House of Commons, Catholic Emancipation, and laws governing safety at work, which were passed many years later in the Factory Acts. Most radically of all, however, he promoted the abolition of all forms of hereditary privilege, including all monarchies.

Andrew Carnegie's direct descendants still live in Scotland today. William Thomson CBE, the great grandson of Andrew, is Chairman of the Carnegie Trust Dunfermline, a trust which maintains Andrew Carnegie's legacy.

Andrew Carnegie's father had worked as a jobbing hand loom weaver. This involved receiving the mill's raw materials at his cottage and weaving them into cloth on the primitive loom in the cottage. In the 1840s, a new system was coming into being, the factory system. During this era, mill owners began constructing large weaving mills with looms powered at first by water wheels and later by steam engines. These factories could produce cloth at far lower cost, partly through increased mechanisation and economies of scale, but partly also by paying mill workers very low wages and by working them very long hours. The success of the mills forced William Carnegie to seek work in the mills or elsewhere away from home. However, the radical views of Andrew Carnegie's father were well known, and he was not wanted.

He chose to emigrate. His mother's two sisters had already emigrated, but it was his wife who persuaded William Carnegie to make the passage. Making the passage was not easy, however, for they had to find the passage money. They were forced to sell their meagre possessions and borrow some £20 from friends, a considerable sum in 1848.

That May, his family emigrated to the United States, sailing on the Wiscasset, a former whaler that took the family from Broomielaw, in Glasgow to New York. From there they proceeded up the Hudson River and the Erie Canal to Lake Erie and then to Allegheny, Pennsylvania, where William Carnegie found work in a cotton factory.

Young Andrew Carnegie found work in the same building as a "Bobbin boy" for the sum of $1.20 a week. His brother, Thomas, eight years younger, was sent to school. Andrew Carnegie quickly grew accustomed to his new country: three years after arriving in the United States, the young Carnegie began writing to his friends in Scotland extolling the great virtues of American democracy whilst disparaging and criticising "feudal British institutions". At the same time, he followed in his father's footsteps and wrote letters to the newspapers including the New York Tribune on subjects such as slavery.

Early career

Andrew Carnegie's education and passion for reading was given a great boost by Colonel James Anderson, who opened his personal library of 400 volumes to working boys each Saturday night. Carnegie was a consistent borrower. He was a "self-made man" in the broadest sense, insofar as it applied not only to his economic development but also to his intellectual and cultural development. His capacity and willingness for hard work, his perseverance, and his alertness, soon brought forth opportunities.

In 1851, he became a telegraph messenger boy in the Pittsburgh Office of the Ohio Telegraph Company, at $2.50 per week. This, to the young Carnegie, seemed a fortune. In addition to providing him with an increase in income, the job also provided him with a lifelong love of William Shakespeare's works. He was frequently required to deliver messages to a theatre, and he often managed to contrive appearing just as the curtain had been raised on a performance. Using a charm that was to pay even greater dividends in the future, Carnegie was then usually able to convince the theatre's manager to allow him to stay and watch the performance for free. When Carnegie was not at the theatre or improving his mind with a book, he would spend time listening to the telegraph instrument itself. The electric telegraph transmitted its signals along the wires that traversed the nation. When they were received into the telegraph office, they were transcribed into readable script on a long paper tape with the aid of an elaborate machine. He quickly learned to distinguish the differing sound the incoming signals produced and learned to transcribe it by ear without having to write it down. At the time, Andrew Carnegie was one of only two or three persons so gifted in the entire country. Having learned Telegraphy, he was noted by Thomas A. Scott of the Pennsylvania Railroad Company, who employed him as a secretary/Telegraph operator starting in 1853, at the princely salary of $4.00 per week. Carnegie was sixteen and soon began a rapid advancement through the company, eventually becoming the Superintendent of the Pittsburgh Division.

During the pre-war period, Andrew Carnegie had formed a partnership with a Mr. Woodruff, an inventor. Woodruff's invention was the sleeping car. The great distances transversed by railways had meant stopping for the night at hotels and inns by the railside, so that passengers could rest. The sleeping car sped up travel and helped Americans settle the American west. The investment proved a great success and a source of great fortune for Woodruff and Carnegie. The young Carnegie, who started work at an early age as a bobbin boy in a cotton mill, and, who was, a few years later, engaged as a telegraph clerk and operator with the Atlantic and Ohio Company, now became the superintendent of the western division of the entire line. In this post, Carnegie was responsible for several improvements in the service. When the American Civil War opened in 1861, he accompanied Scott, the Assistant United States Secretary of War, to the front. where he was "the first casualty of the war" when he pulled up telegraph wires the confederates had buried. he gained a scar on his cheek from when the wire came up too fast and cut him. he would tell the story of that scar for years to come.

Following his good fortune, Carnegie proceeded to increase it still further through fortunate and careful investments. In 1864, Carnegie invested the sum of $40,000 in Storey Farm on Oil Creek, in Venango County, Pennsylvania. In one year, the farm yielded over $1,000,000 in cash dividends, and oil from oil wells on the property sold profitably. Carnegie was subsequently associated with others in establishing a steel rolling mill.

Aside from Carnegie's investment successes, he was beginning to figure prominently in the American cause and in American culture. With the Civil War raging, Carnegie soon found himself in Washington. Carnegie was selected by his boss at the Pennsylvania Railroad Company, Thomas A. Scott, who was now Assistant Secretary of War in charge of military transportation, to join him in Washington. Carnegie was appointed Superintendent of the Military Railways and the Union Government's telegraph lines in the East and was Scott's right hand man. Carnegie, himself, was on the foot plate of the locomotive that pulled the first brigade of Union troops to reach Washington. Shortly after this, following the defeat of Union forces at Bull Run, he personally supervised the transportation of the defeated forces. Under his organization, the telegraph service rendered efficient service to the Union cause and significantly assisted in the eventual victory. During his work "in the field", Carnegie fell ill and needed treatment for sunstroke.

The Civil War, as so many wars before it, brought boom times to the suppliers of war. The U.S. iron industry was one such. Before the war its production was of little significance, but the sudden huge demand brought boom times to Pittsburgh and similar cities and great wealth to the iron masters.

Carnegie had some investments in this industry before the war and, after the war, left the railroads to devote all his energies to the ironworks trade. Carnegie worked to develop several iron works, eventually forming The Keystone Bridge Works and the Union Ironworks, in Pittsburgh. Although he had left the Pennsylvania Railroad Company, he did not totally sever his links with the railroads. These links would prove valuable. The Keystone Bridge Company made iron train bridges, and, as company superintendent, Carnegie had noticed the weakness of the traditional wooden structures. These were replaced in large numbers with iron bridges made in his works. As well as having good business sense, Carnegie possessed charm and literary knowledge. He was invited to many important social functions, functions that Carnegie exploited to his own advantage and to the fullest extent.

In the late 1860s and into the 1870s, Carnegie was "out and about and all over the place". Carnegie now had new investments aside from the iron venture, the Keystone Bridge Company. Carnegie had added to his investments in Pennsylvania oil investments in Texas, which earned him a small fortune, and, after the war, undertook several trips to Europe selling railroad securities on a commission basis for, among others, the London firm of Junius S. Morgan & Company. The last of these trips was in 1872, the commission earned being $150,000. Andrew Carnegie's multiple successes in bond selling, oil trading, and bridge building were so rapidly successful that the conservative Pittsburgh business community regarded him with a certain circumspection. It was during these trips to Europe and to Britain, in particular, that Carnegie came into contact with British steel makers, then the world leaders. He obtained a working knowledge of the Bessemer process of steel making and became a friend of its inventor, Sir Henry Bessemer.

In 1868, he introduced the Bessemer steel making process into the U.S.A. and, in 1873, decided on a now famous gamble. He decided to "put all his eggs in one basket, and then watch the basket." That year he staked all his wealth on steel making. His fellow Americans did not realize it at the time, but the day Carnegie decided to take this gamble was the day the eventual industrial supremacy of the U.S.

became certain. It took Andrew Carnegie only a matter of a few years to become the principal owner of the Homestead & Edgar Thompson Steel Works, and only a short time more to be heading the firms of Carnegie, Phipps & Company and Carnegie Bros. & Company, as well.

1880–1890: Carnegie the Scholar and Activist

Whilst Carnegie continued his business career, some of his literary intentions were fulfilled. During this time, he made many friends in the literary and political worlds. Among these were such as Matthew Arnold and Herbert Spencer as well as being in correspondence and acquaintance with most of the U.S. Presidents, statesmen, and notable writers of the time. Many were visitors to the Carnegie home. Carnegie greatly admired Herbert Spencer, the polymath who seemed to know everything. He did not, however, agree with Spencer's Social Darwinism which held that philanthropy was a bad idea.

In 1881, Andrew Carnegie took his family, which included his mother, then aged 70, on a trip to Great Britain. They toured the sights of Scotland by coach having several receptions en-route. The highlight for them all was a triumphal return to Dunfermline where Carnegie's mother laid the foundation stone of the "Carnegie Library". Andrew Carnegie's criticism of British society did not point to a dislike of the country of his birth, on the contrary, one of Carnegie's ambitions was to act as a catalyst for a close association between the English speaking peoples. To this end, he purchased, in the first part of the 1880s, a number of newspapers in England, all of which were to advocate the abolition of the monarchy and the establishment of "the British Republic". Surprisingly, Carnegie's charm aided by his great wealth meant that he had many British friends, including Prime Minister Gladstone.

In 1886, tragedy struck Carnegie when his young brother Thomas died at the early age of 43. Success in the business continued, however. At the same time as owning steel works, Carnegie had purchased, at low cost, the most valuable of the iron ore fields around Lake Superior. The same year Andrew Carnegie became a figure of controversy. Following his tour of Great Britain, he wrote about his experiences in a book entitled An American Four-in-hand in Britain. Although still actively involved in running his many businesses, Carnegie had become a regular contributor of articles to numerous serious minded magazines, most notably the Nineteenth Century, under the editorship of James Knowles, and the North American Review, whose editor, Lloyd Bryce, oversaw the publication during its most influential period.

That year, 1886, Carnegie penned his most radical work to date, entitled Triumphant Democracy. The work, liberal in its use of statistics to make its arguments, was an attempt to argue his view that the American republican system of government was superior to the British monarchical system. It not only gave an overly-favourable and idealistic view of American progress, but made some considerable criticism of the British royal family. Most antagonistic, however, was the cover that depicted amongst other motifs, an upended royal crown and a broken sceptre. Given these aspects, it was no surprise that the book was the cause of some considerable controversy in Great Britain. The book itself was successful. It made many Americans aware for the first time of their country's economic progress and sold over 40,000 copies, mostly in the U.S.A.

In 1889, Carnegie stirred up yet another hornet's nest when an article entitled "Wealth" appeared in the June issue of the North American Review. After reading it, Gladstone requested its publication in England, and it appeared under a new title, "The Gospel of Wealth" in the Pall Mall Gazette. The article itself was the subject of much discussion. In the article, the author argued that the life of a wealthy industrialist such as Carnegie should comprise two parts. The first part was the gathering and the accumulation of wealth. The second part was to be used for the subsequent distribution of this wealth to benevolent causes.

But all this was only a preliminary to the success attending his development of the iron and steel industries at

Pittsburgh, Pennsylvania. Carnegie made his fortune in the steel industry, controlling the most extensive integrated iron and steel operations ever owned by an individual in the United States. His great innovation was in the cheap and efficient mass production of steel rails for railroad lines.

In the late 1880s, Carnegie Steel was the largest manufacturer of pig-iron, steel-rails, and coke in the world, with a capacity to produce approximately 2,000 tons of pig-metal a day. In 1888, he bought the rival Homestead Steel Works, which included an extensive plant served by tributary coal and iron fields, a railway 425 miles long, and a line of lake steamships. An agglutination of the assets of he and his associates occurred in 1892 with the launching of the Carnegie Steel Company.

By 1889, the U.S. output of steel exceeded that of the U.K., and Andrew Carnegie owned a large part of it. Carnegie had risen to the heights he had by being a supreme organiser and judge of men. He had the talent of being able to surround himself with able and effective men, while, at the same time, retaining the control and the direction of the enterprise. Carnegie's businesses were uniquely organised in that his belief in "democratic principles" found itself interpreted into these businesses. This did not mean that Carnegie was not in absolute control, however. The businesses incorporated Carnegie's own version of profit sharing. Carnegie wanted his employees to have a stake in the business, for he knew that they would work best if they saw that their own self interest was allied to the firm's. As a result, men who had started as labourers in some cases, eventually ended up millionaires. Carnegie also often encouraged unfriendly competition between two of his workers and goaded them into outdoing one another. These rivalries became so important to some of the workers that they wouldn't talk to each other for years. Carnegie maintained control by incorporating his enterprises not as joint stock corporations but as limited partnerships with Carnegie as majority and controlling partner. Not a cent of stock was publicly sold. If a member died or retired, his stock was purchased at book value by the company. Similarly, the other partners could vote to call in stock from those partners who underperformed, forcing them to resign.

The internal organisation of his businesses was not the only reason for Andrew Carnegie's rise to pre-eminence. Carnegie introduced the concept of counter-cyclical investment. Carnegie's competitors, along with virtually every other business enterprise across the globe, pursued the conventional strategy of procyclical investment; manufacturers reinvesting profits in new capital in times of boom and high demand. Because demand is high, investment in bull markets is more expensive. In response, Carnegie developed and implemented a secret tactic. He shifted the purchasing cycle of his companies to slump times, when business was depressed and prices low. Carnegie observed that business cycles alternated between "boom" and "bust". He saw that if he capitalized during a slump, his costs would be lower and profits higher. During the years 1893 to 1897, there was a great slump in economic demand, and so Carnegie made his move. At rock bottom prices, he upgraded his entire operation with the latest and most cost effective steel mills. When demand picked up, prosperity followed for the Homestead & Edgar Thompson Steel Works, the Carnegie, Phipps & Company, and Carnegie Bros. & Company as a flood tide of profit. In 1900, the profits of Carnegie Bros. & Company alone stood at $40,000,000 with $25,000,000 being Carnegie's share.

Carnegie's empire grew to include the J. Edgar Thomson Steel Works Pittsburgh Bessemer Steel Works, the Lucy Furnaces, the Union Iron Mills, the Union Mill the Keystone Bridge Works, the Hartman Steel Works, the Frick Coke Company, and the Scotia ore mines. Also, Carnegie, through Keystone, supplied the steel for and owned shares in the landmark Eads Bridge project across the Mississippi River in St. Louis, Missouri. This project was an important proof-of-concept for steel technology which marked the opening of a new steel market.

In 1901, Carnegie was now 65 years old and was wanting to retire. He reformed his enterprises into conventional joint stock corporations as preparation to this end. Carnegie, however, wanted a good price for his stock. There was a man who was to give him his price. This man was John Pierpont Morgan.

Morgan was a banker and perhaps America's most important financial deal maker. He had observed how efficiency produced profit. He envisioned an integrated steel industry that would cut costs, lower prices to consumers and raise wages to workers. To this end he needed to buy out Carnegie and several other major producers, and integrate them all into one company thereby eliminating duplication and waste. Negotiations were concluded on 2nd March with the formation of the United States Steel Corporation. It was the first corporation in the world with a market capitalization in excess of $1,000,000,000.

The buyout, which was negotiated in secret by Charles M. Schwab was the largest such industrial takeover in United States history to date. The holdings were incorporated in the United States Steel Corporation, a trust organized by J. P. Morgan, and Carnegie himself retired from business. His steel enterprises were bought out at a figure equivalent to twelve times their annual earnings; $480 million, which at the time was the largest ever personal commercial transaction. Andrew Carnegie's share of this amounted to a massive $225,639,000 which was paid to Carnegie in the form of 5%, 50 year gold bonds. The letter agreeing to sell his share was signed on the 26th February, 1901. On the 2nd March 1901, the circular formally filing the organisation and capitalisation of the United States Steel Corporation actually completed the contract. The bonds were to be delivered within two weeks to the Hudson Trust Company of Hoboken, New Jersey in trust to Robert A. Franks, Carnegie's business secretary. There, a special vault was built to house the physical bulk of nearly $230,000,000 worth of bonds. It was said that "....Carnegie never wanted to see or touch these bonds that represented the fruition of his business career. It was as if he feared that if he looked upon them they might vanish like the gossamer gold of the leprechaun. Let them lie safe in a vault in New Jersey, safe from the New York tax assessors, until he was ready to dispose of them...."

As they signed the papers of sale, Carnegie remarked, "Well, Pierpont, I am now handing the burden over to you." In return, Andrew Carnegie became one of the world's wealthiest men. Retirement was a stage in life that many men dreaded. However, Carnegie was not one of them. He was looking forward to retirement, for it was his intention to follow a new course from then on.

Besides steel, Carnegie's companies were involved in other areas of the railroad industry. His company, Pittsburgh Locomotive and Car Works, was noted for its building of large steam locomotives at the turn of the 20th century. His associates and partners included Henry Clay Frick and F. T. F. Lovejoy.

He owned 18 English newspapers, which he controlled in the interests of radicalism.

At the height of his career, he was the second richest person in the world, behind only John D. Rockefeller.

Azim Hasham Premji

Depending on how you want to look at it, the tag of the world's richest Indian sits heavily or lightly on Azim Hasham Premji, the CEO of Wipro Corporation. Heavily, because he feels it a burden and like "an animal in a zoo," and lightly, because he feels untouched by the whole thing. Premji's most oft-quoted line is, "We concentrate on doing our jobs."

This legendary person's lifestyle is legendary in its simplicity. It is common knowledge that he shuns anything that even remotely borders on the ostentatious. He prefers traveling economy class, avoids staying in five star hotels, and yes! he can be labeled a true-blue Indian - he prefers clothes, watches and cars that are made in India. You don't need a more vivid picture of the man, do you?

Premji would rather talk about his corporation and the Indian business scenario than about his personal wealth. He very strongly advocates the use of IT at all levels of society.

At an international conference in Bangalore recently, he said: "Though IT is on its way to become the largest export earner for India, I think its contribution is more fundamental. It has transformed our international image from being a land of "snake charmers" to a land of leaders in Information Technology. Our IT engineers have earned this respect not only in the US, which was the first to spot Indian talent, but in many other countries as well who have opened their doors wide to them. Many successful entrepreneurs in IT all over the world are Indians. This is also an historic opportunity for India to reclaim its earlier glory. In an age where the power of the mind offers a phenomenal new global competitive advantage, we are poised like never before to lead the way."

Premji continued, "We must recognize, however, that there are challenges to surmount. If we have to succeed as a nation, industry alone cannot do it. We need a shared Vision that will ignite the imagination of all the partners - the Industry, the Government and the Educational Institutions. The Industry will have to bring in the entrepreneurial spirit, the Government will have to contribute the appropriate infrastructure and legal support and the Educational Institutions must build the talent base."

For the man to have reached this stage, his beginnings were very simple. He was forced to leave his studies in Stanford at the age of 21 to take over the family business of vegetable oils when his father suddenly passed away in 1966. He has since completed his degree in Electrical Engineering from Stanford University. Originally called Western India Vegetable Products, the company then diversified to making vanaspati, later bakery fats, ethnic ingredient based toiletries, hair care soaps, baby toiletries, lighting products and hydraulic cylinders. The shift from soaps to software has been very focused. Now Wipro has rocketed from a market capitalization of just over $2 million when Premji took over to its present status of $13 billion in June 2000.

For Premji, no matter how high the company is or where his personal wealth is headed, there are certain things which will never change. Like setting high standards, and practicing them, remaining focused and always willing to learn. A combination that has taken him to where he is today.

There are other legendary attributes to this legendary man. Integrity is a great value with him and he is known to be a stickler for it. A little gentle prodding and he will probably recount the tale of how the company had to wait for 18 months to get a substation for the vanaspati unit because Wipro refused to bribe the concerned people. It was run on captive generation for nearly 20 months and cost the company dearly, but Premji preferred that to breaking his values. This is a clear indication of Premji's eminence as a no-nonsense man.

He also makes it a point to deal directly with customers as much as possible. He heads a very loyal team and together he and his employees practice the values Wipro has articulated - Human Values, Integrity, Innovative Solutions and Values for Money.

But, despite all the brouhaha created by his rapidly rising fortune, Premji is a person who has a very sane head on his shoulders. He has no illusions that investment in training and research will continue to keep Wipro in the forefront of performance.

Azim Premji (born July 24, 1945) is an Indian businessman and Chairman of one of the largest software companies in India, Wipro Technologies (Bangalore). He was rated the richest person in the country from 1999 to 2005 by Forbes.

He was an undergrad student in Electrical Engineering at Stanford University, USA but couldn't complete his degree due to the sudden demise of his father, he was called upon to handle the family business. In, 1966, after his father's death, when he was just 21, Azim Premji joined Wipro, his father's vegetable oil business.

In 2000, he was conferred an honorary doctorate by the Manipal Academy of Higher Education in India. He was also adjudged the Business Man of the Year 2000 by Business India. He is a member of the Prime Minister's Advisory Committee for Information Technology in India.

Wipro, a company that initially dealt in hydrogenated cooking fats and consumer products, expanded into computer software under Premji and from a 1.5 million USD company, is now ranked among the top 100 technology companies globally with turnover exceeding 2.3 billion USD. Wipro is world largest independent R&D Service provider

In 2000, he was voted among the 20 most powerful men in the world by Asiaweek. He was also among the 50 richest people in the world from 2001 to 2003 according to Forbes. According to a 2003 BBC report, he is "regarded as an Indian Bill Gates". In April 2004, he was rated among the 100 most influential people in the world by Time magazine. His assets include 84% holding in Wipro Technologies (the remaining belonging to the cofounder of Wipro). In January 2006, he was the 10 richest man in the world.

In 2005, Premji was awarded the Padma Bhushan.

Azim Premji Foundation says it "Aims at making a tangible impact on identified social issues by working in active partnership with the Government and other related sections of the society". The Foundation was set up with financial resources contributed by Azim Premji. It believes that "Education is the vital element in the development and progress of our nation".

Programmes of the Azim Premji Foundation focus on "creating effective and scalable models that significantly improve the quality of learning in the school and ensure satisfactory ownership by the community in the management of the school". Azim Premji Foundation says it "dedicates itself to the cause of Universalization of Elementary Education in India."

Learning Curve is a newsletter from the Azim Premji Foundation. The aim behind this Foundation's involvement in schools isn't merely to promote Information Technology education, but rather to improve the quality of general education, specially in rural schools.

Citing a technology initiative, the Foundation reported: "Think of a single PC with three display terminals, three keyboards and three 'mouses', which can be simultaneously used as if they are three independent computers". This innovative idea from the Azim Premji Foundation is being deployed in the computer aided learning centre at the Byatarayanapura Higher Primary School in Bangalore South District and in another school. Cost of installation and maintenance is lower because of a single CPU (central processing unit). Total cost of ownership -- including power consumption, UPS capacity and battery backup -- is reported to be "substantially lower" compared to regular personal computers.

Five new titles of educational CDs for Indian schools have also been produced earlier in 2005. They are: Friendly Animals and Journey on the Clouds (English), Swatantra Divas, Fun with Chinchoo in Mathematics and Khel-Mel (Hindi), released in February 2005. This makes the total number of master titles available at 70. There are now 68 titles in Karnataka, 42 for Andhra Pradesh, 35 for Tamil Nadu and Pondicherry, 18 for Urdu medium schools, six for Orissa, 14 for Gujarat, 3 for Punjab and 1 for Kerala.

This Foundation is also involved in computer-based assessment in Andhra Pradesh (50,000 students took part in early 2005); a learning guarantee programme; and a policy planning unit in Karnataka.

Buffalo Bill (William F. Cody)

He was born William Frederick Cody in Iowa in 1846. At 22, in Kansas, he was rechristened "Buffalo Bill". He had been a trapper, a bullwhacker, a Colorado "Fifty-Niner", Pony Express rider, wagonmaster, stagecoach driver, Civil War soldier, and even hotel manager. He earned his nickname for his skill while supplying Kansas Pacific Railroad workers with buffalo meat. He was about to embark on a career as one of the most illustrious prairie scouts of the Indian Wars.

From 1868 through 1872 he was continously employed by the United States Army, a record in the hazardous and uncertain scouting profession. He won the congressional Medal of Honor in 1872 and was ever after the favorite scout of the Fifth Cavalry. The men of the Fifth considered Buffalo Bill to be "good luck." He kept them from ambush, he guided them to victory, and his own fame reflected glory on the regiment. Cody considered himself lucky too. He was lucky to have been wounded in action just once, and then it was "only a scalp wound." But mostly he felt lucky to have been in the right place at the right time.

In 1872 he appeared on stage for the first time, playing himself in "Scouts of the Prairie." Thereafter he continued to act in the winter and scout for the Fifth in the summer. The Wild West show was inaugurated in Omaha in 1883 with real cowboys and real Indians portraying the "real West." The show spent ten of its thirty years in Europe. In 1887 Buffalo Bill was a feature attraction at Queen Victoria's Golden Jubilee. At the World's Columbian Exposition in 1893, only Egypt's gyrations rivalled the Wild West as the talk of Chicago. By the turn of the century, Buffalo Bill was probably the most famous and most recognizable man in the world.

The phenomenal success of the Wild West was founded on a nostalgia for the passing frontier which swept the nation in the late 19th Century. But Buffalo Bill himself never looked backward. "All my interests are still with the west - the modern west," he wrote near the end of his life.

He used his fame and public attention as a soapbox for western causes, for the rights of Indians and women, and for conservation. As early as 1879 he cautioned the government to "never make a single promise to the Indians that is not fulfilled." All frontier scouts respected the Indian, he said. "Every Indian outbreak that I have ever known has resulted from broken promises and broken treaties by the government." America was the Indian's heritage, and the Indian had only fought for what was his.

In 1894 a woman reporter asked him whether he thought the majority of women qualified to vote. He was caught offguard but answered, "As well qualified as the majority of men." The women in his Wild West were as skilled and courageous as the men. "If a woman can do the same work that a man can do and do it just as well," he said "she should have the same pay."

Cody recognized very early that a developer in the West was obligated to be a preserver as well. He has spoken out against the hide-hunters of the 1870s and 1880s for slaughtering the buffalo "cruelly, recklessly." In Wyoming and Colorado he worked to establish game preserves and limit hunting seasons. Gifford Pinchot, noted conservationist and head of the Forest Service for Theodore Roosevelt, lauded him as "not only a fighter but a seer."

Cody used his wealth as well as words. Because so few of his investments - in ranching, mining, irrigation, publishing, town building - paid off during his lifetime, he died almost broke.

But he had helped his West to make the transition from a wild past to a progressive future. His was the New West, he wrote, "with its cities, drawing upon the mountains for the water to make it fertile, and upon the whole world for men to make it rich."

The people of Cody have planned a year long celebration to commemorate the centennial of their town and the 150th Birthday of Colonel William F. Cody, the world-famous showman and scout, better known as Buffalo Bill held in February. Every Western event held in Cody in 1996, including the Cody Stampede Rodeo and Parade will carry a centennial theme. Founder's Day was celebrated on the 18th of May, 1996.

A centennial history of Cody titled "Buffalo Bill's Town in the Rockies: A Pictorial History of Cody, Wyoming" is available from the Park County Historical Society. This unique centennial history traces the development of Cody from settlement to present time with special sections on Buffalo Bill, archhaeology and the early history of the region.

Cody is situated in the northwest corner of Wyoming's Big Horn Basin. It was one of the last places in the United States to be settled. Mountain man and fur trapper John Colter, a member of the Lewis and Clark expedition, was probably the first white man to visit the Stinking Water

Valley, while searching for beaver. Later came the miners, cattle kings and flock masters. They had come to encroach on the hunting grounds of the Crow Indians. Once the buffalo were gone, the Crow retreated to their reservation in Montana.

In the 1890s the foundation was laid for irrigation projects in the vincinity of Cody. A few ranches had been developed prior to this time, but irrigation brought the first major colonization and development to the area. Irrigation was the key to the development of the desert land in the Big Horn Basin.

Buffalo Bill Cody advertised through his Wild West Show enticing settlers to come west and take up land under the Cody Canal. There was a sense of excitement and urgency felt by the people moving west. They realized that the Western lands were nearly all settled and if they wanted to be a part of this epic drama they must relocate soon.

Cody, along with a group of investors from Buffalo, New York, and George T. Beck and Holger Alger of Sheridan, Wyoming, formed the Shoshone Land and Irrigation Company and proceeded with plans to locate a town. Cody was established at the present site in 1896.

An earlier attempt to start the town was made in 1895 at the site of DeMaris Springs, slightly northwest of the present site. By 1900, settlement of the Irrigation project picked up and as agriculture expanded in the area, so did the town of Cody. The Burlington Railroad completed a spur to Cody by 1901. Cody poured his own money into the town, building the Irma Hotel, Pahaska and the Wapiti Inn. He also owned the T-E and Carter ranches and had interests in coal mines and gas and oil claims as well as the Canal Company, Buffalo Bill Barn, Cody Enterprise and Cody Trading Company. By 1904 work began on the Buffalo Bill Dam, which would store water from the Shoshone River for hydroelectric power and irrigation use. A system of canals, flumes and dams was constructed to deliver the water to the land. This made it possible for even further settlement.

The founding fathers of Cody realized the potential for tourism. With Yellowstone National Park only fifty miles away and the town surrounded by thousands of acres of wilderness, the city would lure tourists from all over the world. William F. Cody brought many dignitaries and heads of state to Cody to hunt during the off-season of the Wild West Show. The Cody country had abundant game and was developing into a sportsman's paradise. Guiding and outfitting services flourished and guest and dude ranches began springing up to accomodate tourists brought in by the Burlington Railroad.

Another attraction was the reputed healing waters of DeMaris Hot Springs. Cody continued to grow at a fast pace until World War I. The depression of the 1930s brought growth to a halt but the area remained stable. By this time Buffalo Bill had passed on and the town was searching for ways to commemorate his life. The Cody Stampede and Rodeo was founded, along with the establishment of the Buffalo Bill Museum and erection of the famous statue of Buffalo Bill called "The Scout." During this time the gas and oil interests were developed, producing significant economic benefit to the community.

The next era of prosperity was ushered in by the end of World War II. Soldiers came home to establish families and enjoy the good life made possible by their sacrifice. In order to accommodate the needs of the population expansion, more homes were built and business increased. By this time oil, gas and mineral revenue was becoming more important to the economic base of the community than agriculture or tourism. But the community continued to see itself the way it always had. Cody was the last home of the Western hero Buffalo Bill.

Down through the years Cody has gone through a series of economic booms and busts, tied to the major industries of agriculture, tourism and gas and oil.

Bill Gates (William Henry Gates)

Willam Henry Gates III (born October 28, 1955) is the co-founder, chairman, and chief software architect of Microsoft Corporation, the wrld's largest software company as of April 2006. He is also the founder of Corbis, a digital image archiving company. Forbes international rich list has ranked him as the world's richest person for the last twelve straight years. In 1999, Gates' wealth briefly surpassed $100 billion, making him the world's first centibillionaire. When family wealth is considered, his family ranks second behind the Walton family.

Gates is one of the best-known entrepreneurs of the personal computer revolution. He is widely respected for his intelligence, foresight, and ambition. He is also widely criticized as having built Microsoft's business through unfair, illegal, or anticompetitive business practices. Government authorities in several countries have found some of Microsoft's practices illegal, as in *United States v. Microsoft.*

Since amassing his fortune, Gates has pursued a number of philanthropic endeavors, donating large amounts of money to various charitable organizations and scientific research programs through the Bill & Melinda Gates Foundation, founded in 2000. He, his wife Melinda and U2's lead singer Bono were collectively named by *Time* as the 2005 Persons of the Year. That same year he was given the honor of Knight Commander of the Order of the British Empire by Queen Elizabeth II. In 2006, this Foundation has been awarded with the "Premio Príncipe de Asturias en Cooperación Internacional".

Bill Gates was born in Seattle, Washington to William H. Gates, Sr. and Mary Maxwell Gates. His family was wealthy; his father was a prominent lawyer, his mother was the first female Regent of the University of Washington, and his maternal grandfather, J. W. Maxwell, was a national bank president. Gates has one older sister, Kristianne, and one younger sister, Libby.

Gates excelled in elementary school, particularly in mathematics and the sciences. Bill Gates went to Lakeside School, Seattle's most exclusive preparatory school where tuition in 1967 was $5,000. Lakeside rented time on a DEC PDP-10, which Gates was able to use to pursue an interest in computers, a rare opportunity at the time. Gates was a member of the Boy Scouts of America and attained the rank of Life Scout. While in high school, he and Paul Allen founded Traf-O-Data, a company which sold traffic flow data systems to state governments. He also helped to create a payroll system in COBOL, for a company in Portland, Oregon.

According to a press inquiry he scored 1590 on his SATs, and was able to enroll in Harvard University pursuing a Bachelors of Science in Computer Science in 1973, where he met his future business partner, Steve Ballmer. During his second year at Harvard, Gates co-wrote Altair BASIC for the Altair 8800. Gates dropped out of Harvard during his third year to pursue a career in software development. On

December 13, 1977, Gates was briefly jailed in Albuquerque for racing his Porsche 911 in the New Mexico desert.

Microsoft

After reading the January 1975 issue of *Popular Electronics* that demonstrated the Altair 8800, Gates called MITS (Micro Instrumentation and Telemetry Systems), the creators of the new microcomputer, to inform them that he and others had developed a version of the programming language BASIC for the platform. This was untrue, as Gates and Allen had never used an Altair previously nor developed any code for it. Within a period of eight weeks they developed an Altair emulator that ran on a minicomputer, and then the BASIC interpreter. Allen and Gates flew to MITS to unveil the new BASIC system. The demonstration was a success and resulted in a deal with MITS to buy the rights to Allen and Gates's BASIC for the Altair platform. It was at this point that Gates left Harvard to found Micro-Soft, which later became Microsoft Corporation, with Allen.

In February 1976, Gates published his often-quoted "Open Letter to Hobbyists". In the letter, Gates claimed that most users were using "stolen" pirated copies of Altair BASIC and that no hobbyist could afford to produce, distribute, and maintain high-quality software without payment. This letter was unpopular with many amateur programmers, not just those few using copies of the software. In the ensuing years the letter gained significant support from Gates' business partners and allies which gave rise to a movement that led to closed-source becoming the dominant model of software production. Despite Microsoft's reliance on closed source, Gates has said that he collected discarded program listings at Harvard and learned programming techniques from them.

It has been pointed out that Microsoft often produces products that incorporate ideas developed outside Microsoft, such as GUIs, the BASIC programming language, or compressed file systems, without paying royalties to the companies that developed them. Some of these matters have gone to court. Apple v. Microsoft concluded that Microsoft had not infringed Apple's intellectual property; Stac Electronics prevailed in its claim against the DoubleSpace file system. The BASIC question has not been litigated, but the trend in US law is that copyright does not extend to publicly documented programming languages.

When IBM decided to build the hardware for a desktop personal computer in 1980, it needed to find an operating system. Microsoft did not have any operating system at this point. The most popular microcomputer operating system at the time was CP/M developed by Digital Research in Monterey. CP/M allowed software written for the Intel 8080/ Zilog Z80 family of microprocessors to run on many different models of computer from many different manufacturers. This device-independence feature was essential for the formation of the consumer software industry, as without it software had to be re-written for each different model of computer. Bill Gates referred IBM to Gary Kildall, the founder of Digital Research, but when they did not reach immediate agreement with him they went back to Gates, who offered to fill their need himself. He licensed a CP/M-compatible OS called QDOS from Tim Paterson of Seattle Computer Products for $56,000, and IBM shipped it as PC-DOS.

Later, after Compaq licensed Phoenix Technologies' clone of the IBM BIOS, the market saw a flood of IBM PC clones. Microsoft was quick to license DOS to other manufacturers, calling it MS-DOS. By marketing MS-DOS aggressively to manufacturers of IBM-PC clones, Microsoft went from a small player to one of the major software vendors in the home computer industry. Microsoft continued to develop operating systems as well as software applications. In the early 1980's they created Microsoft Windows which was similar to Apple Computer's Macintosh OS graphical user interface, both based on the human interface work at Xerox PARC. The first versions of the Windows OS did not sell well as stand-alone applications but started to be shipped pre-installed on many systems, reducing the incentive of users to buy competing products regardless of quality. Because of this, by the late-1980s Microsoft Windows had begun to make serious headway into the IBM-compatible PC software market. The release of Windows 3.0 in 1990 was a tremendous success, selling around 10 million copies in the first two years and cementing Microsoft's dominance in operating systems.

By continuing to ensure, by various means, that most computers came with their software pre-installed, Microsoft eventually went on to become the largest software company in the world, earning Gates enough money that Forbes Magazine named him the wealthiest person in the world for several years. Gates served as the CEO of the company until 2000 when Steve Ballmer took the position. Gates continues to serve as a chairman of the board at the company and also as a position he created for himself entitled "Chief Software Architect". Microsoft has thousands of patents, and Gates has nine patents to his name.

Since Microsoft's founding and as of 2006, Gates has had primary responsibility for Microsoft's product strategy. He has aggressively broadened the company's range of products, and wherever Microsoft has achieved a dominant position he has vigorously defended it. Many decisions that have led to antitrust litigation over Microsoft's business practices have had Gates's approval. In the 1998 *United States v. Microsoft* case, Gates gave deposition testimony that several journalists characterized as evasive. He argued over the definitions of words such as "compete", "concerned", "ask", and "we." BusinessWeek reported, "early rounds of his deposition show him offering obfuscatory answers and saying 'I don't recall' so many times that even the presiding judge had to chuckle. Worse, many of the technology chief's denials and pleas of ignorance were directly refuted by prosecutors with snippets of e-mail Gates both sent and received."

Gates meets regularly with Microsoft's senior managers and program managers. By all accounts he can be extremely confrontational during these meetings, particularly when he believes that managers have not thought out their business strategy or have placed the company's future at risk. He has been described shouting at length at employees before letting them continue, with such remarks as "That's the stupidest thing I've ever heard!" and "Why don't you just join the Peace Corps?" However, he often backs down when the targets of his outbursts respond frankly and directly. When he is not impressed with the technical hurdles managers claim to be facing, he sometimes quips, "Do you want me to do it over the weekend?"

Gates's role at Microsoft for most of its history has been primarily a management and executive role. However, he was an active software developer in the early years, particularly on the company's programming language products. He has not officially been on a development team since working on the TRS-80 Model 100 line, but he wrote code as late as 1989 that shipped in the company's products.

In 2000, Gates founded the Bill & Melinda Gates Foundation, a charitable organization, with his wife. The foundation's grants have provided funds for college scholarships for under-represented minorities, AIDS prevention, diseases prevalent in third world countries, and other causes. In 2000, the Gates Foundation endowed the University of Cambridge with $210 million for the Gates Cambridge Scholarships. The Foundation has also pledged over $7 billion to its various causes, including $1 billion to the United Negro College Fund; and as of 2005, had an estimated endowment of $29.0 billion. He has spent about a third of his lifetime income on charity. Journalist Greg Palast suggests that the Gates Foundation is used to make tactical donations to hide media sensitive humanitarian side effects of treaties, such as the Agreement on Trade-Related Aspects of Intellectual Property Rights, which Gates has supported. TRIPS requires countries to agree to respect drug and other patents, therefore preventing the local manufacture of existing pharmaceuticals still under patent such as AIDS drugs in Africa.

Gates has received two honorary doctorates, from the Royal Institute of Technology, Stockholm, Sweden in 2002 and Waseda University in 2005. Gates was also given an honorary KBE from Queen Elizabeth II of the United Kingdom in 2005, in addition to having entomologists name the Bill Gates flower fly, *Eristalis gatesi*, in his honor.

Microsoft's CEO Steve Ballmer has stated that Gates is probably the most "spammed" person in the world, receiving as many as 4,000,000 e-mails per day in 2004, most of which were junk. Gates has almost an entire department devoted to filtering out junk emails. In an article, Gates himself has said that most of this junk mail "offers to help get out of debt or get rich quick", which "would be funny if it weren't so irritating".

Gates is widely considered one of the world's most influential people. Time magazine named him one of the 100 people who most influenced the 20th century, as well as one of the 100 most influential people of 2004, 2005 and again in 2006. Gates and Oprah Winfrey are the only two people in the world to make all four lists. He was listed in the *Sunday Times* power list in 1999, named CEO of the year by *Chief Executive Officers_magazine* in 1994, ranked number one in the "Top 50 Cyber Elite" by *Time* in 1998, ranked number two in the *Upside* Elite 100 in 1999 and was included in *The Guardian* as one of the "Top 100 influential people in media" in 2001. Gates has been number one on the "Forbes 400" list from 1993 through to 2006 and number one on *Forbes* list of "The World's Richest People" from 1995-2006. In 2004, he became a director of Berkshire Hathaway, the investment company headed by Warren Buffett, the second wealthiest person in the world according to Forbes and a long time friend of Gates.

Since 2000, Gates's wealth has declined due to a fall in Microsoft's share price and the

multi-billion dollar donations he has made to his charitable foundations. According to a 2004 *Forbes* magazine article, Gates gave away over $29 billion to charities from 2000 onwards. These donations are usually cited as sparking a substantial change in attitudes towards philanthropy among the very rich, as philanthropy eventually became the norm for the very rich. The Gates received the "Spanish Nobel" prize - the Prince of Asturias Award for International Cooperation - on May 4, 2006, in recognition of their world impact through charity giving.

Gates has not generally engaged in conspicuous consumption beyond his lavish home, with its gardens and art collection. Gates also rents or leases a home on Mustique, an exclusive island in the Grenadines, and owns a 300 foot yacht named Ice. In contrast, his former associate Paul Allen has used his wealth in perhaps a more typical manner—owning sports teams, vintage airplanes, and multiple residences. Gates also claimed, in 2005, that he has gone to work every day since 1975, which in recent years includes both his role at Microsoft, and his leadership position at the Gates Foundation.

In May 2005, Gates said in an interview that he wished that he wasn't the richest man in the world, the stated reason being that it was a very irratating ordeal to be looked upon as the world's richest man.

Clarence Birdseye

Born in Brooklyn in 1886 to Clarence Frank Birdseye, a lawyer, and Ada Underwood, the daughter of a noted inventor and manufacturer, Clarence Birdseye was one of eight children. He lived summers with his family on a large Long Island farm where he spent most of his time outdoors in the fields or at the seashore. In his outdoor explorations he noticed a large number of muskrats in the area, and at age 10, through contacts at the Bronx Zoo, he trapped and sold muskrats to a customer in England. He used his profits to purchase a single-barreled shotgun. An outdoorsman and an adventurer, Birdseye also studied and practiced taxidermy as a youth.

With the move of his family to Montclair, New Jersey, where Clarence Birdseye went to high school, he showed an interest in food preparation and attended a cooking class. After graduation from high school in 1908, he worked as an office boy for a Wall Street firm in the summer before starting college. It was during this time that he developed a personal shorthand system that he used throughout his life in his private scientific journals. This shorthand system was based on his study of a portion of a mail-order course that he found on the sidewalk.

Off to college, Clarence Birdseye followed the tradition established by his father and brothers and attended Amherst. The Birdseye family finances were such that he had to work to help pay his college expenses. He used his interest in the outdoors and wildlife to earn money for college expenses, trapping and selling black rats to a geneticist at Columbia University and selling live frogs for use as reptile food to the Bronx Zoo. The nickname "Bugs" came about as a result of his interest in biology and other science courses while at Amherst. Money grew tighter and in 1910, after completion of his second year at Amherst, he left college to start work. Although his formal education ended there, Amherst later awarded him an honorary Master of Arts degree in 1941.

Birdseye continued his interest in animals and the environment. His first job after leaving college was as a naturalist with the U. S. Department of Agriculture's Biological Survey, collecting specimens of animals and birds of New Mexico and Arizona. Here he proved himself willing to eat such unusual meats as rattlesnake and is credited with making and eating a soup from mice, chipmunks, gophers, and packrats.

In this 1910-1912 period, he continued this work on the Biological Survey in the summers and during the winters held a variety of jobs-New York insurance firm work and a snow checker for the New York Department of Sanitation. He also purchased bobcat and coyote skins from traders in the Southwest and sold them to New York furriers. In the winter of 1911, he worked for the government in Washington, D. C. with his summer work taking him to Montana to study the deadly Rocky Mountain spotted fever by collecting ticks and their animal hosts. Upon return from Montana, he resigned from his job with the government to go on a six-week cruise of Labrador waters with the famous medical missionary Sir Wilfred Grenfell.

Learning on his arrival in Labrador of the phenomenal profits being made from the breeding and trapping of foxes, he left the expedition in 1912 to spend the next five years traveling by dog sled and collecting furs for sale. During this period in Labrador, Birdseye and the former Eleanor Gannett were married in 1915. In 1916 he moved his wife and their five-week-old son to Labrador where they lived in a three-room cabin situated 250 miles from the nearest doctor.

His work in Labrador required that he travel distances by dog team buying furs. Always somewhat adventurous in his eating habits, Birdseye tried starlings, blackbirds, whale, porpoise, lynx, alligator, and larger lizards. "I ate about everything...beaver tail, polar bear and lion tenderloin. And I'll tell you another thing-the front half of a skunk is excellent."

He noted that duck and caribou frozen in the extreme cold of midwinter were better than those frozen in the spring or fall. He noticed how easily food was preserved in the arctic climate. He watched the Eskimos' rudimentary quick-freeze methods, a process by which items are frozen at such a speed that only small ice crystals are able to form, and noted that quickly frozen fish retained flavor and texture better than fish frozen slowly. In an early experiment in freezing vegetables, Birdseye, in order to provide fresh vegetables to his family in this remote area, froze cabbage for later use.

In 1917 when the United States entered World War I, the Birdseye family returned to the United States, settling first in Washington, D. C. where Birdseye worked for the firm of Stone and Weber. In 1919 he moved on to work for the U. S. Housing Office as an assistant purchasing agent. Then from 1920-1922, he was employed as an assistant to the president of the U. S. Fisheries Association. He entered the wholesale fish business in 1922 and experimented with the process of quick freezing food that he had learned while in Labrador. He later said, "My contribution was to take Eskimo knowledge and the scientists' theories and adapt them to quantity production."

In 1923, with an investment of $7 for an electric fan, buckets of brine, and cakes of ice, Birdseye invented and later perfected a system of packing fresh food into waxed cardboard boxes and flash-freezing them under high pressure. "Production of perishable foods, dressed at the point of production and quick-frozen in consumer packages, was initiated, so far as I am aware, in the kitchen of my own home late in 1923 when I experimentally packaged rabbit meat and fish fillets in candy boxes and froze the packages with dry ice."

Birdseye made two major contributions to the concept of freezing food-the importance of freezing food so rapidly that there would be no damage to its cellular structure and freezing food in a package that could be sold directly to the consumer. Birdseye's initial idea was followed by home experiments and then later in experiments with freezing fish at a short-lived company he established in New York. After a year this first company ended in bankruptcy and he established in 1924 the General Seafoods Company. Birdseye with the assistance of financial backers set up shop in Gloucester, Massachusetts for experimental work, developing a series of quick freezing devices with the final result being the development of the first commercially practical freezer. He and his financial partners later organized this business into the General Foods Company, which served as the parent company for General Seafoods.

In 1926, Birdseye had developed a quick-freeze double-belt machine weighing 20 tons. It was later transformed into a more transportable multiple-plate freezer which was to become widely used in the frozen food industry. It became obvious that considerable capital would be required to properly develop this new frozen food industry, and in June 1929, the Birdseye business, by then owned by the General Foods Company, was sold for $22 million to Frosted Foods

Company, a corporation formed and owned by Postum Company and Goldman-Sachs Trading Corporation. The newly-purchased company took the name of General Foods Corporation and changed the Birdseye brand name to Birds Eye. According to Clarence Birdseye, this change in his family name returned it to its original form-Birds Eye. It was reportedly derived when an early ancestor saved the life of an English Queen by shooting an attacking hawk squarely through its eye.

Clarence Birdseye, whose share of the purchase was just under a million dollars, was to remain with the new corporation to head up research and development. He directed 22 chemists and food technicians at the laboratory set up by the new corporation in Gloucester, Massachusetts. This research group came up with the use of coated cellophane as a wrapping to go over the cartons in which the food was frozen. It was at this laboratory that the portable multi-plate freezer was invented and built. This group also developed over a hundred varieties of processed foods which could be successfully frozen.

The sale of Birds Eye frozen foods began March 6, 1930 in test marketing in 18 stores in Springfield, Massachusetts. There were 27 items-vegetables, fruits, fish and meats in this initial consumer test. Another consumer test was run in 1934 in Syracuse, New York followed by another in Rochester, New York. From this point, frozen food moved on to nationwide distribution.

Since many retailers couldn't afford to buy freezers during the Depression, Birdseye introduced an inexpensive freezer display case and leased it to them. The ability to distribute and sell frozen foods at the retail level marked the beginning of the frozen food industry. In 1944, Birdseye leased the first insulated railroad cars and nationwide frozen food distribution became possible. In effect, Birdseye created a market for frozen foods. Refrigerator freezer cubic space in home refrigerators grew as the relevance of frozen foods grew over the next decades.

Although primarily known for his contributions to the frozen foods industry, Clarence Birdseye's interests were wide-ranging. He invented a one-man, shoulder-firing, "kickless" harpoon gun for use in hunting whales while participating in the International Whaling Commission study of whale migratory habits.

He considered this work in whaling as a hobby and during this same period he started a small company to create a single unit bulb and reflector for use in display lighting. He also designed more efficient lighting filaments and heat lamps for use in keeping food warm. In 1939, Birdseye sold the Birdseye Electric Company and it later became a part of the Sylvania Company.

In another area of interest, Birdseye developed an electrical fishing reel for use in commercial fishing. It allowed commercial fishermen to fish at deeper levels and catch more fish much more quickly and easily. And then, during the Second World War, Birdseye became interested in dried foods with an eye to improving their quality, appearance and taste. Using experiments in his kitchen at home, he developed a quick drying process for which he obtained patents.

In addition to his genius at invention, Birdseye was known for his ability in expressing his ideas. He wrote articles on everything from fox farming to food drying and while in Labrador wrote and published a fiction piece entitled "Hard Luck on the Labrador." He and his wife also wrote a book, Growing Woodland Plants, based on a long-term hobby of theirs. It was published in 1951.

The last years of Birdseye's life were devoted to the development of better methods of paper manufacture. He worked for two years on a plantation in Peru. There he developed a method of converting sugar cane waste into paper pulp, shortening to12 minutes a process that had previously taken nine hours. This is considered his last major contribution to technology. Over his lifetime he was granted 300 foreign and U. S. patents. He died in 1956 at age 69 from a heart attack. He was survived by his widow, Eleanor, and their four children-two boys and two girls.

Birdseye was a man of many hobbies. "I have more hobbies than the law allows. Some are sissy. Some have hair on their chest." He was known for his enjoyment in cooking, gardening, Chinese checkers, and entertaining. A writer characterized him as "a man with no blisters on his ego. He talks with the simplicity of a cowhand, good humored and frank, and his speech is salty." He impressed the writer as "liking everything and everybody" and "being totally uninhibited."

As to Birdseye's opinion of himself, he said, "I do not consider myself to be a remarkable person. I did not make exceptionally high grades when I went to school. I never finished college. I am not the world's best salesman. But I am intensely curious about the things which I see around me and this curiosity, combined with a willingness to assume risks, has been responsible for such success and satisfaction as I have achieved in life."

Charles Francis Brush

Charles Francis Brush was an American pioneer, inventor and industrialist in the commercial development of electricity. His inventive genius ranked with an elite group of electric pioneers including Thomas A. Edison. Brush designed and developed an electric arc lighting system that was adopted throughout the United States and abroad during the 1880's. He also devised a generator that produced a variable voltage controlled by the load and a constant current.

Charles Francis Brush was born on his parents' farm in Euclid, Ohio, on March 17, 1849. Charles Brush was the youngest of nine children of Isaac Elbert and Delia Williams Phillips Brush. He was an eighth generation American on his father's side, descending from Thomas Brush, who was born in England about 1610. On his mother's side, Charles was a descendent of Rev. George Phillips, 1593-1644. Isaac

Elbert Brush married Delia Phillips on May 2, 1827. Isaac was a successful businessman in the woolen manufacture trade. However, his business did not survive the depression of 1837, which precipitated his move to the Western Reserve in Ohio. He spent five years preparing the land and moved his family in 1846 to the Walnut Hills Farm. At the time Isaac and Delia had seven children. Another daughter and then Charles were born on the farm, which was located about 10 miles east of Cleveland.

Charles' early years were spent on the Walnut Hills Farm. Being the youngest child of nine, Charles probably did not have as many responsibilities on the farm as his older sisters and brothers. Rather than waste his free time on trivial activity, Brush spent it reading about astronomy, chemistry, physics and other areas of science. However, his thirst for knowledge was not satisfied by reading alone. He started to do experiments in the workshop on the farm. Brush was probably most interested in electricity, a source of energy that was poorly understood during the time of his childhood. When he was 12, Brush constructed his first static electric machine, using a bottle, a piece of leather and amalgam from an old mirror. He also made batteries, electromagnets, induction coils and small motors. The fact that he was able to produce such devices from items around the farm was a testament to his ingenuity. He could not afford expensive insulated wire but this did not deter him from making coils. He used rusty wire and shellacked paper for insulation between layers of wire. The rust on the wire, while not being an ideal insulator, provided enough insulation to make a functional coil. During this time Brush learned of Humphrey Davy's 1808 experiment with an arc light. Davy attached two carbon electrodes to a battery and found that he could produce an arc between the electrodes. The arc light held special fascination for Charles but he was not able to construct one with the discarded materials found around the farm. For this he would have to wait until high school, where he would have the necessary materials to assemble such a device.

Brush's parents appreciated the talents of their youngest child and realized that he would benefit greatly from a formal education. They made the financial sacrifice to send him to a high school. In 1863 he entered Cleveland's Central High School. The school was too far from the farm for Charles to live at home so his parents sent him to a boarding house downtown. This boarding house was also the temporary home of other young men soon to make their mark in history, including John D. Rockefeller. Central High provided the environment that Brush needed to develop his interest in science and electricity. It contained the only large public library in the city at the time and there he found printed matter which allowed him to develop his knowledge in frontier areas of science. Furthermore, the science laboratories at the school would provide the facilities he needed to do more advanced experimentation.

During his junior year, Brush fulfilled his boyhood dream of constructing an arc light. Using materials from the school laboratory, he made a zinc-carbon and nitric acid battery and fashioned carbon electrodes from gas retort carbon. He later related that the making of electrodes from retort carbon was quite laborious. Brush's teachers were very impressed with him and he was placed in charge of supervising the electrical apparatus at the school. This also allowed him to have free access to the physical laboratory, which he used to great advantage.

While in high school, Brush learned of Wilde's pioneering experiments with a dynamo and arc light, which were performed in London in 1866. He would incorporate this knowledge into his speech at commencement in 1867, which covered the conservation of energy, following a path from the sun to vegetation, coal, steam, electricity and finally light. By this time Brush surely had a vision for the future of electricity in commercial applications. He graduated from Central High with honors.

Brush now had a good high school education under his belt but this was not enough. He had a strong desire to continue his education at a higher level. But his parents did not have the means to send him to college. They had already spent all they could for his room and board during the high school years. A brother of Charles' mother agreed to finance his education in the form of a loan. The uncle felt that the University of Michigan was a fine institution, which apparently had some influence on Charles' choice for a higher education.

Brush entered the University of Michigan in the fall of 1867 to pursue a degree in mining engineering. At the time the university did not have a course of study in electricity. Furthermore, it did not seem that one could make a living in the area of commercial electricity at the time. Brush felt that mining engineering would give him the practical education that would provide for employment after graduation—much needed employment for repayment of his loan. While the university did not have any course work in electricity, the science courses did provide Brush with the necessary knowledge to be successful in his future endeavors. His course work included history, English, botany, French, rhetoric, chemistry, mathematics, geology, mechanics, machine drawing, metallurgy, civil and mining engineering.

Brush was a very busy young man during his stay at the university. He had worked hard to finish his course of study in a short time, working through the summer months to accelerate his rate of progress. Repayment of the debt to his uncle was part of the motivation for his fast track approach, reasoning that an early graduation would mean earlier employment and resolution of the debt. Somehow he also found time for membership in the social fraternity Delta Kappa Epsilon. He graduated from the University of Michigan in June of 1869, at the age of twenty, with a degree in mining engineering.

After graduating from the University of Michigan in 1869, Brush returned to Cleveland to establish a professional life. The city was developing into a major industrial center and it seemed reasonable that there would be a demand for someone practicing in the field of chemistry. Brush struggled as an analytical and consulting chemist for the first few years of his career. This endeavor did not prove to be very profitable and in 1873 he joined forces with a boyhood friend, Charles Bingham, to market Lake Superior pig iron and iron ore. It was during this time that he became reacquainted with another boyhood friend, George Stockly, vice president and general manager of the Telegraph Supply Company of Cleveland.

The iron ore business turned out to be more profitable for Brush. Now that he was earning a comfortable living his thoughts turned toward marriage. He courted Mary Ellen Morris and they were married on October 6, 1875. They made their home in one of Cleveland's first apartment buildings, located on Prospect Avenue between Cheshire and Huntington. Brush had a private laboratory in the apartment building, where he experimented with electricity. One day there was a loud noise and the inhabitants of the building rushed from their apartments to investigate. Mary explained that there was an accident in the laboratory and her husband had suffered a burn. Brush relocated the laboratory to another building upon the request of the owner but the couple continued to live in the apartment.

In 1873, he began to experiment with electricity. Brush related some of his early experimentation with electricity to Stockly and discussed his vision for the development of arc lighting. The lighting system would need an efficient means of generating electricity, which Brush proposed to do by using a dynamo. Stockly was very impressed with Brush and his ideas and agreed to financially support his effort to construct a small dynamo. The Telegraph Supply Company provided material and facilities needed for preliminary development work.

Dynamo

When Brush was formulating his plans for an arc lighting system he realized that an efficient and economic power source was the key to success. Volta had produced the first battery in 1800 and there were improvements by others in the middle of the century. Nevertheless, Brush did not consider the battery a viable power source for arc lighting. The cost of battery power was simply prohibitive for the lighting systems he wanted to develop. The dynamo seemed to be a promising source of electricity but Brush felt that there was a need to increase the efficiency of existing machines.

Hippolyte Pixii, a French instrument maker, constructed the first direct current dynamo in 1832. The machine contained a permanent magnet which was rotated by a hand crank. The spinning magnet was positioned so that its north and south poles passed by a piece of iron wrapped with wire. Pixii found that the spinning magnet produced a pulse of current in the wire each time a pole passed the coil. Furthermore, the north and south poles of the magnet induced currents in opposite directions. By adding a commutator, Pixii was able to convert the alternating current to direct current.

In 1867 Cooke and Wheatstone produced a dynamo that was clearly superior to Pixii's. Their dynamo was constructed with electromagnets rather than permanent magnets. Electromagnets were found to be superior because they could develop a stronger magnetic field, thereby increasing the electric output. In addition, electromagnets provided a degree of built-in regulation because the field strength would adjust in direct proportion to the output of the dynamo.

Another innovation in dynamo design during this time period was conceived by an Italian scientist, Antonio Pacinotti. He wrapped a ring of iron with a continuous coil of wire to form an armature. The "ring armature" was set to spin between electromagnets. This design produced a fairly steady stream of current because the wire wrappings of the armature were continually passing the electromagnet poles. Pacinotti's machine was the first practical direct current dynamo because it did not produce severely isolated pulses of electric current.

Brush considered the dynamos available in 1875 to be ill-suited to his needs. "The best forms of magneto-electric apparatus at present before the public are unnecessarily bulky, heavy, and expensive, and are more or less wasteful of mechanical power." Nevertheless, Brush was aware of a commercially successful dynamo in use in Europe. This was the machine developed by Zenobe Gramme in 1870. The Gramme dynamo was similar to Pacinotti's in design, containing a ring armature. Brush started with the basic Gramme design and set out to improve the dynamo. In the end the Brush dynamo represented a marked divergence from the Gramme. The ring armature was the only element that Brush retained from the Gramme design.

The initial work on the dynamo was done by Brush on a part-time basis, working after hours while continuing with his sales activity in iron ore. In 1877 Brush quit the iron ore business and devoted his full attention to the dynamo. He assembled his first dynamo in the summer of 1876 while "vacationing" at his old home, Walnut Hills Farm.

At first Brush worked out his designs on paper, considering the weak points of the Gramme design and how he might improve upon it. One major fault of the Gramme was the poor contact of armature coils with the electromagnet fields. The pole shoes of the electromagnets were formed to fit around the circumference of the ring armature. Therefore, only the outside portion of the coils would cut through the strong magnetic field. The wire on the sides and interior of the ring were outside the effective zone of the field. To improve upon this design, Brush would need to find a way to bring a larger percentage of the armature wire close to the magnetic pole shoes. Another weakness of the Gramme was a tendency to retain heat in the armature. The continuous winding acted as an insulating layer that retarded cooling of the armature core. Excessive heating of the armature would result in a drop in the efficiency of current generation.

Brush was an unusual man of many talents. Not only did he possess the scientific and engineering skills needed to create a dynamo, he was also skilled in the mechanical arts needed to fabricate a dynamo. Brush connected the dynamo to a horse-drawn treadmill, the only source of mechanical power available on the farm. At first it appeared that the dynamo could not generate electricity. After some thought, Brush connected the field magnets to a battery, reasoning that this would energize the electromagnets and provide the conditions necessary to initiate current generation. With the battery in place, Brush applied mechanical power to the dynamo and found that it produced a current. After the dynamo started generating electricity, the battery could be disconnected, it was only required to provide the needed starting conditions. Brush had fulfilled his boyhood dream of constructing a dynamo.

Brush returned to Cleveland with his new dynamo and continued development work at the Telegraph Supply Company. By the end of 1877 he had also developed a commercially viable arc lamp and was ready to market his lighting system. At the time Brush was a relatively unknown figure in the emerging electrical industry. He soon found the opportunity to gain recognition for his new dynamo.

The Franklin Institute of Philadelphia announced their desire to obtain a dynamo. In order to select the best model, the institute called upon manufacturers to submit their machines for evaluation. Several manufacturers declined the invitation, fearing adverse publicity if their dynamo was determined to be inferior. Brush felt that the risk of an unfavorable evaluation was offset by the potential benefits of a top evaluation. He submitted a small and large dynamo for consideration. The Wallace-Farmer Company was the only other American manufacturer to submit a machine.

The Franklin Institute was not satisfied with the number of dynamos submitted for testing and sought another machine for comparison. They were able to obtain a Gramme dynamo which had been shipped from Europe for the Centennial Exhibition of 1876. The institute evaluation committee commenced testing of the four dynamos in the spring of 1878, using them to power arc lights for the tests. Test runs were done for 5 hours, evaluating each machine for mechanical efficiency, power, range of currents, sparking, losses due to friction and local action of heat. The tests were completed by June of 1878.

Arc Lamp

Like several inventors during the 1870s, Brush wondered if electricity could be used for lighting. Scientists had known for a long time that they could create a very bright light by passing an arc of electricity between two carbon rods. The light didn't last long, though, because the electric current burned up the carbon rods. Brush invented a way to solve this problem. His invention was called the electric arc light. The arc light was not a new idea but those in existence at the time were not very practical. The chief drawback in lamps was the lack of a good regulating system for the carbon electrodes. As an arc light operates, the electrodes are consumed at their tips, where the electric arc occurs. Extended operation of the lamp requires the maintenance of a specific gap between the electrodes, which can be effected by moving the electrodes during operation with a regulating device. The poor regulation of existing arc lamps resulted in variable light output and unreliable operation.

Brush developed an arc light that was regulated by a combination of electrical and mechanical means. The elegant design, as often is the case, was simple and easy to maintain. An electromagnet was used via a mechanical linkage to move the upper carbon electrode. However, the movement was modulated and limited by a "ring clutch". In hindsight one might think a simple design solution could be conceived quickly; but simple designs are not always obvious until the inventor is successful. Brush's clever design was perfected after a considerable amount of time in the laboratory.

There were other arc lamps before Brush's that utilized electromagnets as part of a regulation system but it was the combination of the electromagnet with the ring clutch that made Brush's design superior in regulating the arc. Brush's lamps featured other design improvements including copper plated electrodes, regulators for operation of multiple lamps connected in series to one dynamo, and double carbon arc lamps for extended operation.

The electrode gap can be maintained with a simple mechanical device actuated by hand. The earliest lamps were of this type. However, it was desirable for the lamp to adjust itself during operation without the need of human attention. Various schemes were developed to regulate the electrode gap automatically but these were typically clumsy, complicated and expensive to manufacture. Furthermore, these lamps usually had poor regulation characteristics. This was the state of the art at the time when Brush began to develop his arc light.

In developing an arc lighting system, Brush initially concentrated on finding an economical source of electric power. His vision was to light America on a grand scale and this would not be possible with expensive batteries. At the time, the only alternative for producing electricity was the dynamo. Brush realized that the dynamo was the key to a successful lighting system and it would represent a great challenge to his inventive skill. Using sound logic, Brush developed a viable dynamo before working on the arc lamp itself.

Brush set forth the following design criteria for his lamp: simplicity, reliability, durability, and automatic regulation. These where the characteristics that would insure wide-scale adoption of the lamp. Initially he experimented with electromagnetic control devices for maintenance of the arc gap. This was not a new idea; several inventors had produced lamps with electromagnetic regulators prior to Brush. However, Brush found that he could not obtain the desired regulation with an electromagnetic device alone. Better control was achieved when Brush combined electromagnetic and mechanical means to control the arc.

The carbon holder rod is sized to freely pass through the central hole of the ring clutch as long as the clutch is perfectly horizontal. Prior to application of electric power, the parts of the lamp are positioned as in figure A. The ring clutch is horizontal and rests upon the bottom of the regulator housing. The upper carbon holder is free to move through the central hole of the ring clutch and the upper electrode is maintained in contact with the lower electrode by the weight of the upper electrode assembly. Initial contact of the electrodes is required to close the electric circuit and provides the conditions required to strike the arc. Immediately after the power is applied, the parts are positioned as in figure B. Upon powering the lamp, a magnetic field is induced by the coil of the solenoid. The magnetic field draws the solenoid core up. As the core moves up, the attached hook lifts one side of the ring clutch, tilting it from the horizontal. As the clutch tilts, it grabs onto the carbon holder. Subsequent upward movement of the core then takes with it the ring clutch and carbon holder. The upward movement of the upper carbon electrode establishes a gap and the arc of the lamp is "struck". The initial gap distance in the control cycle is limited by the limit screw, which arrests the upward movement of the ring clutch. The lamp electrodes and solenoid are wired in series so that electric current always flows through the solenoid coil while the lamp is operating. The solenoid contains an iron core which is free to move up and down inside the coil. The core is hollow and the carbon holder rod can pass freely through it. At the bottom of the core there is an L-shaped hook which provides a mechanical link between the solenoid and the ring clutch. The ring clutch is a disk with a central

As the lamp operates, the carbon at the tips of the electrodes is consumed, resulting in a widening of the gap. As the gap widens, increasing resistance reduces the current flow. This results in a weaker magnetic field in the solenoid and eventually a downward movement of the core. The downward movement reduces the gap. If the current drops low enough, the core will drop to its lowermost position and the ring clutch will then come to rest again upon the bottom of the housing in a horizontal position. When the clutch assumes this position, the carbon holder is released and is free to drop by gravity. As the gap is reduced, higher current flow is established and once again the ring clutch engages the carbon holder to set a proper gap. This regulation cycle repeats itself many times until the carbons are expended.

By utilizing this scheme, Brush was able to create an arc lamp with good regulation characteristics. The light output was fairly stable and of high intensity. The clever ring clutch design allowed the use of relatively long carbon electrodes, which could be fed repetitively in small increments to maintain a proper arc gap. The long electrodes allowed extended operation times of up to 8 hours. Brush tested and refined the design over a period of about one year before he was satisfied with the lamp's performance.

The solenoid and ring clutch regulator represented a breakthrough in arc lamp technology. It provided the basis for a commercially viable lamp. However, Brush was also working on other improvements to the lamp at the same time. Taken together, these improvements would yield a line of lamps eminently suited for commercial use.

Brush also worked on improving the lamp electrodes. Carbon electrodes at the time were commonly made from retort carbon, a material that yields a poor quality electrode. Retort carbon contains a high level of impurities, is soft, and has a high resistance to electric current. Brush needed a better electrode for his new lamp.

Relying on his knowledge of chemistry, Brush developed a new carbon material from still-coke, a by-product of petroleum refining that was readily available from the Standard Oil Company in Cleveland. The still-coke carbon proved to be much higher in quality than the retort carbon. Furthermore, the manufacturing process and raw material were very economical compared to the retort carbon method. Brush was able to produce an electrode of longer length and smaller diameter with the new carbon material. The new electrodes were more efficient because they could yield a longer burn time per unit weight of carbon.

While the new carbon material improved the quality of the electrode, further improvements were needed to provide an electrode suitable for the new lamp. The new carbon material had a high resistance to current flow and was not strong enough to yield the length of electrodes that Brush desired. In a flash of inspiration, Brush quickly devised another method to improve the electrode. By applying a thin layer of copper to the exterior surface of the electrode, Brush was able to improve the conductivity of the carbons and at the same time increase the strength so that longer rods could be manufactured. The copper-enhanced electrodes also yielded a longer burn time because the metal cover reduced the consumption rate of the carbon.

The lamp designs described above were suitable for single-lamp systems, where one dynamo was used to power one lamp. However, these lamps were not optimal for use in series where one dynamo powered multiple lamps. Brush knew that this was a critical limitation in his system. If the arc was extinguished in one lamp due to a malfunction, all lamps in a series circuit would cease to operate.

The addition of the cut-out to Brush's lamp was a critical element in developing a multiple lamp system. This was the system that was used for street lighting, where a number of lamps were powered by one dynamo, housed in a central station. Brush now had a product that could replace the gas lamps used in many cities in America and throughout the world. His superior system of lighting was purchased by many municipalities during the 1880's and his name became known to the general public.

One other limitation in Brush's lamp was the operation time. His single-carbon arc lamp would operate up to 8 hours on a set of carbons. Continued operation required replacement of the electrodes by maintenance personnel. Some cites, like New York, desired a street lamp that would operate from sunset to sunrise without replacement of the carbons. Brush solved the problem by designing a double-carbon arc lamp. This lamp would operate off one pair of carbons until they were expended and then current was transferred to the second pair.

Arc Lighting

Apart from lighting outfits set up for experimental purposes, the first dynamo and lamp actually sold were shipped to Dr. Longworth, father of Nicholas Longworth, at Cincinnati, about January, 1878, and Brush went to Cincinnati to show how the machine should be operated. The light was exhibited from the balcony of the Longworth home on one of the principal residence streets. Brush, who went purposely into the crowd to hear comments, later described the scene: "It was a four-thousand candle power light and, of course, attracted a large crowd. In the gathering were a few men of the type who, if they know nothing about a subject and find others who know nothing about it, will promptly explain it. One man who had collected a considerable audience called attention to the solenoid at the top of the lamp and said, "That is the can that holds the oil," and, referring to the side rod, said, "That is the tube which conducts the oil from the can to the burner." He said nothing at all about electricity—a little oversight apparently unnoticed by his hearers—and they went away happy in their newly acquired knowledge of the electric light."

Brush told also of an exhibit of one of the earliest four-light machines to a number of guests at a large factory in Cleveland: "One man looked the whole apparatus over carefully and then, pointing to the line wire, asked, 'How large is the hole in that little tube that the electricity flows through?'"

A number of indoor installations soon followed. The following year, John Wanamaker hired Brush to install lights in his Philadelphia department store. The lights, described by one observer as "twenty miniature moons on carbon points held captive in glass globes," created a sensation. The age of electrical lighting had been born. Within months, merchants all over the country rushed to have the new lights installed. He was keen to develop further outdoor lighting, an application eminently suited to the power of the arc light. These would be public lighting systems that would replace the gas lamp. At the time the average citizen knew very little about electricity and had no appreciation for its potential as a power source. Brush needed some way to demonstrate the power of his arc lamp to the public. This he did on Cleveland's Public Square, then known as Monumental Park, on April 29, 1879. Twelve arc lamps were positioned around the park and they were powered in series by a dynamo housed in the Telegraph Supply Company nearby. A news article in the Plain Dealer described the occasion: "At five minutes before eight o'clock there was a flicker in the lamp nearest the Telegraph Supply Company's headquarters and immediately the twelve lights beamed forth from their various stations. The lamp posts are much higher than the gas posts, making the electric lamps like beacon lights."

Thousands of people gathered to witness the scene and as the light shot around and through the Park a shout was raised. Presently the Grays Band struck up in the Pavilion and soon afterward a section of artillery on the lake shore began firing a salute in honor of the occasion.

The light varied some in intensity at intervals, when shining brightest being so dazzling as to be painful to the eyes to look long at a lamp. In color it is of a purplish hue, not unlike moonlight, and by contrast making the gaslights in the store windows look a reddish yellow. Some people had raised their expectations too high and were disappointed because it was not as light as day but most people seemed struck with admiration, both by the novelty and brilliancy of the scene.

The reaction of the crowd must have been pleasing to Brush and confirmed his vision of the utility of the arc light. Soon cities across America would place orders for the Brush arc lights, and his name became known to many. Before the end of 1881 Brush arc light systems were illuminating the streets of New York, Boston, Philadelphia, Baltimore, Montreal, Buffalo, San Francisco and other cities. Arc lights changed life in American cities greatly. Nighttime activities became more popular with the new form of lighting. Streetlights made it safer to be out after dark. Electrical lights in factories even made it possible for people to work at night.

Brush's inventive genius gave him his opportunity, but it may have been his knowledge of human psychology that enabled him to turn that opportunity into wealth and power. When the electric lighting of city streets was first proved practical, neither the new lights themselves, nor the inventor was popular with corporations that sold gas. They did all they could to discourage use of the new invention. They might have done more harm than they did if Brush had not quietly explained to them why they were wrong, even from their own selfish viewpoint, in fighting electric lights. His knowledge of crowd psychology was superior to theirs when he predicted: "Electric lights will increase rather than decrease use of gas. People have been living in darkness so long that they have organized their lives on that basis. But when they get used to light, they are sure to want more of it. After seeing brilliantly lighted streets and stores, they'll want more light in their homes and will burn more gas. As they use more gas for lighting, you can make gas cheaper and that will open up almost limitless industrial uses."

Another problem was to educate the public itself. Brush knew how conservative are the masses. He did not underestimate the slowness and tediousness of overcoming public suspicion of novelty. A frequent argument against the new lighting was that it would ruin eyesight. People stared at the brilliant arc and then complained that it was too dazzling.

"After looking at it, everything else looks dark," they said. "We'll ruin our eyes." To which Brush calmly retorted: "The same objection may be raised against the sun!"

The habit of staring at the arc hung on for many years and continued to be used as an argument against electric lighting. Scientists themselves had promoted foolish beliefs. As late as 1873, Deschanel's Natural Philosophy, a well-known textbook, said: "The light of the voltaic arc has a dazzling brilliancy, and attempts were long ago made to utilize it. The failures of these attempts were due not so much to its greater costliness in comparison with ordinary sources of illumination, as to the difficulty of using it effectively. Its brilliancy is painfully and even dangerously intense, being liable to injure the eyes and produce headaches."

One reason people stared was that they wondered where the light really came from. They thought there must be some trick to it. The light must come from oil, and where was the oil supply?

Another early problem was that users of an electric-light apparatus could not be induced to let it alone. This was especially true when outfits were sold to cities for street lighting. Someone mechanically inclined was sure to try to "improve" the device. Nearly every workman thought he knew more about the mechanism than the inventor did. Complaining of a lamp which had not worked properly, one man said; "I've had it all apart four times, and still it doesn't work." If the lamps didn't work, and news of this became widespread, it would wreck the business. Brush saw that he must make the whole mechanism as nearly foolproof as possible. He put it together without screws or bolts of any kind that could be taken out and lost. All necessary adjustments were made at the factory when the lamp was tested and then the parts were riveted, to make further testing or tinkering impossible. Also they were assembled a little like a Chinese puzzle.

The high-tension dynamos for series lighting that came later did not suffer so much tinkering because, as Brush used to say, they were powerful and "able to look out for themselves; they discouraged familiarity."

Nevertheless, it was impossible entirely to eliminate difficulties caused by trivial accidents and the lack of trained men to install or operate lighting plants. Poorly insulated lines led to "short circuits." Since commercial electricity was just starting, not many experts were available to whom Brush could delegate important work, and he himself used to go about as trouble man. Once he traveled fifteen hundred miles to take a common double-pointed tack from the bottom of a dynamo where it had short-circuited a field magnet. Occasionally damage appeared to have been done maliciously—perhaps by an employee who disliked the mechanism because unable to understand it. Long, fine wire nails were sometimes discovered in the field-magnet coils.

Brush used to tell of one lot of sixteen lamps sent back to the factory by a Boston agent with a letter stating that no one was able to make them work. "I examined and tested the lamps carefully, " said Brush, "and found them all right. Without making any change or adjustment whatever, except to change the numbers to conceal their identity, I sent the lamps back, with a letter stating I had personally examined and tested this lot and could guarantee them to be all right. They were put back in their original places, and worked beautifully, so the agent said; and he requested me as a personal favor to look over all lamps he might order in the future before they were shipped. He wanted to know what was the matter with the first set, but I never told him."

Perhaps it was his experience, in the early days of lighting, with the seeming stupidity of a great mass of human beings that made Brush, all the rest of his life, dubious if not contemptuous of the intelligence of the average man. But no matter how much he may have doubted the average man's wisdom, he always retained his sympathy and kindliness and never lost the common touch. Certainly there was nothing intolerant or haughty about him. He never shut himself off from the public. True, he was fairly inaccessible, but he could always be seen by almost anyone who had a semblance of an excuse to take up his time.

In order to keep pace with the rapidly increasing demand for Brush lighting systems, the Telegraph Supply Company of Cleveland underwent significant restructuring, giving birth to the Brush Electric Company in the summer of 1880. The new company constructed a 200,000 square foot factory located between Belden and McHenry streets at their intersection with Mason St. This new facility would thrive for a short time in the 1880's before it was closed due to the merging of Brush Electric with competitor Thompson-Houston Electric Company in 1889 and in turn with the Edison General Electric Company in 1891 to form the General Electric Company still known by the same name today.

These mergers marked Brush's exit from the emerging electrical industry. He sold his interest in Brush Electric and moved on to other fields of endeavor, never to return to the electric industry. Nevertheless, his innovations were an essential part of the development of electricity for commercial use.

Clyde Vernon Cessna

Aviation owes much to a farm boy whose name became synonymous with monoplanes and played a major role in making Wichita the "Air Capital of the World." Clyde Vernon Cessna had been a successful Overland automobile dealer in Enid, Oklahoma for several years until 1911 when he was struck with flying fever. Fascinated by the frail but efficient Bleriot XI monoplane that traversed the English Channel in 1909, Cessna eventually left Oklahoma for New York City, where he worked briefly for the Queen Aeroplane Company and learned about airplanes and how they were constructed. Cessna dubbed his first airplane the "Silverwing." It was an American-built copy of the Bleriot XI, and would eventually teach Cessna the art of aviating. Powered by a two-stroke, four-cylinder Elbridge "Aero Special" engine that developed 40 hp. at 1,050 RPM, the Elbridge was a marine powerplant that had been converted for aviation use. In Throughout 1911

Cessna made many flights in the airplane on the Great Salt Plains near Jet, Oklahoma in an effort to teach himself how to fly. He and Silverwing suffered numerous accidents, but in December 1911 Clyde made a highly successful, five-mile flight near Enid that included turns and ended with a safe landing at the departure point.

Flushed with success, Cessna severed his ties with the automobile business and devoted his time, energy, and money to exhibition flying. It was a lucrative endeavor for any pilot who could keep his airplane aloft for only a few minutes at holiday events and county fairs. During 1912-1915 he built several monoplanes, all of them powered by six-cylinder Anzani radial engines that developed 40-60 hp. Although successful, the Cessna Exhibition Company only whetted Clyde's appetite to become more involved in the fledgling aviation business. Flying was fun and profitable, but what he really wanted to do was manufacture and sell airplanes of his own design to the public. In 1916 he set up shop in a vacant building in Wichita, Kansas and built a new airplane for the 1917 exhibition season. Cessna also established a flight school at the "factory" and enrolled five young men as students. When the United States declared war on the Central Powers in April 1917, Cessna's exhibition flying ground to halt. Instead, he returned to farming at his home near Rago, Kansas and harvested wheat to help feed the "doughboys" fighting in France.

Clyde's interest in aeronautics never faded during the war, and he dreamed of returning to Wichita and resuming the manufacture of airplanes. Cessna continued flying, however, and bought a new Laird "Swallow" biplane that he flew during the early 1920s. He used the OX-5-powered Swallow to give his favorite nephew, Dwane Wallace, an introduction to the world of aviation. Late in 1924, Cessna was visited by Lloyd Stearman and Walter Beech, who had been key employees of the Swallow Company under leadership of the cantankerous Jacob M. "Jake" Moellendick. The two young men, in concert with a few other people, had split from Swallow and planned to form a new business to be known as the Travel Air Manufacturing Company. Stearman urged Cessna to join them, chiefly because Lloyd knew he and Beech needed Cessna's expertise in aviation as well as his money and equipment. It was a hard sell, but Cessna agreed.

In return for his participation and investment, Clyde was named president. The infant company began life in a cramped, 30x30-ft. space in the rear of a planing mill in downtown Wichita. Travel Air's first product was an attractive, two-bay biplane designed by Stearman and was dubbed the "Model A." It made its first flight in March 1925. At a price of more than $3,000, the OX-5-powered Model A was expensive compared with the plethora of war-surplus Curtiss JN-4 and Standard J-1 biplanes that still were available, but it outperformed them both and gradually sales increased to 19 airplanes the first year. The company introduced the improved Model B biplane in 1926 that featured the new, 200-hp. Wright J4 air-cooled radial engine. That year Cessna convinced Walter Beech that the company should offer a monoplane with an enclosed cabin for use by small airlines. Beech agreed, and the Travel Air Type 5000 was based largely on a monoplane designed and custom-built by Cessna earlier in 1926. A slightly larger and more powerful version of the prototype airplane was ordered by National Air Transport, and 8 eventually were delivered to the airline.

Despite the success of the Type 5000, Cessna was restless. In January 1927 he sold his stock and resigned from Travel Air to build a full cantilever monoplane he named the "Phantom." It was a graceful, three-place machine powered by a 90-hp. Anzani radial engine and flew well. In 1927 Cessna and Victor Roos joined forces to found the Cessna Aircraft Company on the west side of Wichita. With help from his talented son Eldon and other company engineers, in 1927-1929 Clyde marketed a succession of 4- and 6-place monoplanes designated Model AA, Model BW, and the popular Model AW series. With the advent of Wall Street's collapse in the autumn of 1929, Cessna and other manufacturers soon found themselves without customers for their products. To spur sales, Cessna slashed prices but to no avail. Faced with the prospect of bankruptcy, in 1931 the board of directors of the Cessna Aircraft Co. voted to oust Cessna and close the factory doors. It seemed as though Clyde's involvement in aviation was over, but he never gave up. Undaunted, Cessna and Eldon rented vacant facilities in the abandoned Travel Air complex on East Central Ave. and created the C.V. Cessna Aircraft Co. that specialized in building diminutive, custom racing airplanes. The most successful of these was the CR-3 owned and flown by the great air-racing pilot Johnny Livingston. In the wake of losing his company to the stockholders in 1931, Cessna was dealt another blow in 1933 when his close friend Roy Liggett died in the crash of the CR-2 racer built by Clyde and Eldon. Cessna's grief ran deep. He withdrew from aviation and retreated to his farm near Rago.

In 1934 his nephew Dwane Wallace, armed with a degree in aeronautical engineering and with help from his brother Dwight Wallace, wrested control of the defunct Cessna Aircraft Company from the stockholders and introduced the classic Cessna C-34 monoplane. Clyde agreed to participate in the new venture only in a ceremonial capacity, and was not involved directly in the day-to-day operations of the company. The C-34 was a success and was named the world's most efficient airplane. Dwane Wallace went on to guide the company through the turbulent 1930s, oversaw development of the twin-engine T-50 that became the famed Cessna "Bobcat" of World War Two fame, and introduced the Model 190/195, Model 120/140 into the post-war market. Later, these airplanes were followed by the ubiquitous Model 150 and 172 Skyhawk as well as the sleek Model 310 made famous by the Sky King television series. After more than 40 years in the aviation business and incalculable contributions to aeronautics, Clyde Cessna died in November 1954 age 74. He never held a pilot's license and had received only a rudimentary education, but his genius with airplanes coupled with an unshakable determination to succeed has made his name and legacy an icon in the history of flying.

Dhirubhai Ambani

Dhirubhai Ambani, Indian businessman, was born in Chorwad, Gujarat, on December 28, 1932. He died in Bombay on July 6, 2002, aged 69. Dhirubhai Ambani is survived by his wife, two sons and two daughters. His two American-educated sons have been in day-to-day control of the company since he suffered a stroke in 1986. He suffered a further stroke 12 days ago from which he never recovered.

Dhirubhai Ambani - Entrepreneur who built up the only Indian business to feature in the Forbes 500 One of India's most dynamic and flamboyant entrepreneurs, Dhirubhai Ambani was head of the multibillion-dollar Reliance group of industries with extensive interests in textiles, petrochemicals, energy and telecommunications. Combining a keen sense of business with a razor-sharp ability to negotiate his way through the labyrinth of the Indian political establishment, Ambani single-handedly built a business empire that in just three decades outgrew corporate houses such as the Tatas and Birlas which had dominated the country's industrial landscape for nearly a century.

Reliance is the only Indian private company to make the Fortune 500 list of the world's largest corporations, and Ambani was listed by Forbes as the 138th richest person in the world this year.

The son of a petty trader from a remote village in rural Gujarat, Dhirajlal Hirachand Ambani – known as Dhirubhai – moved to Aden as a teenager in order to seek his fortune. He started work as a petrol station attendant before taking up a clerical position for an oil company that was the sole distributor of Shell products there. While in Aden, home to many Gujarati expatriates, he realised that a discrepancy between the rial-sterling exchange rate and the intrinsic value of the silver content in Aden's coinage afforded an excellent opportunity to make money. This arbitrage generated some $3,000 in seed money for the modest trading enterprise that Ambani set up when he returned to Bombay in 1958.

The trading house Reliance Commercial Corporation began by importing polyester yarn and exporting spices. This was the era of India's infamous "licence-permit raj", when businessmen with political connections could corner export, import and manufacturing licences and accumulate huge fortunes.

Sensing an opportunity in the textile industry – higher disposable incomes were leading to Indians buying better, more expensive clothes – Ambani sought and received the necessary clearances to manufacture cloth from polyester fibre. He opened his first textile mill in Naroda, near Ahmedabad, in 1966 and then concentrated on quietly building up his business. Vimal, the textile brand he established, flourished and remains a household name in India today.

Though Reliance was a profitable enough concern, Ambani quickly calculated that further expansion –

especially into related sectors – would depend on access to a cheap source of capital. Rather than turning to the banking system, he decided to tap Bombay's fledgeling stock exchange, pioneering an equity cult that was to transform the corporate financing system in India. Reliance's initial public offering in 1977 saw 58,000 investors buying shares; eventually, the number of Reliance shareholders was to climb to some three million.

To Indian middle-class salary-earners, Ambani held out the promise of instant enrichment through the stock market. But he was no fly-by-night operator: Reliance shares offered genuine value, and those fortunate enough to have had faith in the company in the early years eventually became millionaires. Annual general meetings were held in sports stadiums where Ambani would be treated by shareholders with adulation and even reverence.

In 1982 Ambani began the process of backward integration, setting up a plant to manufacture polyester filament yarn. He subsequently diversified into chemicals, gas, petrochemicals, plastics, power and telecom services.

By the late 1980s the Reliance group was one of India's most influential and profitable concerns. However, the phenomenal growth of Reliance owed as much to Ambani's acumen as to the ease with which he was able to get official rules and regulations – including import tariffs – introduced, amended or scrapped in order to undercut his rivals and push his own business interests. His methods earned him many bitter enemies in India's corporate world. Ambani nevertheless forged ahead, cultivating friends in virtually every Indian political party and managing the media in such a way that critical stories about Reliance's unconventional business methods seldom made it into the newspapers.

The final phase of Reliance's diversification occurred in the 1990s when the company turned aggressively towards petrochemicals and telecommunications. But, like most business people, Ambani had rivals, the most bitter of whom was Nusli Wadia, of Bombay Dyeing, a patrician entrepreneur whose company was well established in the textile industry.

Ambani was also anxious to encourage the spread of information technology among India's poor. Through Reliance Industries he arranged computer education and training for thousands of students in schools in Bombay. "You are getting an opportunity. Make the best use of it," he told children in December during one of his last public speeches. "Be daring. Think big. You can be the best. If you believe in this, you will be the best."

Ambani also saw the Indian Government's privatisation programme as a means of further growth. Two months before his death, Reliance successfully bid for the giant public sector Indian Petro-Chemicals.

His two American-educated sons have been in day-to-day control of the company since he suffered a stroke in 1986. He suffered a further stroke 12 days ago from which he never recovered.

Dhirubhai H Ambani rose from humble beginnings to become chairman of India's largest private sector company. In one of his more candid moments, the otherwise reticent tycoon summed up the secret of his remarkable success story. Even those who question his business dealings... readily concede that Ambani had a vision and matchless business acumen

Think big, think fast and think ahead. Born in 1932 to a school teacher father in the small village of Chorwad in western Gujarat state, Ambani followed this advice all his life. He dreamt big even as a small boy when he used to sell hot snacks to pilgrims outside a temple in his native village. And he did not stop dreaming big even when he went to Aden as a petrol pump attendant at the age of 17 to help support his family. It was this desire to make it big in life which prompted his return to India in 1958. Ambani came to Bombay and started his first company, Reliance

Commercial Corporation, a commodity trading and export house.

The company was set up with an investment of 15,000 rupees (about $375). Forty-four years later Reliance has grown into a conglomerate with an annual turnover of $13.2bn. It is the only Indian private sector firm in the Fortune 500 list. In the process, the company has also acquired one of the world's largest groups of shareholders, with over four million investors putting their faith in its stock. In 1966 the Reliance group opened its first textile mill in Naroda in Ahmedabad. The textile mill won accolades in 1975 from a World Bank technical team, who described it as "excellent by developed country standards".

Two years later the company went public, evoking a tremendous response from investors. That made Ambani something of a revered figure among the stock investors' fraternity, who held him in awe from then on. They credit the Reliance chairman with introducing a stock market culture in the country. In the 25 years since it went public Reliance has become more than just a textile industry player. It now has interests in power, telecoms, petrochemicals and life sciences as well. Under Ambani's guidance it became one of the biggest first-generation success stories in Asia. Its founder will go down perhaps as the most controversial industrialist in India's corporate history.

He was known for assiduously cultivating those in positions of power. Many observers attribute his phenomenal rise to his close contacts with the Congress leadership in the 1970s and 1980s. But even those who question his business dealings - especially in the earlier years of Reliance - readily concede that Ambani had a vision and matchless business acumen. While he and his family may have begrudged what they thought was insufficient recognition from his peers and the press till the 1980s, all that changed in the last decade, during which the Reliance family really flourished. Asiaweek magazine voted Ambani amongst the 50 most powerful men in Asia - not once but three times, in 2000, 1998 and 1996.

The federation of Indian chambers of commerce and industry (FICCI) conferred on him the Indian entrepreneur of the 20th Century award. A poll conducted by The Times of India in 2000 voted him "creator of wealth in the century". And in December 2000 Ambani was honoured at a civic reception by the municipal corporation of Bombay. His sons, Mukesh and Anil, both of them groomed in business by their father, have turned into great business leaders in their own right. Rags to riches is click that is often applied to describe the climb up the ladder of even modestly successful businessmen. But it could hardly be more appropriately used than to trace the meteoric rise of Dhirubhani Ambani, Chairman of high flying Reliance Industries, rated among the top three business groups in India today.

From an initial investment of a mere Rs. 15000 in 1958 to start a trading house, followed by the setting up of his own tiny manufacturing facility in Gujarat in 1966, Ambani, Son of a rural school teacher, has managed to build up a synthetic yarn, textiles and petrochemicals empire that is today the third largest private sector mega corporation.

For the year ended March 1991, Reliance Industries is understood to have recorded a sales turnover of Rs. 2,300 crores (more than US $ 1 billion), making it the third largest private corporation in the country to day. Those who predicted that he was a conman, a confidence trickster, have had to eat their words. " I am the dubble that burst!" chortles Dhirubhai, sarcastically referring to the negative headlines that greeted his forays into the primary capital market in the early- 1980s.

Success on such a gigantic scale inevitable excites jealousy and enmity; and Ambani, today 58, has had to deal with his share. Reliance's have been the subject of several exposes in the press. But these have neither fazed the tycoon extraordinaire, nor halted the inexorable progress of his march forward towards his goal of becoming the undisputed No.1 in the country.

To any sort of sniping in the press, Dhirbhai has responded with stoic silence. Rarely has he reacted to even the most stringent media criticism. In the last couple of years, though, he has taken a leaf out of industrialist-cum press baron Ramnath Goenka's book. He has taken the precaution of shoring up his own strength in the media, not minding the expenditure of huge sums of money, and timing the launches of his products to a nicety.

Though not as physically hardy as before, Dhirubhai has not let the permanent handicap of the paralytic stroke blunt the edge of his razor-sharp brain. It is still from his fourth floor office in Maker tower IV at Nariman point that all major policy decisions which affect the future of the Reliance group are taken. The routine running of the organization is left to Mukesh and Anil, who nevertheless consult him in all key matters.

There are some opinion-makers, like well-known newspaper editor Vinod Mehta, who have referred in print to Dhirubhai Ambani as 'the embodiment of evil; However, to the Gujarati business community, he has assumed the status of demi-god. To al aspiring small-time entrepreneurs, he has become a sort of benchmark they aim at. And so, with each succeeding day, the legend to Dhirubhai Ambani continues to gather spice.

Ernest Bevin

Ernest Bevin (9 March 1881 - 14 April 1951) was a British labour leader, politician, and statesman, born in a small village in Somerset, England. His father, whom he never knew, was an agricultural labourer and his mother was a housemaid who died when he was eight. He had little formal education, leaving school in Crediton, Devon in 1890. At the age of eleven he went to work as a labourer, then as a truck driver in Bristol. In 1910 he became secretary of the Bristol branch of the Dockers' Union, and in 1914 he became a national organiser for the union.

In 1922 Bevin was one of the founding leaders of the Transport and General Workers Union, which soon became Britain's largest trade union. He was elected the union's general secretary, making him one of the country's leading labour leaders. Politically, he was a moderate socialist, strongly opposed to communism and direct action. He took part in the General Strike in 1926, but without enthusiasm.

On the other hand he had no great faith in parliamentary politics, although he was a member of the Labour Party from the time of its formation. He had poor relations with the first Labour Prime Minister, Ramsay MacDonald, and was not surprised when MacDonald defected and allied with the Conservatives during the economic crisis of 1931. He was a pragmatic trade unionist who believed in getting material benefits for his members through direct negotiations, with strike action to be used as a last resort.

During the 1930s, with the Labour Party split and weakened, Bevin co-operated with the Conservative government on practical issues. But during this period he became increasingly involved in foreign policy. He was a firm opponent of fascism and of British appeasement of the fascist powers. In 1935 he made a blistering attack on the pacifists in the Labour Party, leading to the resignation of Labour leader George Lansbury and his replacement by Clement Attlee.

In 1940 Winston Churchill formed an all-party coalition government to defend the country in the crisis of World War II. As part of this he appointed Bevin to the position of Minister for Labour and National Service. He was determined to make his mark in office and quipped "They say Gladstone was at the Treasury from 1860 until 1930. I'm going to be at the Ministry of Labour from 1940 until 1990." In this post he became the virtual dictator of Britain's wartime domestic economy. The Emergency Powers Act gave him complete control over the labour force and the allocation of manpower. During this period Bevin was responsible for diverting nearly 48,000 draftees away from military service to work in the coal industry. These workers became known as the Bevin Boys. Shortly after his appointment Bevin was elected unopposed to the House of Commons for a London constituency.

Bevin remained Minister of Labour until 1945 when Labour left the Coalition government. After the 1945 general election, Attlee had it in mind to appoint Bevin as Chancellor and Hugh Dalton as Foreign Secretary, but then changed his mind and swapped them round. Some claim that he was persuaded by King George VI to do so; but others note that whoever was Chancellor would have to work with Herbert Morrison, whom Bevin did not get on with. Bevin became Foreign Secretary at a time when Britain was almost bankrupt as a result of the war and could no longer afford to maintain its overseas Empire. Bevin was unsentimental about the Empire and approved an immediate British withdrawal from India and other territories.

In 1945, Bevins advocated creation of a United Nations Parliamentary Assembly, saying in the House of Commons that "There should be a study of a house directly elected by the people of the world to whom the nations are accountable."

He was also a determined anti-Communist, and was a strong supporter of the United States in the early years of the Cold War. Two of the key institutions of the post-war world, the North Atlantic Treaty Organisation and the Marshall Plan for aid to post-war Europe, were in part the result of Bevin's labours during these years. Bevin defined his foreign policy as being "that I can go to Victoria station and buy a ticket to anywhere I damn please".

Bevin's principal failure was in the British Mandated Territory of Palestine, where he opposed the plans of the Zionist movement to create a Jewish state. When dealing with the Middle East situation, he lacked diplomatic finesse, and had a tendency to make a bad situation worse by ill-chosen abrasive remarks, and obstinacy in adhering to policies which were a public relations disaster. He was infuriated by Zionist terrorism and attacks on British troops, but Britain's economic weakness, and its dependence on the financial support of the United States, compelled him to yield to American pressure and allow the United Nations to determine Palestine's future, resulting in the creation of Israel.

Bevin in office showed the same pragmatism combined with stubbornness that had characterised his years as a trade union leader. Like Churchill he was an old fashioned English patriot, which was why the two leaders worked well together. But he was also an internationalist, a supporter of the American alliance and European unity. He saw clearly that Britain's days of imperial greatness were over, something he did not regret since, he said, the working class had never benefitted from the Empire. His health failing, Bevin moved to become Lord Privy Seal in March 1951 but died, worn out from his labours, the following month. Such was his devotion to office that he died still holding to key to his red box.

Ezra Cornell

Ezra Cornell was an American businessman and, with Andrew Dickson White, was the founder of Cornell University.

He was born in Westchester County, New York, the son of a potter, Elijah Cornell. He was a first cousin, five times removed of Benjamin Franklin on his maternal grandmother's side. Having travelled extensively as a carpenter in New York State, Ezra, upon first setting eyes on Cayuga Lake and Ithaca, decided Ithaca would be his future home.

After settling in at Ithaca, Ezra quickly went to work proving himself as a carpenter. Colonel Beebe took notice of the industrious young man and made him the manager of his mill at Fall Creek.

Ezra Cornell was a birthright Quaker, but was later disowned by the Society of Friends for marrying outside of the faith to a "world's woman," a Methodist by the name of Mary Ann Wood. Ezra and Mary Ann were married March 19, 1831, in Dryden, New York.

On February 24, 1832, Ezra Cornell wrote the following response to his expulsion from The Society of Friends due to his marriage to Mary Ann Wood:

I have always considered that choosing a companion for life was a very important affair and that my happyness or misery in this life depended on the choice...

The young and growing family needed more income than could be earned as manager of Beebe's Mills. So, having purchased rights in a patent for a new type of plow, Ezra began what would be decades of travelling away from Ithaca. His territories for sales of the plow were the states of Maine and Georgia. His plan was to sell in Maine in the summer and the milder Georgia in the winter. With limited means, what transported Ezra between the two states were his own two feet.

Happening into the offices of the Maine Farmer in 1842, Ezra saw an acquaintance of his, one F.O.J. Smith, bent over some plans for a "scraper" as Smith called it. Smith had purchased a share of the telegraph patent held by Samuel F.B. Morse, and was attempting to devise a way of burying the telegraph lines in the ground in lead pipe. Ezra's knowledge of plows was put to the test and Ezra devised a special kind of plow that would dig a 2 1/2 foot ditch, lay the pipe and telegraph wire in the ditch and cover it back up as it went. Later it was found that condensation in the pipes and poor insulation of the wires impeded the electrical current on the wires and so hanging the wire from telegraph poles became the accepted method.

Ezra made his fortune in the telegraph business as an associate of Samuel Morse, having gained his trust by constructing and stringing the telegraph poles between Washington, D.C. and Baltimore, Maryland, as the first ever telegraph line of substance in the U.S. After joining with Morse, Cornell supervised the erection of many telegraph lines, earning a substantial fortune as a founder of the Western Union company.

Cornell was a Republican member of both the New York State Senate and Assembly.

Cornell retired from Western Union and turned his attention to philanthropy. He endowed the Cornell Library, a public library for the citizens of Ithaca. A lifelong enthusiast of science and agriculture, he saw great opportunity in the 1862 Morrill Land-Grant Colleges Act to found a university that would teach practical subjects, as opposed to the classics as favored by more traditional institutions. Andrew Dickson White helped secure the new institution's status as New York's land grant university, and Cornell University was granted a charter through their efforts in 1865.

Ezra Cornell entered the railroad business, but fared poorly due to the Panic of 1873. He began construction of a palatial Ithaca mansion, Llenroc to replace his farmhouse, Forest Home, but died before it was completed. Llenroc was maintained by Cornell's heirs for several decades until being sold to the local chapter of the Delta Phi fraternity, which occupies it to this day; Forest Home was sold to the Delta Tau Delta chapter and later demolished. Cornell is interred in Sage Chapel on Cornell's campus, along with Daniel Willard Fiske and Jennie McGraw.

A prolific letter writer, Ezra corresponded with a great many people and would write dozens of letters each week. This was due partly to his wide travelling, and also to the many business associates he maintained during his years as an entrepreneur and later as a politician and university founder. Cornell University has made the approximately 30,000 letters in the Cornell Correspondence available online.

In 1990, G. David Lowe, graduate of Cornell University and Space Shuttle astronaut, took with him into outer space a pair of tan silk socks worn by Ezra'Cornell on his wedding day in 1831.

Gerhard Herzberg

Gerhard Herzberg was born in Hamburg, Germany, on 25 December, 1904. He was married in 1929 to Luise Herzberg neé Oettinger and has two children. He was widowed in 1971.

Herzberg received his early training in Hamburg and subsequently studied physics at the Darmstadt Institute of Technology where in 1928 he obtained his Dr.Ing. degree under H. Rau. From 1928 to 1930 he carried out post-doctorate work at the University of Göttingen under James Franck and Max Born and the University of Bristol. In 1930 he was appointed Privatdozent and senior assistant in the Physics Department of the Darmstadt Institute of Technology.

In August 1935 Herzberg was forced to leave Germany as a refugee and took up a guest professorship at the University of Saskatchewan, for which funds had been made available by the Carnegie Foundation. A few months later he was appointed research professor of physics, a position he held until 1945. From 1945 to 1948 Herzberg was professor of spectroscopy at the Yerkes Observatory of the University of Chicago. He returned to Canada in 1948 and was made Principal Research Officer and shortly afterwards Director of the Division of Physics at the National Research Council. In 1955, after the Division had been divided into one in pure and one in applied physics, Herzberg remained Director of the Division of Pure Physics, a position which he held until 1969 when he was appointed Distinguished Research Scientist in the recombined Division of Physics.

Herzberg's main contributions are to the field of atomic and molecular spectroscopy. He and his associates have determined the structures of a large number of diatomic and polyatomic molecules, including the structures of many free radicals difficult to determine in any other way. Herzberg has also applied these spectroscopic studies to the identification of certain molecules in planetary atmospheres, in comets, and in interstellar space.

Herzberg has been active as President or Vice President of several international commissions dealing with spectroscopy. He was also Vice President of the International Union of Pure and Applied Physics from 1957 to 1963. He held the offices of President of the Canadian Association of Physicists for the year 1956-57 and President of the Royal Society of Canada for the year 1966-67.

Herzberg was elected a Fellow of the Royal Society of Canada in 1939 and of the Royal Society of London in 1951. He was Bakerian Lecturer of the Royal Society of London in 1960 and received a Royal Medal from the Society in 1971. He was George Fischer Baker Non-Resident Lecturer in Chemistry at Cornell University in 1968, and Faraday Medallist and Lecturer of the Chemical Society of London in 1970. He is Honorary Member or Fellow of a number of scientific societies, including the American Academy of Arts and Sciences, the Optical Society of America and the Chemical Society. He is also a Foreign Associate of the

National Academy of Sciences in Washington and a member of the Pontifical Academy of Sciences. He is a Companion of the Order of Canada. He has received many other medals and awards and holds Honorary Degrees from a number of universities in Canada and abroad, including one from the University of Stockholm.

Gail Borden

As an American philanthropist, businessman, and inventor, Gail Borden, Jr. envisioned food concentrates as a means of safeguarding the human food supply. He was the first to develop a commercial method of condensing milk, and the dairy company founded by him expanded and diversified to become a sizable corporation operating in many areas of business.

Gail Borden, Jr. (1801-1874). Gail Borden, Jr., inventor, publisher, surveyor, and founder of the Borden Company, son of Gail and Philadelphia Borden, was born in Norwich, New York, on November 9, 1801. In 1816 the family moved to New London, Indiana, where Borden obtained his only formal schooling, totaling not more than a year and a half. He is thought to have been captain of the local militia when barely twenty years old. In 1822 he was a principal figure in rescuing a freedman from rustlers. Shortly afterward he moved to Mississippi in search of a milder climate to cure a persistent cough. In Mississippi Borden surveyed and taught school. In 1826 he was official surveyor for Amite County as well as deputy federal surveyor.

After arriving at Galveston Island on December 24, 1829, he farmed and raised stock in upper Fort Bend County and spent some time in surveying. By February 1830 he had succeeded his brother, Thomas H. Borden, as surveyor for Stephen F. Austin's colony. In 1832 Borden was named one of three members of the San Felipe committee of correspondence. In the Convention of 1833 he represented Lavaca District . He also assumed many of the duties of colonial secretary for Austin in the absence of Samuel M. Williams.

As early as January 1835 Borden made plans to found a newspaper, but it was October 10 before the first issue of his Telegraph and Texas Register, published in partnership with his brother Thomas and Joseph Baker, appeared in San Felipe. In the meantime he had prepared the first topographical map of Texas and had resumed his responsibilities on the committee of correspondence. Borden published the Telegraph in San Felipe until March 1836, in Harrisburg in April 1836, in Columbia from August 1836 to April 1837, and in Houston in May and June 1837. In October 1835 he was appointed collector for the Department of Brazos, a post he held until 1837. In October and November 1836 he helped lay out the site of Houston.

On June 20, 1837, Borden sold his partnership in the Telegraph to Jacob W. Cruger and became the first collector of the port of Galveston under the Republic of Texas. His first term as collector lasted from June 1837 to December 1838, when Mirabeau B. Lamar removed him for political reasons. His second term lasted from December 1841 to April 1843; he resigned after a dispute with President Sam Houston over evaluation of exchequers.

From 1839 to 1851 Borden was secretary and agent for the Galveston City Company, which owned most of Galveston Island and for which he helped sell 2,500 lots. He invented a "locomotive bath house" for Galveston women who wished to bathe in the Gulf of Mexico. As an alderman he helped to rid the island temporarily of gamblers. He and his first wife reputedly became the first Anglo-Americans to be baptized in the Gulf west of the Mississippi River. He became Sunday school missionary to the poor and to travelers. He was a trustee of the Texas Baptist Education Society, which founded Baylor University. And he was an officer in the local temperance society and deacon and clerk of the local Baptist church. In 1842 Borden directed insular defenses against an expected Mexican invasion.

In the middle 1840s he began inventing. He is supposed to have experimented with large-scale refrigeration as a means of preventing yellow fever and with a terraqueous machine, a sort of prairie schooner that would go on land or water. In 1849 he perfected a meat biscuit, made of dehydrated meat compounded with flour, which he tried to market on a worldwide scale in partnership with Ashbel Smith. Although this project left him deeply in debt, for seven years Borden struggled to sell meat biscuits. For this purpose he moved to New York in 1851 to be nearer trade centers.

In 1853 he sought a patent on a process for condensing milk in vacuum, but it was 1856 before he received American and British patents. He then dropped the meat biscuit to devote himself to condensing milk. He opened a factory in Connecticut in 1856 but failed, then tried and failed again in 1857. Through Jeremiah Milbank, a New York financier, he received new backing and opened another factory in Connecticut in 1858. When the Civil War brought intensified demand for condensed milk, sales grew so much that Borden's success was assured. He opened another factory in Connecticut, two in New York, and one in Illinois and licensed other concerns in Pennsylvania and Maine. He also invented processes for condensing various fruit juices, for extract of beef, and for coffee. After the Civil War he established a meat-packing plant at Borden, Texas, twelve miles west of Columbus, and a sawmill and copperware factory at Bastrop.

After 1871 he spent his winters in Texas because of the milder climate. In 1873 he built a freedmen's school and a white children's school, organized a day school and a Sunday school for black children, aided in constructing five churches, maintained two missionaries, and partially supported numerous poorly paid teachers, ministers, and students. Borden married Penelope Mercer in Mississippi in 1828; they had seven children. In 1845 he married Augusta Stearns, and in 1860 he married Emeline Eunice Church. He died in Borden, Texas, on January 11, 1874; his body was shipped by private car to New York to be buried in Woodlawn Cemetery.

George Bradshaw

George Bradshaw (July 29, 1801 - August, 1853) was an English cartographer, printer and publisher and the originator of the railway timetable.

Bradshaw was born at Windsor Bridge, Pendleton, Lancashire. On leaving school he was apprenticed to an engraver at Manchester, eventually setting up on his own account in that city as an engraver and printer, principally of maps. Bradshaw himself was a religious man. Although far from wealthy, when he was young his parents enabled him to take lessons from a minister who was devoted to the teachings of Emanuel Swedenborg. Later in his life, he joined the Society of Friends and gave a considerable part of his time to philanthropic work. He worked a great deal with radical reformers such as Richard Cobden in organising peace conferences and in setting up schools and soup kitchens for the poor of Manchester.

George Bradshaw married in 1839. While touring Norway in 1853 he contracted cholera and died in August of that year without being able to return to England. He is interred in the cemetery adjoining the cathedral of Oslo.

Bradshaw's name was already known as the publisher of Bradshaws Maps of Inland Navigation, which detailed the canals of Lancashire and Yorkshire, when, on October 19, 1839, soon after the introduction of railways, the world's first railway timetable was published in Manchester. It cost sixpence and was a cloth-bound book entitled Bradshaws Railway Time Tables and Assistant to Railway Travelling, the title being changed in 1840 to Bradshaws Railway Companion, and the price raised to one shilling. A new volume was issued at occasional intervals, a supplementary monthly time-sheet serving to keep the book up to date.

In December 1841, acting on a suggestion made by his London agent, William Jones Adams, Bradshaw reduced the price of his timetables to the original sixpence, and began to issue them monthly under the title Bradshaws Monthly Railway Guide. From then on the book, in the meanwhile familiar yellow wrapper, became synonymous with its publisher: For Victorians and Edwardians alike, a railway timetable was "a Bradshaw", no matter by which railway company it had been issued and whether George Bradshaw had been responsible for its production or not.

The eight page edition of 1841 had grown to 32 pages by 1845 and to 946 pages by 1898. In 1918 a Bradshaw would still only cost two shillings and in 1937 half a crown. When, in 1865, Punch praised Bradshaw's publications, it stated that "seldom has the gigantic intellect of man been employed upon a work of greater utility." At last, some order had been imposed on the chaos that had been created by countless rail companies whose tracks criss-crossed the country and whose uncoordinated network was rapidly expanding. Bradshaw's publications minutely recorded all changes and became the standard manual for rail travel for more than a century. The last Bradshaw, No. 1521, was printed in June 1961.

Glenn Hammond Curtiss

A great deal has been written about the Wrights. Aviation historians are still debating their story, still comparing their efforts with those of other pioneers, even against new claims for the invention of the airplane that have recently surfaced.

Much less has been written about Curtiss, undeservedly, since he almost single-handedly made enormous technical and business contributions to aviation. His is a unique success story; he advanced the state of the art in everything he did in life, and he did many things.

Virtually self-taught, he became the premier designer of aircraft engines in the U.S., perhaps in the world. He built motorcycles of such high quality and refinement that had he chosen to remain in that business, the Curtiss would undoubtedly be one of the leading machines today.

A "natural" engineer, he quickly grasped the secrets of powered flight and produced airplanes of such advanced design that he snatched the lead from the Wrights and took charge of American aviation.

Historians can trace the Curtiss name through many centuries in Kent and Sussex in England, further still to a Norman knight who came to Britain with William the Conquer in 1066.

Our story begins in the last century. Curtiss was born in 1878 in Hammondsport, New York, a small town on Keuka Lake in the midst of the wine country in the Finger Lakes region. The Curtiss logo dates back to 1903.

Hammondsport had been a town of little distinction, when just prior to the Civil War, a newly arrived Episcopal clergyman planted grape clippings carried from the Hudson River Valley. Sun, rain and soil were perfect for grape growing, and soon Hammondsport was overgrown with grapevines in frontyards, backyards or wherever there was room for planting. Here was the beginning of the wine industry in New York State. Soon expert vintners, members of the Masson family, were enticed from France to produce premium wines; the first American champagne came from Hammondsport. Wine is part of the Curtiss story—the Massons and other winemakers helped to finance his fledgling businesses.

Two Curtiss couples arrived in Hammondsport in 1876 under the auspices of the Methodist Episcopal Church: Claudius G. Curtiss and his wife Ruth Bramble, their son Frank Richmond Curtiss and his wife Lua Andrews. Claudius was a clergyman, his son Frank, a harnessmaker. Frank and Lua would have two children, Glenn Hammond and Rutha Luella.

Following is a portion of the Curtiss family tree which includes Glenn's wife, Lena and their two sons Carlton and Glenn H. Jr.

Each town in the area boasted a glen a valley where pleasant summer afternoons were spent swimming, picnicking, pitching horseshoes, etc. Curtiss was named Glenn after this, his middle name after the town where he was born.

Glenn's father and grandfather both died when he was a child, his upbringing taken over by the women in the family. When he was twelve, his mother remarried, and the family moved to Rochester. There his sister, Rutha, who was deaf as the result of childhood meningitis, received special training; Glenn worked as a Western Union bicycle messenger and later for the budding Eastman Kodak Company assembling cameras. He became a good photographer; in fact, he indicated photography as his profession on his marriage license in 1898.

Although not a good student, he finished the eighth grade. His interests in life then, were mathematics and machinery.

He took up bicycle racing, spending his summers in Hammondsport with his grandmother, training hard and competing in local races. He became the champion bicycle rider for western New York State.

Offered a job in the local Hammondsport bicycle shop, he proved his technical and business skills, starting his own shop in town and two others nearby in Bath and Corning only a few years later. He called his product the Hercules.

Curtiss was a natural competitor. Although a daredevil, he sized-up his opponents' skills, equipment, and the track itself and pre-determined a strategy that would win the race for him. He would later do the same with airplanes.

Motorcycles

He saw an early motorcycle on display at an exposition in Buffalo, the Thomas Auto-Bi. The Thomas Company advertised one-cylinder gasoline engine kits appropriate for installation on a bicycle. Curtiss ordered one of these and found that most of the parts were unfinished castings, and machining instructions were poor. With help from a local shop he managed to machine and assemble an engine. No mention was made of a carburetor in the manufacturer's instructions; he designed and made his own from a tomato can. After installing the engine on one of his bicycles, the whole town turned out to witness the first demonstration of a gasoline-powered vehicle in Hammondsport. The year was 1901. Curtiss' motorbike worked, but he had to jump from the uncontrollable machine and almost broke his neck as it roared toward Keuka Lake. He was pleased with this performance; it put everything into perspective. The engine was too heavy the bike frame too light, and the machine lacked controllability. His next models corrected all these and soon included a new engine of his own design which became his production engine. Curtiss was a genius with engines. His first single-cylinder was powerful, lightweight and amazingly reliable for the day.

By 1902 he was manufacturing motorcycles in two locations and extended his bicycle trade name, Hercules, to both motors and motorcycles. One of his innovations was the invention of the twist-grip handlebar control, still standard today on virtually all motorcycles.

Soon there would be many competing machines in the U.S.; more than twenty-five brands appeared early in the century with varying degrees of technical success.

In 1901 a mechanic named Oscar Hedstrom built an excellent motorcycle in Springfield, Massachusetts. It worked so well that a local businessman, George Hendee, bought the design and put it into immediate production, building 143 units in 1902. He called his machine "Indian".

A motorcycle gained fame by winning races and other competitive events, which were becoming very popular throughout the US Curtiss was ready for competition; he had demonstrated the reliability of the Hercules by completing an uneventful 200-mile run in New York State on unimproved roads. He entered his first motorcycle race on Labor Day 1902 in Brooklyn and was beaten by the Indian.

He was nevertheless complimented for the excellence of his machine and was rewarded with a rash of new orders, now from as far away as Australia.

His business was growing so rapidly, capital was needed to expand the factory. His was the G.H. Curtiss Manufacturing Company rescued by the investment of local townsfolk, the mayor, the Masson family and other wine producers.

Curtiss, the competitor, was raring to get back on the racetrack with a more powerful motorcycle. He designed the first two-cylinder machine in the US, took it to Riverdale on Memorial Day 1903 and made the Indians eat his dust. In the afternoon he motored to Yonkers and easily won a ten-mile race there and was suddenly the American motorcycle champion.

As a note of interest, simultaneously with Curtiss' and Indian's motorcycling efforts, a group of mechanics and draftsmen were struggling in Milwaukee to make their first motorcycle.

Bill Harley, three members of the Davidson family, a German draftsmen who knew European engines, and Ole Evinrude of outboard motor fame built the first Harley-Davidsons in 1903, single-cylinder 3 HP machines not yet ready to enter the competitive arena. By the end of 1905 only 16 Harley's had been built.

Soon after the Hercules name became well known, a California company, which had copyrighted the name, advised Curtiss that he was infringing and would be sued if the name weren't dropped. Discussing this problem during a haircut, his barber, Claude Jenkins, suggested he use his own name and designed the logo which endured through the Curtiss Propeller Division era.

Curtiss did not realize it at the time but his engines were drawing a great deal of interest, not only with motorcyclists, but with aviation enthusiasts as well. His engines were the lightest per power output that could be obtained anywhere;

the two-cylinder was of very advanced design, with roller-bearing crankshaft and connecting rods and pressure lubrication—unique features for that time. But Curtiss had virtually no exposure to or interest in aviation. Shortly after he won motorcycling honors in 1903, the Wrights made their first flight which, although reported widely in US newspapers, did not receive much attention in Hammondsport.

Enough said about motorcycling, except for Curtiss' supreme masterpiece of motorcycle engineering and racing. In 1907 he drove his monstrous creation, a V-8 powered behemoth on a Florida beach at 136 miles per hour and earned the title, "The fastest man alive". It was the fastest speed achieved in history up to that time.

Captain Thomas Baldwin was a renowned showman of the day, involved in expositions, fairs, circuses. . . a sort of P.T Barnum interested in making money from the sensational. One of his favorite props was a gas-filled balloon which he flew and demonstrated as part of his public shows. He and his brother Sam, in fact, invented the parachute and demonstrated successful jumps from their balloon.

Tom Baldwin wished to motorize his balloon and sought a suitable engine for the purpose. The best he could find was a French engine which, although the lightest available, was overweight. In fact, Baldwin himself was overweight. With him and the French engine in place, his airship would not rise from the ground.

One day a spectator arrived on a purring Curtiss 2-cylinder motorcycle. When Baldwin spied the engine, he knew it was the one he needed for his airship. He wired Hammondsport, ordering an engine for immediate delivery. Curtiss did not have a new one in stock, but polished up a used engine taken from one of his motorcycles. Baldwin installed this, and together with the hiring of a flyweight balloonist, successfully powered his airship, which he called the California Arrow.

At the first opportunity, Baldwin visited Hammondsport, met Curtiss and announced plans for new larger airships with Curtiss motors. This resulted in a new V-4 of 16 horsepower. When the San Francisco earthquake destroyed Baldwin's facility there, he moved to Hammondsport and built his airship #4 with Curtiss' close supervision of the engine installation. The success of Baldwin's airships led to a US Army contract in 1908 for Dirigible No. 1, the Army's first airship.

When Baldwin's airship No. 4 was completed, Curtiss was invited to take it up. He did, controlling it perfectly, and got his first taste of the excitement of flying.

Curtiss' business was thriving. There were many purchasers for aircraft engines, a lucrative business—an engine bringing twice the price of a complete motorcycle. Curtiss became involved in propeller design for Baldwin's airships; he built a propeller-driven "wind-wagon", a tricycle vehicle with engine and prop mounted behind the driver. He skittered around the byways of Hammondsport, testing propellers, usually barely under control.

John Jacob Astor

John Jacob Astor was not born a wealthy fur trader. Instead, he was born in Baden, Germany in 1763, the third son of a butcher. One brother, Henry, left for New York, while another, George, travelled to London to open up business in musical instruments. John followed his brother George first, working with him in London. However, in 1783, Astor left for New York, whre, during the voyage, he met another immigrant who told him about prosperous fur trading opportunities in America. Astor was in New York by 1784, married in 1785, and had opened a shop by 1786. He would purchase furs and sell musical instruments of his brother's initially. Soon, Astor established connections in the rising industry, and, along with Montreal fur traders, began to look East to the Orient, whre American furs were in high demand. This is where the story of Astoria begins to take shape.

Astor, in the late 1790s, paid great attention to the stirrings of Peter Pond, Alexander Mackenzie and other "prophets" who foretold the possible benfits of a western trade empire. He also met Alexander Henry, a businessman in Montreal, who furthered his education concerning the ideas of western trading posts. As Astor began to formulate how he could cash in on this opportunity, it became clear that the plan was not exclusively financial and technical, but political as well. Thus Astor would have to court local and national governmants, as welll as fur companies of America and Canada.

His first connection came with New York Governor DeWitt Clinton, nephew of the Vice President. Astor revealed to Clinton his plan of a chain of fur trading posts in the Pacific Northwest. He didn't meet with Clinton, though, just to talk. He wanted first the approval and chartering of his comapny, the Pacific Fur Company. The charter was granted him in April of 1809. What he was mostly after, though, was the affect that Governor Clinton could impose on his uncle, the vice president. Astor wanted "approbation" from the federal government, a fairly vague term which meant full or part approval. Astor realized that in such a venture he would want governmental approval and protection. He recieved some help in 1808 when his letter was delivered to Vice President Clinton. Now Astor could move farther up in the government ranks in his seeking of approbation.

Astor's next step was to meet with President Jefferson, which he did in summer of 1808 in Washington, DC. Jefferson promised "general support", and also that of protection from hostile actions of the North West company. In the fall, Astor went to Montreal, where he hoped to buy the Michilimackinac Company, which trapped in the Great Lakes region. He wanted to create a boundary line with Canadian fur traders - with control of this company he could be in control of the southern Great Lakes areas. However, his offer was rejected. Stern competition would continue with the Canadians.

By 1809 the North West Company was back to their old ways by sending explorers to the west after a few years of inactivity. Simon Fraser and David Thompason both ventured west, and Astor forced himself to act in response to these activities. His plan was for a ship to sail to the mouth of the Columbia first, build a fort and then be joined by an overland party which would depart from St. Louis. He panned for Wilson Price Hunt to lead this overland group - leaving as soon as spring of 1810. Hunt was a man fascinated with the west, a merchant who had met Lewis and Clark. Astor would need more governmental support.

Astor wrote a letter to Secretary of the Treasury Gallatin, which in turn was read to Secretary of War Eustis and eventually President Madison. He asked for increased support and recognition of his Pacific Fur Company. However, Washington promised only "economic nationalism", meaning that they would go no further than they had already in supporting Astor. Thus, Astor ventured to Montreal to see if a deal could be made with the North West Company. In Fall of 1809 a cooperation of mutual interest was attempted, but the deal fell through. Astor would have to act almost entirely on his own.

However, soon after Astor hired three North West men to be members on the expedition. These men arrived in New York in March 1810. The rest of the men were hired and signed the Articles of Agreement, which included the goals and responsibilities of the Astorians. The main goal was for a fort at the mouth of the Columbia, and accompanying trading posts in the region. With his plan coming together, Astor once again sought support. No Canadian support came. However, in July 1810, when the plan was aready in action, the North West company accepted his deal and sent David Thompson to meet the Astorians with a partners in cooperation plan. However, this plan would never really develop, as the Astorians were well along in their own dealings when Thompson arrived in July, 1810.

In early 1810 the final piece of the Astoria plan came into place. This was Astor's dealings with the Russians of the Pacific coast. As early was the 1780s, Russian "promyshlenniks" had been in Alaska. These voyages were led by Gregorii Shelikhov. However, Catherine the Great never really saw the value of Russian assertion in the Pacific fur regions. By 1797, though, the various Russians dealing in furs merged to form the United American Comapny, and in 1799 Emperor Paul formed a twenty year monopoly with the fur traders under the name of the Russian American Comapany. A colony at New Archangel was led by Alexander Baranov. In fall of 1809 Baronov met with Astor to deal. Indians had been harassing the Russians with weapons attained from the seventy two American ships which traded in the Pacific from 1787 to 1806. Baronov also was unable to trade with China. Astor proposed that the Russians and Americans squeeze the British out of the west. There was little Astor could do about the Indians, but, in return for Baronov's cooperation, he would deliver New Archangel supplies, then carrying their furs to the East and trade the furs in the Orient for a higher profit. In 1811 Astor sent son in law Adrian Benton to St. Petersburg, who rejected the plan. Astor would decide to then deal directly with the Russian American Company. The final plan called for cooperation between Astor and Baronov's traders, no selling of Astorian weapons to the Indians, a monoploy on Astor's supplies being purchased by the Russians, and Astor's carrying of the Russian furs to Canton, China. This plan was finally approved in late 1812. But before all of these plans could become reality, Astor would have to establish his fort at the Columbia.

By spring 1810 the expeditions were being put together. Wilson Price Hunt met in Montreal to choose men. Two other leaders of the overland party were McKay and Donald Mackenzie. Clerks were needed. Thus Gabriel Franchere and Alexander Ross were hired. This expedition, the first American of its kind since Lewis and Clark, left Montreal in July of 1810 as a party of 16. They travelled through the Great

Lakes, down the Mississippi, and to St. Louis, their "jumping off" point. Leaving in March of 1811, the crew followed Lewis and Clark's route for a bit but opted for a southern pass through the continental divide. Their hardships were evident the whole trip, as they had to eat horsemeat at the Snake River junction. Travelling down the Columbia, the men arrived to find a fort built at Astoria, the mouth of the Columbia. They had finished the journey in Febuary of 1812. The seaward contingent had arrived much earlier.

Astor purchased his sailing vessel, the Tonquin, in August of 1810 for $37,860. It was 94 feet long, 25 feet wide, and 12 feet deep. Having two Pacific voyages to it's name, Astor thought he had made a wise decision. He hired Captain Jonathan Thorn to lead. Thorn, a hot tempered Navy lieutenant, would prove to be an able yet negative aspect of the trip. The relations between him and the men were poor at best. Along with the sailing Astorian laborers were four specialized men: Johann Koaster, a carpenter, George Bell, a cooper, Job Aitkem, a boat builder, and Augustus Roussel, a blacksmith.

The Tonquin departed New York Harbor in September, 1810. An escort was requested for protection from British ships who had been impressing American sailors, but the actual outcome of this request remains a mystery. While some of the men claim that the USS Constitution escorted them, nowhere in the Constitution's manifest is this evident. The voyage was unpleasant for the men. Thorn especially hated the Canadians, and thought the clerk's journals were secret enemy documents. Thus, the men, many of whom were Scots Irish, spoke amongst themselves in either French or Scots Irish, neither of which Thorn could understand.

By December 1810 they were around the Cape Horn of South America. By Febuary of 1811 they were in Hawaii, the normal breaking point of the journey. There they met and traded with King Kamehameha. The ship was restocked with supplies, and goat's, pigs, and other livestock were purchased. Twelve Hawaiians were signed up for service at

Astoria. The Tonquin left Hawaii in March, and by March 22 was at the mouth of the Columbia. The mouth of the Columbia is an extremely dangerous place for large vessels. The colliding of the river and ocean creates a punchbowl of high waters. High winds contribute to turbulent seas, and sandbars make navigation a nightmare. The Columbia claimed the lives of eight Astorians before the fort was even established. John Fox, leading a longboat crew into the river towards land, capsized and drowned.

The Astorians met the Chinook Indians and thus trade began. The fort site was selected, a fort erected, and thus Astoria was established. It would be almost a year until the overland crew would arrive and Astoria would be at full force. Despite the hardships that both the overland and seaward expeditions endured, both arrived at Astoria in shape enough to carry on their business enterprise. However, the stormy beginnings of Astoria would be a foreboding of things to come.

John Logie Baird

1996 was the seventieth anniversary of the birth of television. John Logie Baird, the father of this pervasive technology, first publicly demonstrated television on 26 January 1926, in his small laboratory in the Soho district of London. Although large companies with great financial support were also working on the problem of television, Baird managed to surpass them all with very little money, a handful of unpaid helpers and equipment pieced together using rather unconventional materials. For example, Baird's choice of mechanical scanning as the most effective way of achieving true television required the use of spinning discs – which of financial necessity were made of hatboxes and mounted on a coffin lid. This short account, written for the anniversary of the invention of television, not only recounts the events that led up to the first demonstration of television by John Logie Baird, but also describes some of the Scottish inventor's many areas of investigation.

John Logie Baird was born on 14 August 1888, the fourth child of Jessie and the Reverend John Baird. His family lived in a large house called "The Lodge" in Helensburgh, a coastal town which lies 25 miles northwest of Glasgow. By the turn of the century, this house had seen the development of a telephone exchange, had been supplied with electric lighting and had been the site of an early flight experiment, all of which were the work of the imaginative youngest child.

A telephone exchange was quite an achievement for a young schoolboy. Other children played with tin cans and pieces of string, but John Baird had tried this method and was dissatisfied. Instead, he made an electric exchange and connected his home to those of four of his friends. Unfortunately this telephone service was not in use for very long, as one of its low hanging wires caused the driver of a hansom cab to have an accident. This driver's protests soon led to the removal of the telephone wires from their various positions around the neighbourhood. Never one to waste resources, the boy then used the wires from his telephone exchange to set up a lighting system for The Lodge. Run by a petrol powered generator in the back garden, this activity made his parents' home the first in Helensburgh to have electric lighting.

John Logie Baird was also conducting experiments in other areas of research. The first year of this century saw the young inventor standing on the roof of his parents' house with a home-made glider. This experiment took place on a flat section of the roof of The Lodge, and had a rather strong impact on the rest of Baird's life. The glider was constructed with the assistance of his friend Godfrey Harris, but may not have been as well designed or constructed as some of his later machinery. Baird describes this incident in his autobiography *Sermons, Soap and Television*:

I had no intention of flying, but before I had time to give more than one shriek of alarm, Godfrey gave the machine one terrific push, and I was launched shrieking into the air. I had a few very nauseating seconds while the machine rocked wildly and then broke in half and deposited me with a terrific bump on the lawn.

Fortunately, Baird was not seriously hurt by this fall, but elements of this particular experiment would surface again in his life. Just as he collaborated with young Godfrey Harris, he would always be ready to enlist the help of others. In later life, Baird's experiments would associate him with a diverse range of people, from a bright teen age radio enthusiast named Victor Mills to Winston Churchill's chief scientific advisor Frederick Lindemann.

This glider incident gave Baird a great fear of flying, which would prevent him from travelling easily, and also foreshadowed the great difficulty he would have in maintaining his physical well-being. Even as a child, from the time he suffered an undiagnosed illness at the age of two, Baird's health was never good. Later on, as well as incurring various minor injuries in the early days of his work on television, he would also suffer from repeated physical breakdowns. After falling victim to a heart attack, Baird had time to write his autobiography while he was convalescing, but lived only another five years. He died on 14 June 1946, at a time when he was about to reinstate Britain as a world leader in television technology.

A healthy social life and an inventive nature seemed to be at variance with Baird's school career. The twelve year old boy is described in his school report as "very slow," "timid" and "...by no means a quick learner." Nevertheless, Baird was not discouraged by his academic record, and in 1906 entered a diploma course in electrical engineering at the Glasgow and West of Scotland Technical College. He graduated from this course on 1 October 1914, and then entered Glasgow University to upgrade his diploma to a Bachelor of Science. Unfortunately, World War One broke out, and Baird never completed his degree. Baird, now 26 years old, tried on many occasions to enlist with the army, but was repeatedly rejected as unfit for army service. He therefore continued his various investigations, including work on television.

The earliest suggestion of Baird's interest in television technology is an experiment which he conducted at his parents' house in 1903. This experiment involved the attempted construction of a selenium photo-electric cell, but was unsuccessful, and Baird burnt his hands in the process. Although John Logie Baird suggests that he first started work on a complete television system in Hastings, there is evidence that he actually began ten years earlier. In 1976, Peter Waddell wrote an article which quoted sources suggesting that Baird first experimented with a complete television system between 1912 and 1915, while living in Yoker and working towards his electrical engineering diploma at the Glasgow College. R.W. Burns reinforces this suggestion in his 1986 book *British Television: The Formative Years.* In 1996, Malcolm Baird said that his father's work in Yoker can now be considered a definite possibility.

The most fully substantiated evidence for Baird's early television work is found on the south coast of England, in Hastings in 1923. Even here, there is a certain amount of controversy, for Baird himself writes that he travelled directly from London to Hastings, where he then started work on television. This statement is untrue, for although Baird did travel to the south coast, it was not first to Hastings but to another seaside town called Folkestone. Since this new information has been released, a plaque has been placed on 26 Guildhall Street in Folkestone, in order to commemorate Baird's early television work there. According to R.W. Burns, Baird was definitely in Hastings during the winter of 1922 to 1923. This situation therefore suggests that Baird was simultaneously renting accommodation in Folkestone and Hastings.

In order to tackle the problem of television, John Logie Baird chose a system which employed mechanical scanning. There were various methods available to achieve this, and Baird selected a system which used the Nipkow disc as being the most promising. Invented by Paul Nipkow in 1884, this disc had a series of apertures cut into it, which could then be used to scan an image. This disc was combined with other discs, and produced a very different television set from the ones we use today, for Baird's system did not use the cathode ray tube which is the most common method of displaying an image on modern television equipment Baird was quite capable of inventing his machines, but he was not quite so capable of their construction. For this reason, he enlisted the help of two young Hastings boys, Victor Mills and Norman Loxdale. Mills assisted Baird in the refinement of his electronics and Loxdale made various components, including a Nipkow disc with two spirals of apertures which were covered with orange-red and blue-green filters. Loxdale later described his surprise at Baird's experimentation with this disc, as at that time the inventor had not yet achieved a television picture. This surprise can be more easily understood when one realises that this disc was capable of producing colour and/or three dimensional pictures.

Other experiments conducted by Baird at this time involved the transmission, reflection and detection of radio waves which determined the distance of an object. According to Loxdale, Baird did some of these experiments in his laboratory at 8 Queen's Avenue in Hastings, and the inventor later conducted further experiments of a similar nature from a local hilltop. The significance of these tests is that they were very early examples of experimentation with a technology that was later to become famous during World War Two – namely, radar.

Although Baird was not accepted into military service at the beginning of World War One, there is evidence that he joined the military services. On 1 June 1976, a Mr. James Heath wrote a letter to Helensburgh library, stating that he saw Baird in 1928 or 1929, dressed as "...a Lieutenant in the Supplementary Reserve of Officers... was conducting experiments in several types of army field communications and new systems." Heath suggests that these new systems involved "...an invention to send pictures through the atmosphere." In other words, this statement implies that John

Logie Baird was not only working on television for public use, but also for use in secret signalling for the armed forces.

Tom McArthur and Peter Waddell report the above information in their book *The Secret Life of John Logie Baird*, which was published in 1986. These authors have uncovered a remarkable amount of previously undisclosed work which connects John Logie Baird with radar and secret signalling, and more information will eventually be published by Peter Waddell and Douglas Brown on this subject.

There were two main problems which Baird would have to overcome in order to achieve television: the problem of the insensitivity of the photo-electric cell, and also the difficulty of obtaining a clear image. At first, he could only produce pictures of the outline of shapes, known as "shadowgraphs." C.F. Jenkins in America and D. von Mihaly in Hungary were also working on the problem of television, and had also produced shadowgraphs. However, Baird was able to solve his main difficulties and go beyond these two inventors in achieving true television.

To overcome his first problem, Baird worked with an assistant in Tunbridge Wells on the development of a photo-electric cell. The experimentation was successful, and he eventually produced a cell that "...was entirely different from existing cells on the market. The second problem was solved by Baird's refinement of his electronics. Douglas Brown suggests that Baird's system was as poor as everyone else's, but it was his use of a technique called "sharpening" that finally produced a television picture. Sharpening is an electronic method which brings a picture into focus in the same manner in which a normal lens focuses an image.

Almost eleven years to the day after graduating with an electrical engineering diploma from the Royal Technical College in Glasgow, John Logie Baird first achieved a recognisable television image. In his autobiography, Baird describes this historic occasion.

The image of the dummy's head formed itself on the screen with what appeared to be almost unbelievable clarity...I ran down the little flight of stairs to Mr. Cross' office, and seized by the arm his office boy William Taynton, hauled him upstairs and put him in front of the transmitter...

After paying Taynton two shillings and sixpence to stay in position, Baird finally saw a human face recognisably reproduced on his apparatus. Baird waited four months, until 26 January 1926, before demonstrating his achievement to the Royal Institute and a reporter from *The Times* newspaper.

John Logie Baird's achievement of television brought him great recognition. He went on to become a well known public figure in Great Britain. In 1931 married the concert pianist Margaret Albu. The couple had two children, Diana and Malcolm. Diana is a retired schoolteacher living near Glasgow, and Malcolm is a professor in chemical engineering at McMaster University in Hamilton, Ontario, Canada, as well as a Baird historian in his own right.

Baird's work did not stop with his achievement of true television. He went on to develop television for cinemas, both colour and three dimensional television, and also investigated further into secret signalling and radar technology. The fall edition of *Kinema* will contain a complementary article by Malcolm Baird, examining his father's work following the first demonstration of television.

The first public demonstration of television, in the cramped London attic room in January 1926, marked a turning point for Baird. One of the scientists at the demonstration was heard to comment "Well, he got it right. It's only a matter of .s.d. to carry on developments." Public interest was immense and the small company that had been formed six months earlier, Television Limited, was able to expand. One of its first recruits was the business manager, a genial Irishman called Oliver Hutchinson. He and the outspoken journalist Sydney Moseley fed the public interest by writing optimistic articles in the press, to the effect that television would soon take its place in the home along with radio; but the plain truth was that television had some way to go before this could happen. Early television pictures were about the size of a business card and because of the low definition, the pictures were limited to head and shoulders. As Dr. Samuel Johnson said in another context, "the wonder is not that 'tis done well, but that 'tis done at all." Despite the limitations of these early images, it was possible to recognize individuals and to pick up changes of expression. This past April in Toronto, visitors to the "Watching TV" exhibition at the Royal Ontario Museum had an opportunity of checking for themselves, by viewing a reconditioned Baird "Televisor" of 1930.

Seventy years ago, public broadcasting in Britain was only legally possible through the BBC. Its domineering and puritanical director, Sir John Reith, was afraid of television and his technical staff took their lead from the top and quibbled about the picture quality. It was only after much pressure from Hutchinson and Moseley, and a parliamentary committee hearing, that the BBC agreed to begin experimental transmissions in 1929. During this period of pressure politics, Baird himself continued to focus on research and development. Although the news media were enthusiastic about television, Baird was criticised in the prestigious British scientific journal *Nature* for not giving out enough technical details of his invention. In reply, he pointed out that such details were the subject of patent applications and would be released in due course.

Baird's worldwide monopoly of television was broken in April 1927 when the Bell Telephone Co. sent a mechanically televised message from Herbert Hoover by phone lines from Washington to New York, a distance of 200 miles. This event acted as a challenge to Baird and over the next few years he achieved a remarkable series of "firsts" in television history. In May of 1927 he ran a television transmission from London to Glasgow by phone lines — a distance of 435 miles, more than twice that of the Bell transmission.

Later that year, Baird was joined by his first engineering assistant Ben Clapp, who was experienced in the new techniques of short wave radio. Radio waves of about 40 metres length could be sent over very long distances because they were reflected around the earth's curvature by the ionosphere, under climatically favourable conditions. Early in 1928, Clapp and Hutchinson sailed to New York with crates containing a television receiving apparatus; this was set up at the home of a radio enthusiast in Hartsdale, just north of New York City. After some initial disappointments, the first television pictures from London were received at Hartsdale on 8th February. This caused a sensation on both sides of the Atlantic, and the *New York Times* compared the event to Marconi's sending of the letter "S" by radio across the Atlantic, 27 years earlier.

In July 1928, Baird demonstrated colour television; this still employed the mechanical scanning method, but the scanning wheels contained three spirals of holes with three filters in the primary colours. In this way, three separate coloured pictures were transmitted in rapid succession; the persistence of vision caused the eye of the viewer to "mix" the three primary pictures, so that a coloured moving picture was perceived. Later, a primitive system of stereoscopic television was demonstrated, and it was also shown that television could be recorded on a wax disk and replayed. Some of the old plastic pressings for the disks were played back over 50 years later, using special equipment.

The early television pictures were only a few square inches in area and Baird was under pressure to provide something more comparable in size with the cinema screen. This was achieved in 1930 in a demonstration of "large screen television" from the Baird studio to an audience at the London Coliseum Cinema. The screen consisted of an array of 2100 small flashlamp bulbs. Celebrities beat a path to the studio to appear on the new medium, and the cinema drew packed houses. A year later, the Derby horse race was televised and sent by phone line to the Baird studio and to the experimental BBC transmitter. This was the first public "outside broadcast" of television.

The hesitations of Britain's monopoly broadcaster, the BBC, led Baird's company to explore international possibilities. In 1928 a Baird subsidiary was set up in the USA where there were already many experimental TV stations, and in 1931 Baird made his first and only visit to the USA. He received a VIP reception in New York, and entered negotiations for a joint TV venture with Donald Flamm, owner of radio station WMCA. The license application was at first well received by the Federal Radio Commission, but it was eventually rejected after an appeal from a rival radio station on the grounds that no "foreign influences" should be allowed in the broadcast media! If the FRC had accepted the application, Baird might have stayed on in the USA and the history of television would have been very different. However, his American visit was not entirely wasted, since Baird invited his girlfriend Margaret Albu over from England, and they were married before a judge. No relatives from either side were present at the ceremony, but the marriage was a happy one lasting until Baird's death in 1946.

In Germany, the authorities' approach to television was much more sympathetic than that of the BBC. In 1929 a company called Fernseh AG was formed with 25% ownership assigned to each of three German companies, and 25% to Baird's Television Limited. For a few years there was a useful collaboration and experimental transmissions were sent from Berlin to a specially built receiving station in North London, near Wembley Stadium. Relations between Baird and Fernseh became difficult after the Nazis came to power, and essentially broke off in 1935 when all television research in Germany was abruptly placed under military control.

On his return to London from his American visit in January 1932, Baird found that his company had changed hands. The new majority shareholder was Isodore Ostrer, who also owned the Gaumont British chain of cinemas. This led to a growing emphasis on large screen projection television in cinemas. Ostrer and many others in the cinema industry believed that television was an opportunity, rather than a rival to be feared. The public could be attracted to the theatres by a live telecast which could then be followed by a regular feature film.

The 2100-lamp screen which had been demonstrated in 1930 was replaced by a "flying spot" method, with the picture being traced out in strips by a powerful beam of light deflected on a rotating mirror drum. This technique was successfully used in the live showing of the 1932 Derby at the Metropole Cinema, Victoria. The overall picture size was 9 ft wide by 7 ft high and it was formed by joining three pictures 3 x 7 ft sent over three separate telephone lines. By the late 1930s electronic projection television receivers had been developed by Baird, but cinema television was stopped after the start of World War II. It was resumed in some of the London theatres for several years after World War II, under the aegis of the Rank Organization; but the demand for cinema television fell off as the private ownership of television sets increased. Although television has not been adopted in movie theatres, the showing of films on television has become a big business; Rank Cintel is one of the leading manufacturers of telecine equipment.

In June 1908, the Scottish scientist Alan Campbell Swinton wrote a letter to the journal *Nature*, suggesting that the newly discovered properties of the electron could provide a means for "Distant Electric Vision." Three years later, he gave a remarkably prophetic lecture in which he outlined a detailed scheme on these lines. The proposed system was to be entirely electronic with the receiver featuring a cathode ray tube in which a beam of electrons can be deflected by a varying electrical field, with their motion being visible as lines on the phosphorescent screen of the tube. The specification of the camera was more vague. Although Campbell Swinton's ideas were only theoretical, they pointed to an obvious advantage of electronic television, namely that a beam of electrons can move essentially instantaneously without any of the mechanical problems associated with rotating disks. But experimental progress towards electronic television was painfully slow, and as late as 1924 Campbell Swinton stated that electronic television would be so costly to develop that it would be hardly worthwhile! It is known that Baird read this article which may have confirmed his belief that the most feasible ways to the first television picture was through mechanical techniques. His main competitor in this area was the American pioneer, Charles Francis Jenkins.

While Baird was gaining headlines in the late 1920s, two individuals in the USA were starting to make real progress with electronic television. The Russian-born Dr. Vladimir Zworykin had obtained the financial and technical backing of the Radio Corporation of America for his researches on an electronic camera, the Iconoscope. A more colourful character was Philo T. Farnsworth, a largely self-taught young man from Utah, who obtained funding from private investors for his image dissector camera. By 1929, Farnsworth was sending silhouettes through his camera, with the pictures being received on a cathode ray tube. This marked the beginning of years of rivalry and patent litigation between Farnsworth and RCA, the David and Goliath of electronic television. After many years, Farnsworth won his case against RCA, but his small company could not compete as a television set manufacturer and Farnsworth died an embittered man in 1971. RCA went on to gain a dominant position in the United States television industry despite the loss of face involved in having to license Farnsworth's technology.

Britain declared war on Germany on September 3 1939. Two days earlier, BBC television had been abruptly shut down, and the British television industry was out of action for the duration of the war. Baird Television Ltd. went into liquidation, and Baird found himself to be, in his own words, "a free agent." Sydney Moseley and Donald Flamm urged Baird to move with his family to the United States where he could continue his research in better conditions, but he politely declined. However his first concern was to move his family out of London, and my mother and sister and I went to Cornwall, 250 miles west of London, where we stayed until 1945. Baird himself had become very interested in high definition colour television and he continued to work, at his own expense, in a small private laboratory next to the house at Sydenham. He retained the services of two technicians, W. Oxbrow and Edward Anderson; later in the war, only Anderson remained. Most of his other technical staff had been conscripted for service in the new radar stations being set up around the southern and eastern coasts of England.

Baird set his sights on a picture definition of 600 lines. Scanning was carried out by an electronic "flying spot" method, similar to that used a few years earlier in cinema television demonstrations. Some "mechanical" operation was still included, in the form of a set of 3 rotating primary colour filters, on the same principle as the first colour television in 1928. This was demonstrated to a few reporters on a 2.5 by 2 foot screen in December 1940. Publicity was however minimal, as this was in the darkest time of World War II. Another idea from 1928, stereoscopic television, was also developed on high definition in colour, and successfully demonstrated in late 1941. This technique did not require the wearing of special glasses by the viewer; but it was necessary for the viewer's head to stay in one position to get the best stereoscopic effect!

Baird's crowning achievement in colour television was the Telechrome, which was the first colour tube to dispense entirely with mechanical devices. The Telechrome tube was spherical, with a flat mica screen in the middle. One side of the mica was coated with an orange-red fluorescent coating, and the other side with a blue-green fluorescent coating. Pictures were formed electronically on each side of the sheet, and a colour picture was visible because of the transparency of the mica. The Telechrome was publicly demonstrated in the summer of 1944; press coverage was very favourable, but the event was considerably dwarfed by other news such as the D-day invasion of Europe, and falling of flying bombs on London. I remember seeing the Telechrome early in 1945 and the picture was comparable in quality to today's colour television. After Baird's death in 1946, no one else continued the work at Sydenham. The house was sold, Anderson moved to the USA and the equipment seems to have disappeared.

The year 1926 marked the breakthrough for television, but in that year Baird also took out a patent on something slightly different. The specification called for the scanning of an object with a directional beam of ultra-short radio waves; the reflected waves were then picked up by a suitable receiver and the amplified signal was combined to form a picture of the object. This is what we now describe as radar, with the ability to see objects through darkness, cloud and fog. Why was this discovery not publicized by Baird on a par with television?

The question has been answered by Dr. Peter Waddell of the University of Strathclyde, who has found files of official correspondence from the 1920s and 1930s, formerly classified, describing visits of Air Ministry and Admiralty personnel to Baird's laboratories. There is little doubt that Baird was placed under a "gag order" on many aspects of his research. However, a few pieces of firm information have emerged. In 1939, Baird Television fitted out a French bomber with an airborne television camera for reconnaissance purposes. This used a miniaturised version of the intermediate film process, which provided not only a television signal for transmission to the ground base, but also a filmed record of the observations from the aircraft.

Baird's refusal to move to the USA at the outbreak of World War II may well have been due to his involvement in secret work. During the war he received £1,000 per year from Cable and Wireless Co., the crown corporation which controlled all official communications in Britain. The services performed for this fee are still not known exactly, but his work is believed to have been on the use of television methods for high-speed coded signalling. Research is continuing on this aspect of Baird's life.

The public image of John Logie Baird has fluctuated in the 50 years since his death. In 1952 a biography appeared by Baird's old friend Sydney Moseley, an outspoken journalist who put his viewpoint into everything he wrote. The subtitle of his book was "...the Romance and Tragedy of the Pioneer of Television." Moseley's theme was that Baird's life had been romantic but ultimately a failure, because his mechanical system was replaced by electronic television. This theme was taken up by others. In 1957 an attempt to convert the family home in Scotland to a public museum of television was thwarted by some powerful figures in the British government who said bluntly that "Baird did not invent television." The chorus of denigration was taken up by one of Baird's former engineers who had since risen to a high position in the BBC. The tide began to turn when the right to use "Baird" as a tradename passed to Radio Rentals, which had made a fortune with television rentals in the post-war years.

John Baskerville

John Baskerville was born in 1706 at Wolverley in Worcestershire. He was a man with a lifelong passion for beautiful lettering and books. By 1723 he had become a skilled engraver of tombstones and was teaching writing. He moved to Birmingham in about 1726 and set up a school in the Bull Ring where he taught writing and book-keeping, whilst still maintaining his work as an engraver. In 1738 he set up a japanning business in Moor Street, in which he first showed his mettle as an innovator, 'effecting an entire revolution' in the manufacture of japanned goods, and specialising in salvers, tea trays, bread baskets and the like. Within a decade he had become a wealthy man and had bought an estate of some eight acres and a large house on the site of the present-day Baskerville House.

Whilst keeping on his japanning business, in about 1750 he once again turned his attention to his passion, typography.

He experimented with paper-making, ink manufacturing, type founding and printing, producing his first typeface in about 1754. Never afraid to innovate, he made changes to the way in which metal type was made, enabling him to produce finer, more delicate lettering than any before him had achieved. He invented his own lustrous, uniquely black, opaque ink; he was the first to exploit commercially James Whatman's invention of wove paper, which was much smoother than the traditional laid paper; and he modified the printing process by using heated copper cylinders to dry the ink before it had time to soak too far into the paper. All of these innovations enabled Baskerville to produce printed work of an elegance, crispness and clarity never seen before.

In 1757 he published his first book, an edition of Virgil. This was followed by some fifty other classics. In 1758 he became printer to the Cambridge University Press for which, in 1763, he published his masterpiece. Ironically for a confirmed atheist, his greatest work was a folio edition of the Bible, which represented a monumental advance upon the standards and practices of the time. He established a lasting friendship with the American scientist and statesman Benjamin Franklin, who had built up a successful printing business in Philadelphia, and who visited Baskerville in Birmingham.

John Baskerville's guiding principles in his work were simplicity, elegance and above all, clarity. The typeface that bears his name remains one of the most pleasing of the all-time great classical fonts, vastly superior to the dismal Times Roman which, sadly, has become all too ubiquitous. John Baskerville was a friend of the Boulton family, and a good friend and mentor to the young Matthew Boulton as he was growing up. Defying convention, he lived openly with his partner, Sarah Eaves, whose husband had deserted her; rejected religion, pouring withering scorn upon religious bigots; and indulged his fondness for show, wearing masses of gold lace and riding about in a lavishly decorated carriage.

John Baskerville died in 1775 and was buried in a little mausoleum in his garden.

Joseph Bramah

Joseph Bramah was born in 1748 in the village of Stainborough near Barnsley. His father was a small farmer and Joseph, the eldest of 5 children, was destined for the farm. After a very brief education at the village school he became a farm-hand. As a boy he occupied what little spare time he had by making musical instruments and made some creditable pieces of work with very imperfect tools. When he was 16 years old, he had an accident to his right ankle which made him lame and made it impossible for him to continue farming.

While he was confined at home he spent his time doing woodwork and it occurred to him that as he was now of no use on the farm he might become a mechanic. Accordingly, he was apprenticed to the village carpenter and by the time his apprenticeship was finished had acquired such skill that he determined to try his fortune in London.

Arriving there, having made the journey on foot despite his lameness, he soon found work with a cabinet maker. After some time, he set up in business, in a very small way, on his own. It was then that Bramah made his first successful invention, the modern water closet which he patented in 1778. The merits of his invention were soon recognised and before long he had moved to a larger workshop.

Bramah then turned his attention to locks. Locks had been in general use since the early days of the Egyptians , but they had always been, and still were, of such an imperfect character that they could be picked very easily.

In 1784 he patented his lock which for many years had the reputation of being absolutely unpickable. He offered £200 to anyone who could pick his lock and although many tried it - it was not until 1851 that the money was won by an American, A.C. Hobbs, although it took him 16 days to do it ! Obviously for all ordinary purposes the lock could be regarded as impregnable.

The action of the lock greatly depended upon the precision with which the various parts were made and Bramah soon found that their manufacture called for a better class of workmanship than was generally available. A series of machine-tools would have to be devised if the locks were to be made in the quantity and quality desired.

He tried to get the machines made in London but failed.

Then he was told of a clever young workman at the Woolwich Arsenal named Henry Maudslay.

Bramah sent for him and at first was surprised at Maudslay's youthfulness- he was but 18 years old.

He nevertheless engaged him and within 12 months, so impressed was he by Maudslay's capabilities, made him his works superintendent.

Bramah's spirit of invention was stimulated by the success of his lock and in 1785 he invented his Hydrostatic Machine. This name came into practical use but it was the forerunner of his Hydrostatic or Hydraulic Press which he patented in 1795.

Even the success of this press, however, ultimately depended upon Maudslay, for Bramah, although he had invented the machine despaired of ever bringing it to a state of practical efficiency for he found it impossible to built a matching piston and cylinder with sufficient clearance to enable the piston to move up and down freely and yet sufficiently watertight to withstand the internal force of the pump.

It was Maudslay who solved the problem with his idea of a leather self-tightening collar.

Bramah was a fertile and clever inventor and in 1797 he invented a beer-pump, the four-cock and a quill-sharpener.

In 1802 he obtained a patent for a wood working planer and then used a similar machine for planing the metal parts of his locks, a method that was the forerunner of modern face-milling.

Bramah never seemed to be at a loss for inventions. Thus, when the Bank of England asked him to construct a machine for more quickly and accurately numbering bank notes, he proceeded to invent it in one month.

He then turned his attention to the writing implements of the day and invented a machine for making quill pens which continued in use until the steel nib was invented.

The last patent of his versatile genius was that taken out in 1814 for the purpose of applying Roman cement to timber to prevent dry rot.

For some time prior to his death Bramah had been employed in the erection of several large machines for sawing stones and timber to which he applied his hydraulic power with great success.

He was occupied with superintending one of his presses at Holt Forest, in Hampshire where some 300 trees were to be torn up by the roots when he caught a severe cold. This turned to pneumonia and he died suddenly on December 9th 1814.

Joseph Bramah was deservedly honoured and admired as one of the earliest mechanical geniuses of his day.

From his workshop came Maudslay and Clements and many more first class mechanics who carried the mechanical arts to still higher perfection.

Jim Bridger

James Bridger was one of the greatest frontiersmen of Utah and American history. During his lifetime he was a hunter, trapper, trader, Indian fighter, and guide, and one of only a few trappers to remain in the Rockies after the demise of the fur trade.

Bridger spent his first year with the company on the upper Missouri until Blackfoot Indian hostilities forced the expedition back down river in the spring of 1823. Bridger then accompanied Henry's brigade to the Yellowstone River, where, en route, Hugh Glass was attacked by a grizzly. Evidence would indicate that Bridger volunteered as one of Glass's caretakers, but that he abandoned Glass believing he would not live. Glass miraculously survived and apparently exonerated Bridger's desertion due to his youth.

Bridger spent the fall of 1823 and the following winter and spring of 1824 trapping and wintering in the Bighorn region as part of John Weber's brigade. By summer's end, he had pushed west across South Pass to trap the Bear River. The brigade assembled in "Willow Valley" to winter on Cub Creek near present Cove, Utah. Allegedly during that winter of 1824-25 a dispute arose concerning the Bear River's course south of Cache Valley. Bridger was selected to explore the river to resolve the question. His journey took him to the Great Salt Lake, which he believed was an arm of the Pacific Ocean due to its saltiness. For years, Bridger was recognized as the first documented discoverer of the great "Inland Sea"; however, more recent evidence seems to indicate that this honor should be given to Etienne Provost.

The following spring, Weber's brigade spread along the Wasatch Front to trap. In May, Bridger was probably at the Ogden-Gardner trappers' confrontation near present Mountain Green; however, there is no documentation that indicates he participated in the proceedings. That summer Bridger attended the Randavouze Creek rendezvous, just north of the Utah-Wyoming border near the present town of McKinnon, Wyoming.

The winter of 1825-1826 was spent by Bridger and most of Ashley's men in the Salt Lake Valley in two camps: one at the mouth of the Weber River and one on the Bear. Bridger continued to trap the regions of the Wasatch Front for approximately the next four years, spending some of his winters in the Salt Lake Valley. He was present at all the rendezvous, including the Cache Valley rendezvous of 1826 and the rendezvous of 1827 and 1828 on the south shore of Bear Lake at present-day Laketown, Utah.

In 1830 Bridger and four other partners formed the Rocky Mountain Fur Company; however, exhausted fur reserves and increased competition from John Jacob Astor's American Fur Company forced the company to venture north into hostile Blackfoot territory. The Rocky Mountain Fur Company was dissolved in 1834 and by the end of the decade the fur trade itself was over.

During the final years of the fur trade, Bridger, with partner Louis Vasquez, planned and constructed what was to be Fort Bridger, located on Black's Fork of the Green River. This new enterprise was to become one of the principal trading posts for the western migration, established specifically to serve the wagon trains heading to the far West. Bridger's post served many immigrants heading west, including the ill-fated Donner-Reed party.

In June 1847 Bridger had his first encounter with the Mormon pioneers near the mouth of the Little Sandy River. At this gathering, Bridger and Brigham Young discussed the merits of settling in the Salt Lake Valley. Also during this meeting Bridger drew his map on the ground for Young depicting the region with great accuracy and conveyed to the Mormon leader his misgivings regarding the agricultural productivity of the Salt Lake area. This first meeting between the Mormons and Bridger appears to have been pleasant, yet this relationship was to become a bittersweet one for Bridger.

The coming of the Mormons increased the number of immigrants at the fort. However, the Mormon settlements attracted away a significant portion of Bridger's trade, including that of the Indians, causing economic hardships for the post.

In 1850 Bridger consulted and guided the Stansbury expedition, which established a road much of which would later become the route of the Overland Stage and the Union Pacific Railroad. The same year, the territory of Utah was created; it included under its jurisdiction the Fort Bridger area.

Animosity between Bridger and the Mormons festered in the summer of 1853. Mormon leaders were convinced that Bridger was engaged in illicit trade with the Indians, especially guns and ammunition, and that he had stirred hostility among the Native Americans against the Mormons. Mormon leaders revoked Bridger's license to trade and issued a warrant for his arrest; however, before the posse's arrival Bridger had fled.

By the end of 1853, the Mormons had begun to move in and secure control of Bridger's Green River Basin, opting to establish Fort Supply rather than occupy Fort Bridger. Bridger had gone to the east, but returned to the mountains in 1855. That summer, Bridger sold his fort to the Mormons for $8,000. The Mormons paid Bridger $4,000 in gold coin that August; however, the final payment was not made until 1858, when Vasquez received the remaining $4,000 in Salt Lake City.

The Mormons took possession of Fort Bridger in 1855, making much-needed improvements, including erecting a large cobblestone wall around the fort. However, in 1857, the fort was destroyed by the Mormons to hinder the advance of Albert Sidney Johnson's Army, which was being guided by none other than James Bridger. The army occupied the fort until 1890. Bridger tried to deal with the army regarding leasing the fort under the premise that the Mormons had forced him out and stolen it from him. During the 1870s and early 1880s, Bridger inquired about the army's lease, but without success.

Bridger died in July 1881. After his death, the government paid his widow for the improvements of the post, which consisted of thirteen log structures and the eighteen-foot-high cobblestone wall, which, ironically, were built by the Mormons.

John Chuang

At the age of 31 John Chuang isn't far from the days of using a door as a table to save a few bucks. That was back in 1986 when he was running a tiny print shop above a convenience store in Harvard Square. The Harvard sophomore was in the perfect place to spot his clients' growing need for trained Macintosh operators. That was the seed of his $75 million MacTemps, barely a decade old, which saw sales of over $50 million in 1995. During its most recent three years the fast-growing temp agency has averaged 40% annual growth with a solid profit margin.

"Back then all I knew was I wanted to create a company that would be scaleable and that could be replicated in other cities," says Chuang. "The Mac computer became our niche in the market, because most companies were focused on using PCs. The Mac was still small and not everyone used it." But those customers that Chuang wanted were using the Macintosh.

"We ran a small ad in a computer newsletter that basically asked, 'You don't use any computer. Why use any computer specialist?' recalls Chuang. "The phone rang off the hook."

"We were the only game in town." Within three months there was an office in New York City, and two months after that, Los Angeles. "We were the staff and the owners, so we were sending ourselves out on jobs as well as trying to run the company." The company developed a training program for new temps and quickly began hiring the best Mac computer gunslingers it could find. In the first year of operation, 5 offices opened across the country. "Sooner or later somebody would have started this company, but we were the first." John Chuang had brought popcorn to the movies and the results were predictably spectacular.

Originally, the company began opening offices quickly because they had made a unique marketplace discovery. Others began imitating the idea and unless MacTemps opened their own offices they were in danger of losing at their own game. "We were the first," says Chuang, "and now we're the largest." Recently the company expanded internationally, opening offices in London, Paris and Melbourne, Australia in 1995, bringing their worldwide total to more than 40 offices.

In any given MacTemp week 2,300 temps are on assignment, 70 percent in graphics, 20 percent in networking and another 10 percent in administrative capacities. Confirming the company's success, Inc. magazine placed MacTemps on its list of America's 500 fastest-growing privately held corporations in 1992 and 1993. Chuang himself was named "Entrepreneuer of the Year for Service" in New England by Inc. Magazine/Ernst & Young and Merrill Lynch. John also received the "Excellence 2000" award from the United States Pan Asian American Chamber of Commerce, the only national award of its kind. Chuang says modestly that his company "performs very well," but recent figures reveal that the company enjoyed sales of over 50 million dollars in 1995. Over the last three years, the company has enjoyed a steady 40% growth and a rock-solid profit margin.

By 1996 MacTemps had developed two entirely new and thriving units – Portfolio and 1-800-Network. Portfolio specializes in high-end creative graphic arts personnel, art directors, designers and illustrators. Currently, the company is number two in the country for graphic arts specialists and Chuang predicts a number one ranking by the end of the year. Since its inception, nine months ago, Portfolio has opened offices in New York, Atlanta, Chicago, Houston, Los Angeles, San Francisco, San Diego and Detroit, each within a month of each other and the company continues to expand.

The other new unit is a techical support staffing company for Network and LAN systems. It provides personnel for all aspects of network operations, from original design to administration to trouble shooting of Windows, NT and Novell systems. It also has eight offices nationwide in Detroit, Atlanta, Dallas, Denver, Los Angeles, Seattle and Boston. "With each new unit we create," says Chuang, "we examine the marketplace first to see if the market has a need for our service and can sustain it." Once that is completed, the company moves swiftly to capitalize on its opportunities in each new market.

MacTemps is also experimenting with two new additional units—Montage, a company which specializes in the rapidly-expanding world of Multimedia, and MacTemps Technical, which, as the name implies, will offer technical support for Mac users on-site as well as by telephone. Montage is currently up and running only in the Seattle area, and Mactemps, according to a spokesperson, is currently on the drawing board.

John Chuang was born and raised in the Queens district of New York City. He attended Stuyvestant High School before moving to Cambridge, Massachusetts to attend Harvard University and receive his MBA. "I always knew I would be in some kind of business for myself," says Chuang. "My parents never really pushed me in any one direction or another. My father was in business and my mother was a librarian."

Chuang chose his career path while still at Harvard, when he and two dorm mates beat the bushes among friends and family to raise the $5,000 needed as startup capital for their small Mac-based printing company. When Chuang saw how few of his clients had the broad base of Macintosh computer experience to truly benefit from their use, Mac Temps was born.

"We have a unique advantage in our company, because when we first started, we had an idealistic vision of what a company should be like and we've been able to keep to that over the years," Says Chuang. "Most of our major managers have never worked anywhere else, so we've been able to create a homegrown vision. This is a very flat-structured company. There isn't a lot of hierarchy. We have only one manager in each market who deals with the clients, the employees and the headquarters. There is no middle person. What we try to do is replace control mechanisms with a lot of trust, not people looking over your shoulder all the time. Every manager, for example, has the ability to make monetary decisions without going through various levels of approvals. For example, if a customer is unhappy with the service for whatever reason, or if adjustments need to be made on any account, that staffer can take care of it right there." Any staffer can also see that a temp is reimbursed for any training he or she enrolls in.

Chuang wants to make Mactemps a very special place for people to work. Which is all the more important when one realizes that not everyone gets to work there. "Unlike a lot of temp agencies, we don't hire just everyone. The testing and screening is very tough. We want someone who has a mastery of skills, not just a cursory knowledge. Then we look for a certain attitude. Someone has to want to do this job, not just be looking for something in between other jobs."

"We also interview each candidate in person," he adds. "We know what our people can do, and we also offer services like a software library to help our temps improve their skills."

Though the original idea for MacTemps was to capitalize on the Mac graphics revolution, the company has since expanded to include PC/Windows experts as well. However, it's from the Mac that the company receives its unique flavor. The Macintosh and its software are the tools of choice for most of the leading design, graphics and multimedia companies in the world. Thus, if one hires a Mac-based work force, one hires a creative work force. No one really uses a Mac to do its spreadsheeets. They use them to create. A company filled with Mac experts will be filled with artists and people who bring a unique vision to any assignment.

"We want to treat our temps like employees and individuals," says Chuang, "not just names on a roster. We seek the best assignments and we want them to do interesting work, great design work, and learn and be challenged." Thus Chuang enjoys a very loyal work force. Oftentimes the company will sponsor daylong training sessions at no expense to the temps, to sharpen and hone their skills, or on the flip side, the company will simply schedule an impromptu get-together for its employees. Thus their loyalties are rewarded. "A while back," says Chuang, "we took all of the employees who'd been here at least 3 years to Cancun."

In March of 1993, John Chuang revolutionized the temp employee industry by introducing the company's innovative health, 401 retirement and vacation benefits plans for its employees. The New York Times called the plan "..the envy of many permanent workers." Those employees working 300 hours in a ten-week period are eligible for conmprehensive long-term health care coverage, full disability insurance and complete dental converage for preventive care. MacTemps pays 60% of the cost for long term health care, and 100% of disabiliity insurance and preventive health care. Employees who manage to work 1,900 hours in a 52-week period will receive full health benefits at no cost. In addition, MacTemps offers family coverage as an option to its employees and in 1995, the company expanded its benefits to include a dependent care reimbursement plan.

"We wanted to redefine the staffing industry, not replicate existing practices," says Chuang. "The benefits program is a major step in that direction."

Obviously John Chuang has learned the lesson that a valued employee is a valuable employee and he has taken that idea and spread it across the nation, indeed around the world, redefining the word "temporary" in the process.

Maurice Félix Charles

An independent-minded French economist, Maurice Allais strove to carry the message of the original Lausanne School of Walras and Pareto into the modern era, through what we have called the Paretian Revolution of the 1930s. Maurice Allais wrote two major treatises in the 1940s, Á la Recherche d'une discipline économique and Economique et interet whose inspiration was to a great part derived "from meditation upon the works of Leon Walras, Irving Fisher and especially Vilfredo Pareto, three great masters who deeply influenced me". As a later commentator put it, had Allais written these two works in English, "a whole generation of economic theory would have taken a different course".

In his 1943 opus, Allais provided the groundwork for much of the Paretian system, including the first proofs of the Fundamental Welfare Theorems in both a static and intetemporal framework. He went on to unveil what are now standard ideas about market failures in a general equilibrium setting. Recognizing the potential implications of natural monopolies, transactions costs and unnatural rents on market efficiency, Allais made several quite "radical" policy proposals. His affinity to the old Lausanne school extended to the points on policy, e.g. sharing the latter's call for the complete nationalization of land and massive income redistribution by capital taxation.

Allais's work on intertemporal equilibrium and capital were extended in his 1947 book and further developed in other articles. Among his contributions in 1947 was the invention of the now-famous "overlapping generations" model. Allais also introduced the "Golden Rule" for optimal growth. The Baumol transactions demand for money rule was also anticipated by Allais in 1947.

The contribution Allais is generally best known for in the Anglo-Saxon world is the "Allais Paradox" in the theory of choice under uncertainty - which he presented in a series of papers in 1953. Succinctly, the paradox claims that the assumptions made in conventional expected utility theory contradict real life decisions - specifically, Allais finds behavior which contradicts the expected utility rule. The idea introduced by Allais is that there is a systematic relationship between the an agent's attitude towards risk and the "degree of certainty", what was later called the "common consequence effect". Discovering this paradox, Allais led the way to new attempts at formulating new theories of decision-making under uncertainty.

In his earlier 1943 book, Allais's introduced several other advances in general equilibrium theory besides welfare theory and the concept of an intetemporal equilibrium: namely, he introduced a unique non-tatonnement process of stability without interim prices. In 1971 and after, Allais called for a re-examination of the foundations of the Neo-Walrasian economics he had helped create, proposing instead a theory of "markets economies" relying on his 1943 process. This process relied on the "search for surplus" in exchange, which eschewed the concept of price as a guiding principle. Equilibrium, Allais claimed, is achieved when surpluses are exhausted and only then can prices be deemed to exist. His theory of surpluses and markets is best outlined in his 1989 treatise, Théorie Générale des Surplus .

Allais's legacy is mixed. Through his two major works and as mentor of two of the most prominent pioneers of Neo-Walrasian theory, Gerard Debreu and Edmond Malinvaud, Allais channeled numerous concerns of the original Lausanne School economists into the post-war General Equilibrium program. Today, he might be best known for his development of the "Allais Paradox" in uncertainty theory, but most of Allais's highly original contributions - notably his surplus theory of exchange and stability and his unique "psychological-relativistic" theory of money - have been either completely ignored or surreptitiously stolen by the mainstream economics establishment without due acknowledgement. His calls for a re-examination of the foundations of Neo-Walrasian theory and his single-handed attempts to reform it have only recently gotten wider attention.

Nonetheless, despite the numerous setbacks during his professional career, Maurice Allais was vindicated by being made an officer of the Legion of Honor in 1977 and a richly-deserved Nobel Memorial prize in 1988. It perhaps also should be mentioned that while Allais's contributions to economics have only been reluctantly recognized, his contributions to physics and history have been better acknowledged!

A graduate of the the École Polytechnique and the École Nationale Supérieure des Mines of Paris, Allais taught at ENSM from 1944 to 1988. He was director of research at the Centre Nationale de la Recherche Scientifique and the Center of Monetary Analysis at the University of Paris.

Matthias William Baldwin

Matthias William Baldwin was born 10 December, 1795, the youngest of five children of William Baldwin senior, an Elizabethtown, New Jersey carriage maker. His father died when young Matt was just four years of age, his mother was left with nothing as the property was broken up through poor business transactions by the executors. His mother strived so he could finish school and he was then apprenticed to Woolworth Brothers, manufacturing Jewellers. In 1817 he was working for Fletcher and Gardiner, Jewellers and Silver-smiths in Philadelphia.

Two years later in 1819 he had established himself as a fine workman in his own business and devised a patent gold plating process, but he left this trade in 1825 to join David Mason, a machinist in the manufacture of engravers and book-makers tools; later expanding into hydraulic presses and forms of copper and steel rolls for the calico printing trade. In 1824 Baldwin had become a founder in the Franklin Institute for the Betterment of Labour. He practiced his philanthropic ideals in establishing a school for black children in 1835 and donated many funds to chapels and churches in the city.

He was for many years county and city .prison inspector. expanded he built a noiseless stationary engine to replace an unsatisfactory one previously purchased. This engine was quite novel and served the works for many years, later being preserved by the company and eventually housed in the collection of the Smithsonian Institute, where it still resides.Mason apparently had reservations about Baldwin's innovations. The partnership was dissolved, Baldwin becoming the sole owner. At this time, in 1827, he married Sarah C. Baldwin a distant cousin. From this union there were three children - one son and three daughters. Philadelphia at this time was the hub of a booming coal mining region, relying on crude wooden railed tramways for transportation to the nearest waterway. This stimulated interest in the development of land transport to the extent Franklin Peale requested Matthias Bald-win to build a demon-stration example of the new form of locomotion for railroad use.On April 25, 1831 Bald-win displayed in Peale's Philadelphia City Museum a model 'Dummy' locomotive; large enough to haul two small carriages, of four people in each, around a circular display track within the building.

Unusual for its day, this loco burnt coal, something that he persisted with for many years where others always used coke, that being the superior heat source and a smokeless fuel.This exhibition aroused the interest of the regional railroads, at that time all still using horses for motive power. The six mile Philadelphia, Germantown and Norristown Railroad ordered its first locomotive from the works. Baldwin and Peale spent some time studying and sketching the recently arrived and still unassembled *John Bull* imported from Robert Stephenson & Co of Newcastle-upon-Tyne, for the Camden and Amboy.

The imported *John Bull* at this time resided in a shed at Bordentown, a Quaker settlement some 25 miles away, having arrived in August 1831 as a kit of parts. It was later assembled by Isaac Dripps a young machinist and marine engineer whom the President of the Camden and Amboy, Robert L. Stevens, had seen working on the largest steamboats then being built.Baldwin also became involved in the assembly of *Delaware,* the original Stephenson Planet type machine for the New Castle and Frenchtown Railroad AS 1907). It appears that this was the engine that became a prototype for his order to the P.G.&N. Railroad. Taking six months to build his early American steamer, with the assistance of Andrew Vauclain, who had acquired his experience with such machines by constructing steam fire pump engines, with 'old' Johnny Agnew of Philadelphia. There were many trials and such skills as were required had to be passed on to the workers. Constructed of iron and timber, this 51/2 ton machine was apparently capable of 28 m.p.h. and drew thirty tons, on fine days. Baptised as "Old Ironsides" it was dismantled for transport to the railroad and tested on 23 November 1832.The initial trials were favourably reported in the *United* States Gazette and *The Chronicle;* and advertisements appeared in Poulsons *American Daily Advertiser,* where it was advised that, "on rainy days it would not appear, for horses were to be used"; clearly indicating such machines were still to be regarded as novelties or experiments.A series of mishaps on its first run all the way to Germantown showed serious defects in wheel and axle arrangements.

These consisted of a cast iron hub with wooden spokes, rims and wrought iron tyres. A driving wheel had slipped upon a hub causing out-of-gauge and locking up of the valve gears, primitive as they were. Other problems became evident since the cylinders had a common exhaust, causing much back pressure in the opposite engine. This arrangement was most unsatisfactory and was quickly modified. The applauded advantage of light weight advocated at the time soon showed that the locomotive suffered from lack of adhesive traction and was incapable of performing an efficient service on adversely graded lines. A dispute arose over the worth of the locomotive such that Baldwin declared he would never build another! However persuasion by other engineers and his own preoccupation with improvement soon brought forth new development. His second locomotive featured a leading four wheeled truck, the style and plan having been devised by John B. Jervis; and in use on the Mohawk and Hudson R.R. This second engine of 1834. the *E.L. Miller,* entered service on the longest railroad in the world at that time, the South Carolina R.R. The 4-2-0 outside framed engine, with 'haystack' type firebox. became a standard Baldwin product improved conservatively over the next decade AS 1907. Where others were building bigger and better to improve haulage capacity, like Long and Norris. They turned out some remarkable machines, unafraid to purchase the patents of others where development had proven itself. Baldwin on the other hand sought to discredit others' inventions, whilst discreetly trying to achieve the same improvements by alternative methods. The Railway Mania' of 1833 was coming to an end. However the standardisation of engines and good workmanship must have given Baldwin an edge over rivals. On the Columbia Railroad, 11 of 27 locos on the roster were Baldwins, and the superintendent's report of 1836 was most scathing in respect of some of his motley collection of other charges. An annual output of forty-odd machines was reached before the financial crises of 1837-40, this being weathered only by the tolerance of the shareholders. They must have been quite taken in by Baldwin's arguments to stick it out and gave him three years to trade out of the mire.

Indeed it is quite amazing that his reluctance to buy others' successful patents, whilst striving to sell his own ultra conservative contraptions was not the complete undoing of the company. From 1842 the six coupled engine developed into the 'Flexible Beam Truck' the following year and this innovation was patented by Baldwin and proven to be of superior haulage power. This device indeed hauled the company out of the financial quagmire of bankruptcy and saved the railroads' increased operating ratios.The early history of what was later to become 'The Standard Railroad of the world'. i.e. The Pennsylvania R.R. from 1847, was closely associated with Baldwin locomotives and the flexible beam truck engine that defied the engineering theory but worked in practice. Of this heavy freight hauler from the l840s and 50s. some survived into the l880s on the Louisville and Nashville R.R. and indeed one was still at work in Cuba in 1906.Other partners from 1839 included Vail to 1842; then

Asa Whitney from the Mohawk and Hudson River R.R., who left in 1846 to specialise in the manufacture of steel car wheels. Whitney was a very thorough business man who did much to manage the administration of the works. Mathew Baird, who had been a foreman within the organisation then bought an interest in the works as partner in 1854. It was Baird who experimented with soft coal burning and developed the brick arch that was adopted by all coal burners from then on.

At Baldwin's suggestion. his first travelling and commissioning Engineer, Andrew Vauclain, was recommended to the Pennsylvania R.R. 's new works at Altoona. where later Andrew's son, Samuel. then became indentured. Baldwin was still in some financial trouble leading up to the Civil War. as a boycott by the south came as a result of his philanthropic ideals, on behalf of the coloured people. His diminishing sales were compensated by the Union Government buying some 33 locos during the hostilities, between 1862 and 1864. By the end of the war, over 1500 engines had been constructed and the works by now had become the largest locomotive builders and exporters in the world. they would keep that title forever more in steam.Baldwin's other interests extended well beyond his engineering establishment. Around 1826 he had become a Sunday school superintendent and conducted bible class for 35 years. Life at home in his residence at Wissinoming. Philadelphia was simple whilst $10,000 a year was donated to charity. During the hostilities of 1860~ 1865. he allocated 10% of the company's annual income to the Civil War Christian Mission. An active man of athletic disposition, a keen archer and equestrian sportsman, he abstained from alcohol and worked up to a few days prior to his final illness and death on 7 September 1866.

Michael Bloomberg

Michael Rubens "Mike" Bloomberg (born February 14, 1942), a Republican, is a prominent Jewish American businessman, the founder of Bloomberg L.P., and the current Mayor of the City of New York.

Bloomberg was born and raised in a Jewish-American family in Medford, Massachusetts, a Boston suburb. He is an Eagle Scout. He attended Johns Hopkins University, where he joined Phi Kappa Psi, and graduated in 1964 with a B.S. degree in electrical engineering. Later he received his MBA degree from Harvard Business School.

Bloomberg was a general partner at Salomon Brothers, where he headed equity trading, sales and, later, systems development. He made his fortune with his own company, Bloomberg L.P., selling financial information terminals to Wall Street firms; the company also began a radio network.

Bloomberg is among the world's richest people. He was ranked no. 34 by Forbes magazine in its list of 400 Richest Americans in September 2004. He was ranked no. 94 in the Forbes List of the 500 Richest People in the World in March 2005.

Forbes and other sources report his net worth at US$5 billion, which, in addition to furthering his political career, has allowed him to engage in substantial philanthropy, including donating over US$200 million to Johns Hopkins University, where he served as the chairman of the board from 1996 to 2002.

His daughters by former wife, British-born Susan Brown, are Georgina Bloomberg and Emma Bloomberg. His younger sister, Marjorie Tiven, is Commissioner of the New York City Commission for the United Nations, Consular Corps and Protocol. His mother, Charlotte Bloomberg, is still alive, in her nineties, and reported to be in good health. His current girlfriend is state banking superintendent, Diana Taylor.

Bloomberg does not reside in Gracie Mansion, the official mayor's mansion, but at his own home elsewhere on the Upper East Side. He maintains his home address in the white pages and is known to ride the subway to City Hall every morning, even during periods of heightened terrorist alert against the subway system.

In 2001 the incumbent mayor, Rudy Giuliani, was prevented by term limits from running for re-election. Several well-known New York City politicians aspired to succeed him. Bloomberg, a lifelong member of the Democratic Party, decided to run for mayor as a member of the Republican Party, reportedly to avoid the crowded field in the Democratic primary.

Voting in the primary began on the morning of September 11. Later that day, however, because of the disruption caused by the attacks on the World Trade Center, the voting was canceled and the primary postponed. In the rescheduled primary, Bloomberg defeated Herman Badillo, a former Congressman, to become the Republican nominee. The Democratic primary did not produce a first-round winner. There was a runoff, in which the nomination went to New York City Public Advocate Mark J. Green.

In the general election, Bloomberg had Giuliani's endorsement. He also enjoyed a huge spending advantage. New York City's campaign finance law restricted the contributions a candidate could accept, but Bloomberg exercised his right to opt out of this law, though this also attracted some criticism. He spent some $73 million of his own money on his campaign, outspending Green by five to one. One of the major themes of his campaign was that, with the city's economy suffering from the effects of the attacks, it needed a mayor with business experience.

In addition to being the Republican nominee, Bloomberg had the ballot line of the Independence Party. The latter proved to be important, as Bloomberg's votes on that line exceeded his margin of victory over Green. Bloomberg won by 50% to 48%.

Bloomberg declined the mayor's salary, accepting renumeration of $1.00 annually. He is considered a liberal Republican, who is pro-choice, in favor of legalizing same-sex marriage and an advocate for stricter gun control laws.

In sharp contrast to the tight central control and preference for the appointment of political appontees favored by the previous Giuliani administration, Bloomberg has chosen to apply a statistical results-based approach to city management, appointing city commissioners based on expertise and only loosely overseeing their policies. In addition, breaking with 190 years of tradition, Bloomberg implemented a "bullpen" open office plan, seating dozens of aides and managerial staff in a large chamber, reminiscent of a Wall St. trading floor - this was designed to promote accountability and accessibility.

On January 30, 2006, Bloomberg fired Edward Greenwood IX, employed as an assistant in the city's lobbying office in Albany, after finding him playing solitaire on a computer in his office. "The workplace is not an appropriate place for games," Bloomberg said. "It's a place where you've got to do the job that you're getting paid for."

His mayoralty coincides with an increase in the mayor's authority over and accountability for the city's public schools. From 1968 through 2000, the schools were run by 25 local school boards who were elected, and overall management was the responsibility of a Board of Education composed by 7 members, two of which were appointed by the mayor. The local boards and Board of Education were abolished and replaced with a mayoral agency, the Department of Education. To head this department, he appointed Joel Klein as Chancellor, and based him out of the Tweed Courthouse near City Hall. During their time in office test scores rose and they have obtained a higher percentage of funding from the state budget. Bloomberg opposes social promotion, and favors after-school and summer school programs to help schoolchildren catch up rather than allowing them to advance to the next grade level unprepared. Despite often tense relations with teachers' unions, he avoided a teacher strike by concluding a contract negotiation in which teachers received an average raise of 15% in exchange for givebacks and productivity increases.

Bloomberg supports the legalization of same-sex marriage in New York, though he has appealed a decision finding the limiting of same-sex marriage unconstitutional because he has stated he wants to ensure it is permitted under New York State law: "My personal opinion is that anybody should be allowed to marry anybody. I don't happen to think we should put restrictions on who you should marry.... What the city doesn't want to have happen is people getting a marriage license and then six months, or one year later, or two years later, finding out it's meaningless."

He supported extending the city's smoking ban to all commercial establishments, removing the last indoor public areas where one could smoke in the city: bars and nightclubs.

The smoking ban took effect in March 2003 and was still being enforced as of 2005.

Under his term, the reduction of crime that started under Mayor David Dinkins has continued .Bloomberg's approach to the issue has been more low-key than that of Giuliani, who was often criticized by advocates for the homeless and civil rights groups.

Since 2003, Bloomberg has become increasingly assertive in demanding that federal homeland security funds be distributed to municipalities based on risk and population rather than any other measure.

Bloomberg, the founder of an information services company, has tried to better citizen access to city information services.

Perhaps Bloomberg's single most popular program has been the establishment of a 311 telephone line. Dialing 311 puts the caller in contact with the city, allowing them to report any crimes, annoyances, trash problems, etc. It also can be used for question-answer purposes.

There has been some opposition from community groups to Bloomberg's plan to open a new waste transfer station in an affluent residential area on the Upper East Side - the intention being to make the distribution of waste storage sites more equitable and to reduce garbage truck traffic, and the criticism being based on concerns for property values and neighborhood quality of life.

In June 2005 Bloomberg signed the Potty Parity bill requiring more women's toilets in newly opened public places such as bars, theaters, stadiums and convention facilities.

Local 100 of the Transport Workers Union went on strike December 20, 2005 forcing a shutdown of the city's bus and subway service. The transit workers are employed by the Metropolitan Transit Authority and the mayor does not directly control the negotiations. However, the mayor is responsible for coordinating the overall response of the city agencies. Showing solidarity with the people of New York who were inconvenienced by the strike, the Mayor crossed the Brooklyn Bridge on the first day of the strike as Mayor Ed Koch did in the 1980 strike.

In the 2001 campaign, he ran on a "no new taxes" platform and criticized Green for refusing to rule out a tax increase, but during his first year in office, Bloomberg proposed a 25 percent increase in the property tax. The City Council approved an increase of 18.5 percent. This was the largest property tax increase in city history.

He was the most visible proponent of the failed New York City 2012 Olympic bid and planned accompanying West Side Stadium, which he had hoped would help extend Midtown westward to the Hudson River. This plan met opposition from neighborhood residents, and was then rejected by Albany government leaders who felt they had not been sufficiently consulted. He has also been a major supporter of the Brooklyn Nets Arena, controversial among other reasons for the planned use of eminent domain to support private development. Generally, Bloomberg's development plans have been criticized by opponents for a perceived top-down approach. He also supports a plan for a new Mets Stadium stadium and a new Yankee Stadium. Despite the support of the Bronx Borough President, Adolpho Carrion, the proposal for the new Yankee Stadium has encountered significant community opposition.

He is a supporter of immigration reform to secure the rights of illegal aliens, who comprise a large part of the population of New York City. He argues that deportation breaks up families and scares illegal aliens away from cooperating with law enforcement or accessing vital social services; as such, he supports proposals like those put forth by U.S. Senators Ted Kennedy and John McCain, which would normalize the status of otherwise law-abiding illegal aliens already present.

While he was mayor, New York City hosted the 2004 Republican National Convention, to the opposition of many locals who felt it inappropriate during the Iraq War. He was particularly criticized for his handling of protest activity, with hundreds being detained at a former bus garage on Pier 57 characterized by opponents as a "Guantanamo on the Hudson".

Bloomberg was re-elected mayor in November 2005 by a margin of 20%, the widest margin ever for a Republican mayor of New York.

Bloomberg had spent over $66 million on his campaign by late October 2005, and was projected to exceed the record early 2005, he gave the Independence Party $250,000 to fund a phone bank seeking to recruit volunteers for his re-election campaign.

Former Bronx Borough President Fernando Ferrer won the Democratic nomination to oppose Bloomberg in the general election; there was no opposition in the Republican primary, as Bloomberg's campaign successfully sued to keep Thomas Ognibene off of the ballot. Ognibene, who ultimately ran on the Conservative Party ticket, accuses Bloomberg of betraying Republican Party ideals.

Bloomberg was the most prominent Republican to oppose the successful confirmation of John Roberts as Chief Justice of the United States. Though a Republican, Bloomberg is a staunch supporter of abortion rights and did not believe that Roberts was committed to maintaining Roe v. Wade.

Besides Republican support, Bloomberg had obtained the endorsements of several prominent Democrats: former Mayor Ed Koch, former governor Hugh Carey, former City Council Speaker Peter Vallone, his son, Councilman Peter Vallone, Jr., former Congressman Floyd Flake, and Brooklyn Borough President Marty Markowitz.

Bloomberg's term as mayor ends on December 31, 2009. He is barred by term limits from running again. The election means that the Republicans have held onto the mayor's office for four consecutive elections, or 16 years. Bloomberg joins

Rudy Giuliani and Fiorello LaGuardia as re-elected Republican mayors in this mostly Democratic city.

One of Bloomberg's top aides, Kevin Sheekey, has indicated that Bloomberg is considering running for President in 2008 as an Independent or a Democrat.

Bloomberg has pledged his support to the GLBT community to support marriage equality.

Michael Cudahy

Michael Cudahy was born in 1924 in Milwaukee, Wisconsin. His father, John, was the son of Patrick Cudahy, a wealthy owner of a meat packing company. Unfortunately, due to Irish tradition, the vast majority of the family fortune went to John's eldest brother, Michael.

Michael's father was a well respected attorney in the city and became close friends with a lot of politicians. One of his friends was James Farley, who served as Postmaster General under President Franklin Delano Roosevelt, and Farley convinced John to become the United States Ambassador to Poland.

The family moved to Warsaw in the early 1932 and lived at the embassy there. Michael found it difficult to make friends due to the language barrier, but he became quite a nuisance to the staff members. On one occasion, he disassembled a turntable in the embassy out of curiosity. On another occasion, he fashioned an explosive cigarette and gave it to a Polish general, who had it explode in his face. The incident made the local news and established Michael as an official brat.

In 1934, the family returned to Milwaukee for a short while and Michael developed his interest in electronics and technology. He credits his grandfather, Harrison Reed, for showing him how to use machine tools and the type of mindset required to repair things. Michael began tinkering around at home and invented some creative things, for example a light that was switched on with a pressure switch. He also invented a way to turn on his radio and pull off the bedsheets with a motor when the alarm clock went off. One time, while disassembling his father's pocket watch, disaster struck when parts flew out of it and he found himself unable to put it back together. Luckily, his mother came to his aid and they had the watch repaired before his father came home.

In 1937, Michael's father was appointed ambassador to Ireland and the family moved to live in the embassy in Dublin. While there, Michael met someone named Paddy McCormack, who had a HAM radio. Michael became absolutely fascinated by the radio and built his own at the embassy. Being able to talk to people around the world was like a dream to him. One day, while attempting to increase the power of his antenna on the roof of the embassy, he fell onto the skylight and broke through, luckily without any injuries.

In 1939, the family returned to Milwaukee again and his father was sent to serve as the ambassador to Belgium. At that time, Hitler was directing the initial phases of the invasion of Europe and it was John's job to communicate Hitler's actions directly to the United States. When Hitler invaded Belgium in 1940, John returned to Milwaukee and began working as a reporter for Life Magazine.

Towards the end of 1941, at the start of the United States' involvement in World War 2, Michael was drafted into

Army's Air Corps. Basic training in Lincoln, Nebraska was quite torturous for him since he had grown up in a pretty leisurely lifestyle. Shortly after starting, he was recalled to Milwaukee to learn that his father had died in a horseriding accident. The incident had a profound effect on Michael and he described it as the time when he realized it was time to "grow up".

After completing basic training, he applied for and was accepted in the Truax Field Radio School in Madison, Wisconsin. His aptitude in radio communication was so high that the Army hired him as a teacher before he was transferred to Chanute Field in Rantoul, Illinois to be trained in RADAR technology. There, he also received high marks and was hired to teach classes. He continued to teach throughout the war, but found himself lacking in the area of money.

To get more money, Michael decided to start a business that involved sneaking women in and out of the military base in the trunk of his car. He charged a premium price for this service and it was used quite frequently. He also used his car as a bus service to Milwaukee and made a decent amount of money.

After the war, he returned to Milwaukee and began wondering what he would do with the rest of his life. He met a woman named Mary Lee and married her in 1947. They had a daughter, Susie, in 1948, but he felt overly confined in his marriage. He longed for the freedom granted by being a bachelor and divorced her in 1950. Later that year, he moved to New York City with another man's wife, but she later returned to Milwaukee to live with her husband.

Michael found work at NBC's Radio City, working as a sound technician. He lived with a man named Dick Chenery in Manhattan and they would frequently throw open house parties. With the advent of magnetic tape recordings, Michael got the idea of putting background music in planes. He sold the idea to Presto Recording Company and soon found himself making trips to airlines to sell the product.

Some time after, he was contacted by a man named Warren Cozzens who represented a railroad company and was interested in the background music technology. The two became close friends and Michael moved to Evanstown, Illinois to work for him. Eventually, they decided to start a company as a partnership that would make RF signal generators. The company would be based in Milwaukee and they named it Marquette Electronics.

The first product of Marquette Electronics was a sound synthesizer for usage by musicians. It was designed as a pedal board that would play different bass notes and could be played at the same time as a piano or keyboard. Unfortunately, the end product was too expensive for musicians to purchase and only one "T-BASS" was sold.

Luckily, their next idea would be more successful. Cozzens received a call from a doctor who had the idea of building a central ElectroCardioGraph machine that would save hospitals time and money. Cudahy and Cozzens bought their first office building and set to work building their machine. After hiring some additional help and a lot of tinkering around, they managed to complete the project and deliver it to their first hospital on December 1, 1964.

Unfortunately, the machine did not work at all upon delivery. It actually took another year before it was finally in tune, but not all was well. 3M engineers had been coming to the hospital and poking around the machine. Later, at the American Heart Association Exposition, Marquette Electronics presented its EKG along with 3M, but fortunately the 3M machine did not work at all and the doctors instead became interested in Marquette's product.

Soon the company was making hundreds of millions of dollars every year and employing thousands of people. Michael continued to work closely with the company and its customers to find out what products the medical field really needed. The company became known for its innovative products that made it increasingly easy for doctors to find out what was wrong with their patients and monitor them after treatment.

As CEO, Cudahy exercised his position in a most unusual manner. Part of his management philosophy was to develop trust in his employees. As a result, he made it a point to get to know every one of his employees and make them feel comfortable around him. Neckties were absent from the company in favor of more casual attire such as shorts and sandals.

Mike also allowed the construction of a daycare facility on-site, making Marquette the first company to do it in the state of Wisconsin. He also made alcoholic beverages available at all times to employees, explaining that it represented his trust in the employees. The company also frequently held plays and other fun activities to increase morale and make everyone feel more at home.

As the 1990s arrived, Mike was beginning to fear for the future of his company. He sought proteges to take over for him, but failed to find any individuals that would work. Towards the end of the decade, he began looking for other companies to merge with his. His favorite choice was General Electric and he contacted Jeffrey Immelt, then leader of GE Medical Systems, to discuss the merger. In late 1998, the deal was sealed after a meeting with GE CEO Jack Welch in New York City. GE agreed to pay nearly twice the market value for Marquette stock and all of the stockholders became rich.

Unfortunately, Cudahy began to realize that his baby, Marquette Electronics, would never be the same under different leadership. When GE took over, many of the long time employees left since they couldn't handle the changes. Despite initial promises to preserve the company's policies, such as beer drinking and an extremely casual atmosphere, GE made a lot of changes that irreversibally changed the atmosphere.

In 2001, Cudahy formed the Cudahy Trust Foundation with the goal of donating money intelligently to local charities and needy organizations. He proceeded to donate millions of dollars to organizations like the YMCA, Boys and Girls Club, Marquette University, and the Milwaukee School of Engineering. He has also become a board member of numerous other companies since his retreat from Marquette.

Oskar Schindler

Oskar Schindler was born in Svitavy, Czechoslovakia on April 28, 1908. His parents were wealthy and owned a machinery business. He married a woman named Emily after becoming an adult, but their marriage crumbled after he began abusing alcohol. He ended up having affairs outside of his marriage and produced two illegitimate children.

In 1929, the stock market crashed and his family wnet bankrupt. His father left his mother, who died shortly afterwards, and Oskar was left without a job. He decided to join the Nazi Party in 1930 and move to Poland, where he worked as a machinery salesman.

After the German invasion of Poland, Schindler moved to Krakow, where he purchased a factory in Krakow, Poland that manufactured enamel kitchenware. He decided to open a small enamel shop outside of Krakow, where he employed mainly Jewish workers. By employing them, he also saved them from being sent to concentration camps elsewhere.

Since Germany was ruled by a fascist government, Schindler was forced to manufacture munitions for the Germany military. However, he instructed his workers to purposefully introduce defects into the weaponry such that it could never fire. He hoped that by doing so, the German Army would more easily be defeated.

In 1942, he witnessed a raid by the Germany military on the Krakow Ghetto and was horrified by the treatment of the Jews. As the Jews were rounded to be sent to the Plaszow concentration camp, he met with Amon Goth, the commander of the camp, to arrange for nine hundred of the Jews to be sent to work at a factory instead.

His activities began to make him look suspicious to the Germans and he was twice charged with conspiracy. However, he managed to avoid being jailed by bribing government officials. As the Red Army advanced, he had all of his 1200 workers transferred to Brunnlitz in October of 1944. Unfortunately, a portion of them were accidentally shipped to Auschwitz, but he was able to save them and have them returned.

After the end of World War 2, he moved to Argentina, where he ended up going bankrupt. He returned to Germany in 1958 and pursued several business ventures, all of which ultimately failed. He died on October 9, 1974 in Hildesheim, Germany and was given an honorable burial at the Christian Cemetery at Mount Zion in Jerusalem, Israel.

After Schindler died, one of his workers told his story to an author, Tom Keneally, who wrote a book called "Schindler's Ark". This book was later turned into a movie, "Schindler's List", which was directed by Steven Spielberg.

Oleg Cassini

Oleg Cassini (April 11, 1913 – March 17, 2006) was an American fashion designer noted for being chosen by Jacqueline Kennedy to design her state wardrobe in the 1960s. His clothing designs also appeared in numerous Hollywood films starring his second wife, the actress Gene Tierney.

Born in Paris, France, the eldest son of Countess Marguerite Cassini and her husband, Alexander Loiewski, Oleg Cassini Loiewski was raised in Italy and moved to the United States in 1936. His father was a Russian diplomat, and his maternal grandfather, Arthur Paul Nicholas Cassini, Marquis de Capuzzuchi di Bologna, Count Cassini, was the Russian ambassador to the United States during the administrations of William McKinley and Theodore Roosevelt. His father later adopted his wife's surname, which they deemed more distinguished, and when the family lost its status and fortune in the wake of the Russian Revolution, the Cassinis moved to Italy, where Marguerite Cassini went to work as a fashion designer.

Cassini took American citizenship and became a second lieutenant in the Army during World War II, at Fort Riley, Kansas. Initially, he joined the Coast Guard but as was indicated in his obituary in The New York Times, he joined the Army cavalry corps because he found it more glamorous.

His brother, Igor Cassini, became a famous gossip columnist known as Cholly Knickerbocker.

On September 2, 1938, in Elkton, Maryland – a Russian Orthodox ceremony took place in New York City on September 16 – Cassini became the fourth husband of Mary "Merry" Fahrney, a daughter of Chicago industrialist Emory Homer Fahrney and his wife, the former Marion L. Hills. She was an heiress to the Dr. Peter Fahrney & Sons patent medicine fortune. In addition to having a small role in the 1934 motion picture Cleopatra, which was directed by Cecil B. DeMille and starred Claudette Colbert, Merry Fahrney was an aviator and parachutist frequently known in gossip columns as Madcap Merry. She had previously been married to and divorced from Hugh Parker Pickering, by whom she had a son, Peter, who was adopted at 15 months of age by his maternal grandparents and given the surname Fahrney; Frank Van Sands Eizsner; and Baron Arturo Berlingieri, to whom she was married from July 31, 1937 until February 3, 1938.

Nearly two months after she and Cassini married, on October 26, her divorce from Berlingieri was reversed on appeal. The Illinois Appellate Court declared the divorce invalid on the grounds that the former Baroness Berlingieri's claim of being beaten up four times on her honeymoon was unproven, that she had not established beyond doubt that the baron tried to extort $200,000 from her, and that as she was an Italian citizen by marriage, the Chicago court had no jurisidiction. The divorce, however, was soon resolved in her favor.

Fahrney's divorce from Cassini, which was granted on February 5, 1940, was equally dramatic. She won her case by proving "marital misconduct" on her husband's part, stemming from evidence presented that Cassini had been in the company of "a scantily clad young woman" in his apartment in the Hotel Lowell in New York City. Curiously, however, Fahrney and her first husband, Hugh Pickering, were reported to have been in an adjoining room with an automobile salesman, spying on the couple. Cassini, for his part, denied he had been unfaithful and attempted to prove that his wife had had extramarital affairs, presenting testimony from his cook and the couple's former butler, who claimed that Merry Cassini had been caught in compromising circumstances on three occasions. Cassini also declared that his wife had bought clothes for another man, socialite La Grand Griswold. In handing down the divorce decree in Merry Cassini's favor, the judge declared the defendant's claims of wifely adultery were "unworthy of belief."

In 1941, Merry Fahrney married her fifth husband, a Swede, whom she divorced the same year. In 1944, she married her sixth husband, Carlos Ojeda, Jr, a son of the Mexican ambassador to Argentina.

Cassini's second wife was the American movie star Gene Tierney, whom he married on July 11, 1941. The Cassinis had two daughters, Antoinette Daria Cassini, who was born deaf, blind, and mentally retarded, due to her mother's bout during pregnancy with German measles, and Christina "Tina" Cassini.

Fraught with problems that included Tierney's serious depression after the birth of the couple's handicapped daughter, Cassinis's marriage was short but volatile. Both husband and wife had extramarital relationships, with Tierney's including affairs with John F. Kennedy, Tyrone Power, and Mohammad Reza Pahlavi, the last Shah of Iran. According to The New York Times of March 11, 1947, Tierney won an uncontested divorce in California that year; the action was withdrawn since the couple reconciled before the divorce was made final. However, another divorce action was filed in Los Angeles, California on February 28, 1952, with Tierney declaring that her husband cared more about his tennis game than his wife; the final decree was granted on April 8, 1953.

After his divorce from Tierney, Cassini was, for a brief period of time, unofficially engaged to the actress Grace Kelly.

Cassini studied studied art under Giorgio de Chirico and eventually gravitated to his mother's career, fashion, when he took a job sketching for the French couturier Jean Patou. In the late 1930s, he worked as an assistant to the costume designer Edith Head and in the early 1940s was hired by Paramount Pictures.

Among the films Cassini costumed was The Shanghai Gesture, a 1941 film by Josef Von Sternberg, which starred Cassini's second wife, Gene Tierney, who eventually would only wear Cassini designs onscreen. As a result, Cassini costumes appeared in The Razor's Edge; The Ghost and Mrs. Muir; That Wonderful Urge; Whirlpool; Where the Sidewalk Ends, in which Cassini appeared as a fashion designer; and The Mating Season and On The Riviera.

After the war, Cassini designed ready-to-wear dresses while continuing to design for television, motion pictures, and Broadway.

Cassini shot to international stardom, however, in the early 1960s, thanks to his association with Jacqueline Kennedy. "We are on the threshold of a new American elegance thanks to Mrs. Kennedy's beauty, naturalness, understatement, exposure and symbolism," Cassini said when his selection as the couturier to shape the entire look of the First Lady was announced.

The fashion industry, however, was shocked at Cassini's selection by the White House. As Women's Wear Daily journalist John Fairchild wrote in his 1965 book The Fashionable Savages, "Everyone was surprised. Oleg Cassini had been around for years. He was debonair, amusing, social, but none of the fashion intellectuals had considered him an important designer."

The publicity that Cassini's work for Jacqueline Kennedy received led women from 18 to 80 to copy the look of simple, geometric dresses in sumptuous fabrics and pillbox hats with an elegant coiffure. Meticulously tailored and featuring oversized buttons and boxy jackets, as well as occasionally dramatic decolletage, it was a style that was inspired by the work of Hubert de Givenchy. Cassini designed a reported 300 outfits for the First Lady, including a much-copied coat made of leopard pelts and a heavy satin gown for the inaugural ball in 1961; the Cassini outfits were paid for by her father-in-law, Joseph P. Kennedy, Sr..

The name recognition that he gained during these years led him to be the first designer to have licensing agreements, with his name adorning everything from luggage to nail polish to a trim package on the 1970s AMC Matador automobile. "All I remember about those days are nerves, and Jackie on the phone 'Hurry, hurry, Oleg, I've got nothing to wear'," he wrote in his 1995 book, A Thousand Days of Magic: Dressing Jacqueline Kennedy for the White House.

His designs were shown at the Metropolitan Museum of Art in 2001 in its exhibit Jacqueline Kennedy: The White House Years, which was curated by Vogue's European editor at large, Hamish Bowles.

His partnership with David's Bridal was formed in the 1990s, and they had a line of his wedding dresses at the time of his death.

He died in Manhasset, New York at 92 years of age. He was survived by his third wife, Marianne, his two children, and four grandchildren. He was predeceased by his brother Igor Cassini. At the time of his death, Cassini lived in a Manhattan townhouse and a house in Oyster Bay, New York whose property once had been part of the estate of Louis Comfort Tiffany.

Peter Cooper

Peter Cooper was born in New York City to Dutch parents on February 12, 1791. Cooper did not attend a great deal of school throughout his youth. Instead, his time was spent working with his father in various industrial settings. During Cooper's youth, trades were considered more useful than education. The trades Cooper became adept in included: hat-making, brewing and brick making, etc. His knowledge of machinery and manufacturing increased throughout the years.

At the age of 17, Cooper became an apprentice to a Coach Maker in New York City. For three years, he was employed in Hempstead, Long Island were he made machines for shearing cloth. Cooper voyaged into entrepreneurship by setting up his own shop providing the same service. This was an important transitional period in Cooper's Life. During the Second War of Independence 1812, business proved to be a success for Cooper but his profits soon declined once the war was over. To stay competitive, Cooper converted his facility to a furniture factory. Eventually Cooper sold the business and took an interest in a grocery business, which was ironic for the fact that it was opposite the future Cooper Union.

Cooper took full advantage of the shortcomings of American society before and during the Industrial Era. He saw that there were not enough skilled workers to supply the manufacturing needs of society. Cooper supplemented this demand for manufactured goods with the power of the machine. American soil was plentiful with many natural resources, which included wood, water, metals, etc. Land was plentiful, so expansion was not an issue. These resources provided the necessary conditions for success and growth for most manufacturing organizations within that era.

Iron has long been regarded as a key element in industrial development and compared to wood or copper, it is extremely strong. By heating it, iron is relatively easy to bend and shape using simple tools. Cooper had always fancied the idea of having his own Iron manufacturing company and this was just another business opportunity for him. Cooper had several Iron business ventures which included: manufacture of charcoal iron near Baltimore, a rolling mill in New York City, and several mines in Jersey and the Andover mine. Realizing the importance of this industry, Cooper purchased Ringwood Manor in 1853 for $100,000. The prospects for this purchase far outweighed Cooper's previous ventures and with this new acquisition, his inventive spirit continued.

His some works are:

Invented a machine for shaping wheel hubs.

Concocted a method of siphoning power from ocean tides.

Invented a rotary steam engine.

Unveiled America's first steam locomotive, known as the Tom Thumb.

Patented a musical cradle.

Concocted a method for making salt.

Obtained the very first American patent for the manufacture of gelatin.

Another one of Cooper's accomplishments involved in laying the first Atlantic cable. Cooper was also president of the New York, Newfoundland & London Telegraph Company and the North American Telegraph Company. Along with a few a of Cooper's colleagues, the project for laying the Atlantic cable was completed. This project involved laying communication cable from Valentia, Ireland to Trinity Bay, Newfoundland, requiring the use of two ships because of the bulk of the 2000 miles of cable. The project was completed in 1858 and telegraph messages were exchanged between North America and Britain over a period of three weeks before technical problems caused the failure of the cable."

"After the two ocean cables had been laid successfully, it was found necessary to have a second cable across the Gulf of St. Lawrence. Our delays had been so trying and unfortunate in the past, that none of the stockholders, with the exception of Mr. Field, Mr. Taylor, Mr. Roberts, and myself, would take any interest in the matter. We had to get the money by offering bonds, which we had power to do by charter; and these were offered at fifty cents on the dollar. Mr. Field, Mr. Roberts, Mr. Taylor, and myself were compelled to take up the principal part of the stock at that rate, in order to get the necessary funds. We had to do the business through the Bank of Newfoundland, and the bank would not trust the company, but drew personally on me. I told them to draw on the company, but they continued to draw on me, and I had to pay the drafts or let them go back protested. I was often out ten or twenty thousand dollars in advance, in that way to keep the thing going. After the cable became a success, the stock rose to ninety dollars per share, at which figure we sold out to an English company. That proved to be the means of saving us from loss. The work was finished at last, and I never have regretted it, although it was a terrible time to go through."

During December 1858, Cooper was in the process of developing a conveyer system for ore mining. This conveyor system stretched three miles from Ringwood Mine to a forge at Boardville. The system was composed of seemingly endless amounts of ore that passed through large drums. The ore was carried by barrels that were suspended from the peak of the system. The barrels were capable of supporting a hefty 160 pounds. This system would prove to be much more efficient than conventional methods of transporting ore. There is not much information that states whether or not the conveyor system was completed.

To a large extent, Cooper's success can be attributed to the early training which awakened his innate mechanical ability that made him revered as a pioneer even today. Cooper was not only concerned with his own success, he also believed that others less fortunate should have the opportunity to educate themselves and be successful as well. Cooper provided this opportunity to others by starting Cooper Union.

Cooper was responsible for most, if not all, of the Cooper Union's design. Construction for the institution began in 1853. Steel I beams were normally used for the development of buildings of this size, but at the present time these beams were not available. Once again, Cooper's inventiveness aided the project. He decided to use railroad tracks which were bolted together as a replacement for the steel I beams. The elevator shaft for Cooper Union was circular because Cooper felt it was the most efficient design. To Cooper's surprise elevators were designed using a square template, but and inventor by the name of Elisha Graves Otis designed a special elevator for the school. Cooper poured over nine hundred thousand dollars into Cooper Union.

Cooper's unselfish devotion and everlasting spirit lives on through his work. Cooper's many ventures in life as an apprentice; mechanic, inventor, and humanitarian continue to affect many of our lives till this day. Cooper gave the less fortunate an opportunity to afford education, he was a great pioneer of The Industrial Era manufacturing steel and was even responsible for laying communication cable across the ocean. With all these accomplishments, Cooper's saga lives on. Below is an article that was posted in "The Jersey City Express"edited by Otis M. Macmillan, after Cooper passed in New York city on the 4th of April 1883.

The death of Peter Cooper had plunged me into a peculiar strain of thought. Here was a man whose grand purpose in life was the elevation of the working classes, and to the realization of this object he devoted his time and money with what results is known to the world. On the other hand there is Wm. H. Vanderbilt, a man who devotes his hours by day and many of his hours by night to the accumulation of wealth. As I reviewed the characters of these men the contras they presented impressed me most forcibly. It would be hard in the whole category of human experience to find men differing in all important essentials more widely. One was a philanthropist, the other is a miser. One was benefactor, the other a stumbling block. One did well; the other is constantly doing harm. One helped his fellow-man - the other is injuring him. The death of Peter Cooper causes sorrow, even tears. The death of Vanderbilt would hardly cause a sigh of regret. And yet, of the two, Vanderbilt was and is the most powerful. His wealth, no matter how gained, is potent, and entrenched behind his bags of gold, his coupons and securities, he is enabled to defy and even to laugh at the will of the people. One was revered, the other is despised. One was loved, the other hated. One gave his wealth to the erection of a building that will prove a lasting monument to his love: the other spends his money on pictures for the artistic merit of which he has no perception, and gives balls for the amusement of his children and friends, the cost of which would keep many people from starvation. As I thought of all these things, I not only marveled at the inequality of human justice but was amazed at the peculiarity of the fate, destiny, or whatever you may it that dispenses favors so indiscriminately, and at the same time I thought here is a lesson by which the workingman will do well to profit. It teaches him that wealth is selfish and in the hands of some men a positive danger. Vanderbilt is the embodiment of the elements of monopoly. He uses his vast possessions for the oppression of the very men whose labor placed it in his coffers. In his person they have an admirable illustration of the effects of the monopolistic evil, an evil against which they should be strongly arrayed. Monopoly means the sacrifice of the rights of the many for the privileges of the few, the enrichment of the few at the sacrifice of the many. It is the modern case of Juggernaut under the ponderous wheels of which are dashed the honest product of labor. The death of Peter Cooper has instituted this comparison and I trust the lesson it so eloquently conveys will not be lost upon the men who toil.

Peter Cooper, inventor, industrialist, and idealist, was born in New York City and raised in Peekskill, New York. Not given the opportunity for a formal education, Cooper developed a mechanical inclination at an early age, which led to his pioneering, inventive, and philanthropic spirit.

At the age of seventeen, Cooper left his country home to become an apprentice to a prominent coach builder in New York City. In the years that followed, he owned and operated a furniture factory, a grocery, and a glue-making factory. The foundation of Cooper's wealth came through the development of a glue-making process which he patented in 1830. During this period he married Sarah Bedell. Their marriage produced six children, of which only Edward Cooper and Sarah Amelia survived.

Cooper's other contribution to the industrialization of America included the first American-built stream locomotive, isinglass, gelatin, and a new method of salt-making. He was also a founding member of the company that laid the first Trans-Atlantic telegraph cable.

Peter Cooper's greatest achievement was the establishment of the Cooper Union School for the

Advancement of the Arts and Sciences in 1854. Cooper Union provided a free education to the gifted working class of New York City. He wanted to "give to the world an equivalent in some form of useful labor for all that I consumed in it."

One hundred and fifty years later, Peter Cooper's legacy of Cooper Union still provides scholarship for those students that excel in the arts, engineering, and architecture.

Peter Cooper died at the age of 92 from pneumonia at his home in New York City. An editorial from The Nation stated that Peter Cooper "was a man that united the highest integrity with the highest success

Peter Cooper Hewitt

Peter Cooper Hewitt bears a family name that has been famous in the business, public and philanthropic life of the country for three generations. His grandfather was the famous Peter Cooper, who founded and endowed the Cooper Institute in New York City and who was as widely known for his other benevolences. His father was one of the most aggressive mayors New York City ever had and also made a notable record as a member of the National Congress. Peter Cooper Hewitt is himself noted for his scholarly attainments and inventions.

Peter Cooper Hewitt was born on March 5th 1861 and died on August 25th 1921 at the age of 60 years. He was born in New York City, the son of Abram Stevens Hewitt and Sarah Amelia Cooper. His father, Abram Stevens Hewitt, the son of Peter Cooper, was an iron manufacturer, a merchant and a politician.

Hewitt attended Stevens Institute of Technology at Hoboken, New Jersey. He then attended Columbia University School of Mines in New York City. With such an education, Hewitt went on to pursue his own interests and used the wealth amassed by his grandfather, Peter Cooper, and his father, Abram Stevens Hewitt, to pursue his own interests. This resulted in much of his adult life being devoted to scientific experimentation & investigation. This dedication won him numerous patents but not until in the late 1980's when he was engaged in an electrical experiment, did his work seem worthwhile.

His 1st major invention was 'The Cooper Hewitt mercury-vapor lamp'. He was experimenting with electric conductivity and he was able to prove that a gas can conduct an electrical charge. By doing this, he was able to pass an electric current through mercury gas sealed in a quartz tube. The following illustration is a later version of this lamp.

What originally drove him to explore this field and invent 'The Cooper Hewitt mercury-vapor lamp' was that the lamps that were used in his time were very waste-full compared to today's standards. The incandescent lamps that were used in the 1890s converted only 5% of the energy used into light and converted the other 95% to heat. This is why Hewitt sought to find ways of producing a better light source and he did.

The Cooper Hewitt mercury-vapor lamp produced an intense, cool, bluish-green light when tested. Also, because more than 5% of the energy used was converted into light, it was more efficient and less expensive to operate. The only drawback was its color but Hewitt had enough proof that this idea was worthwhile to pursue. The light started being used for shop work and situations where color differentiation was not critical. Later on, he solved this problem when he found out that the gas he was using, Mercury, lacked the elements that produced red light rays. He simply analyzed the color spectrum and extrapolated that in order to get white rays from bluish-green rays, you simply add the elements that would produce red rays to the spectrum. The solution to adding the red rays was overcome by devising a transformer that would fill in the red rays.

The result of adding this transformer produced a powerful ultraviolet light that became very useful in numerous applications like therapeutical practices, sterilizing and chemical applications. Within a short period of time, there became a great demand for 'The Cooper Hewitt mercury-vapor lamp'. Then in 1902, Hewitt and George Westinghouse formed the 'Cooper Hewitt Electric Company' to manufacture and sell the new lamps. The product gave rise to the firm 'Westinghouse Cooper-Hewitt' in England and they then manufactured and distributed a variety of electric equipment like Hewitt rectifiers, which were very useful in wireless networks, telegraphy & telephony, as well as the Cooper Hewitt oscillator and the Battery-Operated Locomotive Headlamps. The company grew so well due to Hewitt's inventions that by 1914, General Electric Company had assumed a controlling interest in the Cooper Hewitt Electric Company. In addition to his company's success, Hewitt himself was being recognized for his inventions during the years of 1904 to 1914. The inventions were the static converter/mercury arc rectifier and a gliding craft, but it was the static converter/mercury arc rectifier that Hewitt was nominated for and received the prestigious Elliott Cresson Medal of the Franklin Institute.

The gliding craft was another invention of his that came about when Hewitt turned his passions to automobile. In 1907, he developed a small hydroplane motorboat on the theory that only by lessening or by freeing altogether a ship's hull from the friction of the water through which it passes, it could it be made dramatically faster and more efficient. He later proved it when he tested his hydroplane boat, which was powered by a large eight-cylinder engine of his own design. During testing, the hull of his craft would break loose from the water as the speed increased. It rose up and planed on four small wing-shaped hydrofoils that extended from the hull below the water line.

From this achievement, Hewitt pursued interests of powered flight. He wrote articles for the popular press and in 1908, he predicted that one day aircrafts would be more plentiful and cheaper than automobiles. He further launched investigations into the possibility of helicopter flights, which won him U.S. Patent No. 1,134,386 for a balloon envelope and supporting truss.

Hewitt then went on to serve on the first board of governors in 1910 for the newly formed Inventor's Guild. It was formed in New York City to further the interests and secure the rights of those who made contributions in the fields of science and technology. A measure of the Guild's success became evident in 1915, when it was asked by the secretary of the Navy to recommend individuals to the new Naval Advisory Board, which was newly created in response to the war in Europe. Hewitt was named and he later received three patents Nos. 1,350,454, 1,350,455, and 1,350,456 to build a helicopter, which he had earlier launched investigations into in 1908, but no actual physical prototype actually evolved. However, 1n 1920, Hewitt and another engineer named Francis B. Crocker, constructed a full-size working example. It had two counter-rotating blades, which provided sufficient lift to support the craft plus an additional 225 pounds. This is where the life of the helicopter began for the U.S army and would be the last major invention of Hewitt's Days.

Roger W. Babson

Roger Ward Babson (1875-1967) achieved many successes in his lifetime. His personal and professional accomplishments as entrepreneur, educator, and philanthropist demonstrate the merits of his particular formula for success: the combination of tradition and innovation.

Representing the tenth successive generation of Babsons to live in Gloucester, Massachusetts, Roger Babson valued his heritage. He researched his ancestors, investigating their personalities, professions, and lifestyles. Beginning with Isabel Babson, who came to Massachusetts from England in 1637, Roger Babson discovered a lineage of farmers, merchants, midwives, religious preachers, and sea captains. Believing that personality traits were hereditary, Roger Babson continually looked for opportunities to foster and benefit from his ancestors' individual attributes.

Roger Babson also valued lessons from his childhood, especially the business and investment practices he learned from discussions with his father, Nathaniel Babson, who owned a dry goods store. Despite Roger's interest in business, his father had little faith in colleges and their academic programs. Against Roger's wishes, Nathaniel decided his son would pursue a rigorous, technical education at the Massachusetts Institute of Technology. Feeling that the instruction "was given to what had already been accomplished, rather than to anticipating future possibilities," Roger Babson believed that his professors had failed to foresee the great industries of the 20th century: automobiles, aviation, motion pictures, phonographs and radios. The one aspect of his studies at M.I.T. that he valued throughout his life was learning about the British scientist, mathematician, and philosopher, Isaac Newton. Roger Babson was impressed by Newton's discoveries, especially his third law of motion—"For every action there is an equal and opposite reaction." He eventually incorporated Newton's theory into many of his personal and business endeavors.

While on break from M.I.T., Roger Babson applied his engineering studies to various highway projects throughout Massachusetts. Upon graduating in 1898, Roger knew for certain that he preferred an alternative career. Nathaniel Babson counseled Roger to find a line of work that would ensure "repeat" business indefinitely. After careful consideration, Roger Babson decided to try the world of finance and looked for work as an investment banker.

In 1898, Roger began his business career working for a Boston investment firm where he learned about securities, stocks, and bonds. Inquisitive by nature, Roger Babson soon knew enough about investments to get himself fired. Acting in the best interests of his clients, he had questioned the methods and prices of his employer and quickly found himself out of work. Babson subsequently set up his own business selling bonds at competitive prices in New York City and then in Worcester, Massachusetts. By 1900, he returned to Boston to work once more for an investment house and in

March of that year, he married Grace Margaret Knight and moved to Wellesley Hills, Massachusetts.

In the fall of 1901, Roger Babson contracted tuberculosis. His doctors initially told him that that a cold "had settled on his lungs." When Roger demanded to know the exact nature of his illness, he was given a decidedly gloomy prognosis. The tuberculosis had seriously affected one lung and had begun to attack the other; it was not certain if he would survive. For Roger Babson, resignation was not an option. Demonstrating his characteristically dogged determination, he resolved to fight the disease and live a productive life. Rather than seek a "fresh air" cure in the milder climates of the American Southwest, Roger remained in Wellesley Hills. Cared for by Grace, a nurse by training, Roger gave a great deal of thought to how to continue his investment career away from a city environment. He ultimately decided to start a business based upon his investment expertise. While Roger finalized his business plans, Edith Low Babson, Roger and Grace Babson's only child, was born on December 6, 1903.

Aware that every financial institution employed statisticians who duplicated each other's research efforts, Roger chose to develop a central clearinghouse for information on investment information and business conditions. He would publish his analysis of stocks and bonds in newsletters and sell subscriptions to interested banks and investors. In 1904, with an initial investment of $1,200, Roger and Grace Babson founded Babson's Statistical Organization, later called Business Statistics Organization and then Babson's Reports, which continued to thrive until as Babson-United Investment Reports it closed its doors in 2001. As pioneers who helped revolutionize the financial services industry, the Babson's and their organization realized millions of dollars in annual revenues in the company's first decade.

Having amassed a sizable fortune, Roger Babson was not content to join the idle rich. Instead he shared his business knowledge to protect investors, and invested his own wealth in industries and endeavors that would benefit humanity.

After witnessing a dramatic stock market crash and financial panic in 1907, Roger Babson expanded his investment practice to include counseling on what to buy and sell as well as when it was wise to purchase or unload stocks. Working with M.I.T. Professor of Engineering George F. Swain, Roger Babson applied Isaac Newton's theory of "actions and reactions" to economics, originating the Babsonchart of economic indicators, which assessed current and predicted future business conditions. Although the Babsonchart has since proved to be an imperfect tool, through it Roger Babson earned the distinction of being the first financial forecaster to predict the stock-market crash of October, 1929, and the Great Depression that followed.

Roger Babson extended his interest in the public's welfare beyond investment counseling. He encouraged industries to develop products to improve public health and safety. Among businesses receiving Roger Babson's approval and financial backing were select manufacturers of sanitary paper towels and other hygienic products, fire alarm call boxes, fire sprinklers, and traffic signals.

Roger Babson saw it as his duty to share his insights and experience. An avid reader and writer, he sought to dispense his brand of advice and wisdom beyond the readership of Babson's Reports. From 1910 to 1923, he commented on business and other matters as a regular columnist for the Saturday Evening Post. He also contributed weekly columns for the New York Times and for the newspapers owned by the Scripps Syndicate. Babson eventually formed his own syndicate, the Publishers Financial Bureau, to disseminate his writings to papers across the United States. Over the course of 33 years, he authored 47 books, including his autobiography, Actions and Reactions. Although his writings covered topics as diverse as business, education, health, industry, politics, religion, social conditions, and travel, the primary message behind each work was that individuals and society could and should change for the better.

Beginning in 1908, Roger Babson offered through Babson's Statistical Organization a correspondence course on how to sell bonds. This endeavor was an instant success and courses in economics, finance, and distribution soon followed. He then saw the need for a private college that specialized in business education. In June 1919, in a special letter to clients of the B.S.O., Roger Babson announced the establishment of a school of business administration to provide not only practical but also ethical training for young men wishing to become business executives. On September 3, 1919, with an enrollment of 27 students, the Babson Institute held its first classes in the former home of Roger and Grace Babson on Abbott Road in Wellesley Hills.

From the very beginning, Roger Babson set out to distinguish the Babson Institute from other colleges offering instruction in business. The Institute provided intensive training in the fundamentals of production, finance, and distribution in just one academic year, rather than the standard four. The curriculum was divided into four subject areas: practical economics, financial management, business psychology, and personal efficiency, which covered topics such as ethics, personal hygiene, and interpersonal relationships. The program's pace did not allow time for liberal arts courses and it was assumed that students would learn these subjects elsewhere.

Believing experience to be the best teacher, Roger Babson favored a curriculum that was a combination of both class work and actual business training. Seasoned businessmen instead of career academicians made up the majority of the faculty. To better prepare students for the realities of the business world, the Institute's curriculum focused more on practical experience and less on lectures. Students worked on group projects and class presentations, observed manufacturing processes during field trips to area factories and businesses, met with managers and executives, and viewed industrial films on Saturday mornings.

The Institute also maintained a simulated business environment as part of the students' everyday life. The students, required to wear professional attire, kept regular business hours and were monitored by punching in and out on a time clock. They were also assigned an office desk equipped with a telephone, typewriter, adding machine, and Dictaphone. Personal secretaries typed the students' assignments and correspondence in an effort to accurately reflect the business world. Roger Babson prepared his students to enter their chosen careers as executives, not anonymous members of the work force.

Babson College continues to be one of Roger Babson's greatest achievements. Remaining close to his initial conception of offering practical business and management instruction, the College now offers a graduate business degree and courses in executive education in addition to a four-year undergraduate business program. Roger Babson's success with Babson College led him to establish Webber College in Babson Park, Florida, in 1927. Named after his granddaughter, Camilla Grace Webber, the College initially provided business education to women, similar in many ways to the courses at Babson College. Webber College is now a coeducational institution. To bring practical business instruction to other parts of the United States, in 1946, Roger Babson established a two-year, certificate-granting school, Utopia College, in Eureka, Kansas. Utopia College graduates were invited to complete their baccalaureate degrees at the Babson Institute. Due to declining enrollments, Utopia College closed in the early 1970s.

Following Newton's law of "actions and reactions," as one venture in Roger Babson's life concluded, a new endeavor naturally began. He was never discouraged by setbacks. One of his greatest assets was his willingness to take chances and to rebound when risks overshadowed outcomes. In addition to his pursuits in education and business, Roger Babson actively engaged in religion, politics, and scientific advances.

According to Roger Babson, the greatest experience of his life was his religious conversion at the age of fifteen. Indeed, an unshakable faith in God was one of his primary personal beliefs. From 1936 to 1938, Babson served as National Church Moderator for the General Council on the Congregational-Christian Churches. During his term, he forced the Council to examine itself and its weaknesses as he continually pushed himself, his business colleagues, and the students who studied at the Babson Institute. Using statistics, Babson showed that church development and attendance followed a cyclical pattern that was similar to business trends. He feared that the declining interest in religious activities was a clear and accurate indicator of the declining moral state of society. His appeals to chart a more morally correct course for the church, and for society, were met with defiance and personal threats. Roger Babson's tenure as moderator ended in great disappointment.

However, not one to give up easily, Babson turned his attention to the promotion of an "Open Church." Through a volunteer network, church doors would be unlocked every day, all day, so that persons of any faith could pause for private worship within the spiritual and curative sanctuary of a church. This experiment began in Wellesley in 1938; by 1942, the national Open Church Association was incorporated with its headquarters in Roger Babson's ancestral home of Gloucester.

Roger Babson's religious convictions also extended into the world of politics. In 1940, he ran for President of the United States as the candidate for the National Prohibition Party. Although the church-affiliated party was best known for wanting to outlaw vices such as alcohol, gambling, and narcotics, as well as indecent movies and publications, the party also advocated reducing debt and taxation, conserving natural resources, aiding farmers, and "assuring workers and consumers a fair share of industry's products and profits." Although Roger Babson knew his party would not win the election, he felt it was his duty to bring its moral and religious agenda to the nation. Out of a field of eight candidates, Roger Babson followed third behind Franklin Roosevelt and Wendell Wilkie.

Another risk that Roger Babson took, although he was often ridiculed, was to promote research on gravity. Believing that the scientific community had done very little to expand upon Isaac Newton's studies of gravity, he created the Gravity Research Foundation in 1948. Roger maintained that a conductor could be built, along the same principles as a waterwheel, for harnessing gravity waves as they occur in nature. He hoped that the invention of a perpetual motion machine would solve the world's dependence on nonrenewable fuels. The nonprofit foundation, which still exists today, encourages research and acts as a clearinghouse for studies on gravity.

Throughout his long life and his many enterprises, Roger Babson was able to successfully foresee and foster change while holding fast to fundamental spiritual and ethical values. As a devoted educator, he saw it as his mission to pass along the basic truths that he learned from experience:

"It is not knowledge which young people need for success, so much as those basic qualities of integrity, industry, imagination, common sense, self-control and a willingness to struggle and sacrifice. Most individuals already have far more knowledge than they use. They need inheritance and development of a character which will cause them properly to apply this knowledge. . .Real business success comes through the qualities above mentioned, not through money, degrees, or social standing."

Robert Bacon

Among the representative men of South Otter township none stand forth more conspicuously than does Robert Bacon. Although not one of the first settlers in the township, yet by great industry, coupled with sound practical economy and excellent judgment, he has rightfully assumed a place with the largest farmers and most substantial business men of the county. As exhibiting an example worthy the emulation of all, particularly the young, we herewith present a brief sketch of Mr. Bacon's life and character, feeling as though the history of South Otter township would be incomplete without a notice of that gentleman. He is now the present nominee of the republican party for county treasurer; is a native of England, and was born in Norfolk, near the city of Norwich, on June 10th, 1825. His father, Richard Bacon, was a farmer in comfortable circumstances, and his wife's maiden name was Mary K. Sayers. Robert Bacon was the second of eight children. From the time he was old enough, he was sent to school quite regularly, and laid the foundation for the main part of his education in England before coming to America. He had little opportunity for attending school after coming to this country, and with the exception of the opportunities he had in England, his education is mostly the result of his own efforts. In 1835 his father emigrated with his family to America; came across in a sailing vessel, the voyage occupying about a month, and reached New York June 1st 1835. From New York they went to the city of Troy, where the family remained until the fall of 1837, and then removed to the West. Reaching St. Louis, the family came at once to Carlinville, settling there on the recommendation of Dr. Gideon Blackburn, whom his father had met in Troy. On coming to the county his father moved on Dr. Blackburn's farm, near Carlinville, and lived there one year, and then the family moved to Chesterfield township, and rented the farm now owned by Nicholas Challacombe. While living there, Mr. Bacon's father died, in August, 1839. His mother moved then, with the family, to a farm north of Carlinville, and in the spring of 1840 his mother entered forty acres of land in section 19, town 11, range 7, where she lived for some years, and where the children were raised. Her place was Mr. Bacon's home until he was twenty-four years of age. For a couple of years he worked by the month in Chesterfield township, and the remainder of the time was employed in farming at home, until his marriage, which occurred November 18, 1849, to Miss Mary A. Miller. Mrs. Bacon was born in Floyd county, Indiana, and became a resident of Macoupin county in 1836. Her father was Henry Miller, who came to the county that year and settled on section 30, South Otter township. After Mr. Bacon was married he went to farming on his own account where he now resides, and has ever since been engaged in farming. His farm consists of 240 acres, and a view of his residence is shown elsewhere among the illustrations in this work. Mr. and Mrs. Bacon have had three children: Emily, who married George M. Killam, and is now deceased; Henry R., who died in infancy; and Anna

M., wife of John C. Wiggins. Mr. Bacon began his political life as a member of the old whig party, and cast his first vote for president in 1848. He voted the whig ticket until the dissolution of that party, and when the war broke out he became a strong and earnest republican, and has remained a member of that party sever since. In 1872 he was chosen supervisor of South Otter township, and was re-elected to that position the succeeding year. He was one of the board of supervisors during the period when the trouble became most prominent regarding a levy of a tax with which to pay the indebtedness incurred by the county in building the courthouse. He took a determined stand against paying anything of what he believed to be an unjust claim until the matters had been compromised on a just and equitable basis. As a member of the board, he voted against the levy of a tax in compliance with the mandamus of the United States circuit court, and was one of the seventeen who were fined one thousand dollars each for refusing to comply with the mandamus and levy a tax. In 1876 he was the republican candidate for circuit clerk, and made a race creditable to himself, receiving more votes than the majority of the ticket. In 1879 the republican convention nominated him by acclamation as their candidate for county treasurer. Mr. Bacon is a man who stands well among the citizens of the county. He is a gentleman of personal honor and integrity, and has been influential in the counsels of the republican party in Macoupin county. In conclusion, Mr. Bacon may be relied upon as a sterling business man, quiet in his demeanor, and charitable where there is any just claim. What he has is the result of hard labor, the cumulative proceeds on the earnings of a poor boy.

Richard Branson

Sir Richard Charles Nicholas Branson (born 18 July 1950) is an English entrepreneur, best known for his Virgin brand, a banner that encompasses a variety of business organizations. The name Virgin was chosen because a female friend involved in setting up the initial record label commented "We're all virgins at business".

Sir Richard Branson was educated at Stowe until he was 15 years old, and he began his entrepreneurial activities there by setting up Student Magazine. When he was 17, he opened a Student Advisory Centre, his first charity institution. Branson set up a record mail order business in 1970, started a record shop in Oxford Street, London shortly afterwards, and then in 1972 the record label Virgin Records with Nik Powell, opening a recording studio.

The company's first issue was multi-instrumentalist Mike Oldfield's Tubular Bells, which was to be a best-seller.

Branson's company also courted controversy by signing bands like the Sex Pistols, whose contract more conventional companies had dispensed with. Virgin also introduced Culture Club to the music world. Later, in 1992, Branson sold the Virgin label to EMI, a more conservatively-minded company which had rescinded the contract of the Pistols. Branson is said to have wept when the sale was completed since the record business had been the genesis of the Virgin empire. He later formed V2 Records to re-enter the music business. In the early 1980's he purchased the gay Nightclub Heaven

Branson has rarely worn the conventional businessman's uniform of shirt, tie and suit, preferring a more relaxed image. He was initially known for sporting a wide range of pullovers - which he later discarded after press reports pointed out they were less than fashionable. He then went through a period of wearing predominately black.

Described as "flamboyant" by the mainstream media, Branson's personality can partly be credited for his successful career. Branson is known for his outlandish media events used to promote his businesses. He is keen on playful antagonisms, exemplified by his "Mine is bigger than yours" decals on the new Airbus A340-600 jets used by his airline. Also Virgin Atlantic aircraft displayed a Vargas-designed Scarlet Lady painted near the cockpit. This scantily-clad woman originally held a Virgin headscarf firmly on one hand and the airline's main rival, British Airways' headscarf in the other, which she is discarding. The design has since been adapted to make the image more "British" as she now holds a Union Jack flag.

With balloon designer and builder, Per Lindstrand, in 1987 Branson successfully flew in the first hot air balloon to cross the Atlantic Ocean. The Virgin Atlantic Flyer, was the most advanced hot air balloon ever built, and was then the largest ever flown at 60,513 m^3 volume. Designed as the first hot air balloon to fly in the jetstreams the balloon reached ground speeds in excess of 130 mph. Also in 1987, Branson started Virgin Healthcare Foundation, a charity foundation that helps people with AIDS.

In 1991, again with Lindstrand, Branson crossed the Pacific Ocean from Japan to Arctic Canada in a hot air balloon. They travelled a distance of 7,672 km, but their track took them a claimed 10,885 km. This again broke all existing records with speeds of up to 245 mph in an even larger hot air balloon that remains the largest ever built – measuring 74,000 m³. In December 1998, in an unsuccessful attempt to circumnavigate the world, Branson, partnered by Lindstrand and adventurer Steve Fossett, flew for 7 days and covered over 20,000 km in a Rozière balloon, launching from Morocco and landing in Hawaii.

In July 2003, Branson flew a replica of the first heavier-than-air flying machine, the glider designed by Sir George Cayley, at the original site in Yorkshire. In October in the same year, he announced that he would be lead sponsor for Steve Fossett in an attempt to break the record for a non-stop flight around the world. A new aircraft, the GlobalFlyer, was built specially for the attempt by Scaled Composites, and on March 3, 2005, at 01:50pm CST, Fossett completed the record-breaking flight in 67 hours and 1 minute, with an average speed of nearly 300 mph.

Branson formed Virgin Atlantic Airways in 1984, launched Virgin Mobile in 1999, Virgin Blue in Australia in 2000, and later failed in a 2000 bid to handle the National Lottery.

In 1997 Branson took what many saw as being one of his riskier business exploits by entering into the railway business. Virgin Trains won the franchises for the former InterCity West Coast and Cross-Country sectors of British Rail. Launched with the usual Branson fanfare with promises of new high-tech tilting trains and enhanced levels of service, Virgin Trains soon ran into problems with the aging rolling stock and crumbling infrastructure it had inherited from BR. The company's reputation was almost irreversably damaged in the late 1990s as it struggled to make trains reliably run on time while it awaited the modernisation of the West Coast Main Line, and the arrival of new rolling stock.

Virgin has also started a European short-haul airline, Virgin Express, and a national airline based in Nigeria, called Virgin Nigeria. Another airline, Virgin America, is set to launch out of San Francisco in 2006. Branson has also developed a Virgin Cola brand, but is now retreating only to the UK market, and even a Virgin Vodka brand, which has not been an overly successful enterprise. As a consequence of these lacklustre performers, satirical British fortnightly magazine, Private Eye, has been critical of Branson and his companies.

After the so-called campaign of "dirty tricks" , Branson sued rival airline British Airways for libel in 1992. John King, then-chairman of British Airways, countersued Branson, and the case went to trial in 1993. British Airways, faced with likely defeat, settled the case, giving £500,000 to Branson and a further £110,000 to his airline and had to pay legal fees of up to £3 million. Branson divided his compensation among his staff.

On September 25, 2004 he announced the signing of a deal under which a new space tourism company, Virgin Galactic, will license the technology behind SpaceShipOne to take paying passengers into suborbital space. The group plans to make flights available to the public by late 2007 with tickets priced at $200,000. The deal was mostly financed by Microsoft co-founder Paul Allen, and the modern American space engineer & visionary, Burt Rutan.

Branson has been tagged as a 'transformational leader' by management lexicon, with his maverick strategies and his stress on the Virgin Group as an organization driven on informality and information, one that's bottom heavy rather than strangled by top-level management.

Although Branson says his success was not planned, and it just happened, he has said that he has 10 secrets to success:

1. You've got to challenge the big ones.
2. Keep it casual.
3. Haggle: everything is negotiable.
4. Have fun working.
5. Do the right things for the brand.
6. Smile for the cameras!
7. Don't lead "sheep", herd "cats".
8. Move like a bullet.
9. Size does matter.
10. Be a common, regular person.

He was 9th in the Sunday Times Rich List 2006.

Branson was fêted by the Conservative government in the 1980s, and was briefly given the post of "litter tsar" by Margaret Thatcher – charged with "keeping Britain tidy". He was again seen as close to the government when the Labour Party came to power in 1997. In 2005 he declared that there were only negligible differences between the two main parties on economic matters. He reputedly considered running for Mayor of London in 2004, but decided not to. Branson has described himself as a libertarian.

In 1993, Branson received the honorary degree of Doctor of Technology from Loughborough University.

He became Sir Richard Branson when he was knighted by the Queen in 1999 for "services to entrepreneurship".

He is the Patron of the International Rescue Corps which is one of the few truly independent front-line search and rescue organisations in the world - a UK registered charity, financed solely by donations and their own fund raising, and manned totally by volunteers.

He has guest starred, playing himself, on several television shows, including Friends, Baywatch, Birds of a

Feather, The Daily Show, Only Fools and Horses, The Day Today and a special episode of the comedy Goodness Gracious Me. He also was the star of a reality television show on Fox called The Rebel Billionaire, in which sixteen contestants were tested for their entrepreneurship and sense of adventure. It did not succeed as a rival show to Donald Trump's The Apprentice and only lasted one season. Sir Richard appears at No. 85 on the 2002 list of "100 Greatest Britons".

Richard Boyle, 3rd Earl of Burlington

Richard Boyle, 3rd Earl of Burlington and 4th Earl of Cork (April 25, 1694 - December 15, 1753), born in Yorkshire, was a descendant of Richard Boyle, 1st Earl of Cork.

Lord Burlington, also known as "the architect Earl", was instrumental in the revival of Palladian architecture. He succeeded to the title and extensive estates in Yorkshire and Ireland at the age of ten. Three foreign Grand Tours 1714 - 1719 and a further trip to Paris in 1726 gave him opportunities to develop his taste. His professional skill as an architect was extraordinary in an English aristocrat. He carried his copy of Andrea Palladio's book I Quattro Libri dell'Architettura with him in touring the Veneto in 1719, and made copious notes in the margins.

Burlington never closely inspected Roman ruins or made detailed drawings on the sites; he relied on Palladio and Scamozzi as his interpreters of the classic tradition. Another source of his inspiration were drawings he collected, some drawings of Palladio himself, which had belonged to Inigo Jones and many more of Inigo Jones' pupil John Webb, which Kent published in 1727 as Some Designs of Mr Inigo Jones... with Some Additional Designs that were by Kent and Burlington. The important role of Jones' pupil Webb in transmitting the palladian—neo-palladian heritage was not understood until the 20th century. Burlington's Palladio drawings include many reconstructions after Vitruvius of Roman buildings, which Burlington planned to publish. In the meantime, in 1723 he adapted the palazzo facade in the illustration for the London house of General Wade in Old Burlington Street, which was engraved for Vitruvius Britannicus iii. The process put a previously unknown Palladio design into circulation.

Burlington's first project, appropriately, was his own London residence, Burlington House, where he dismissed his baroque architect James Gibbs when he returned from the continent in 1719 and employed the Scottish architect Colen Campbell, with the history-painter-turned-designer William Kent for the interiors. The courtyard front of Burlington House, prominently sited in Piccadilly, was the first major executed statement of neo-Palladianism.

In the 1720s Burlington and Campbell parted, and Burlington was assisted in his projects by the young Henry Flitcroft, "Burlington Harry"— who developed into a major architect of the second neopalladian generation— and Daniel Garrett— a straightforward palladian architect of the second rank— and some draughtsmen.

By the early 1730s Palladian style had triumphed as the generally-accepted manner for a British country house or public building. For the rest of his life Burlington was "the Apollo of the arts" as Horace Walpole phrased it— and Kent his 'proper priest."

Many of Burlington's projects have suffered, from rebuilding or additions, from fire, from losses due to urban sprawl. In many cases his ideas were informal: at Holkham Hall the architect Matthew Brettingham recalled that "the general ideas were first struck out by the Earls of Burlington and Leicester, assisted by Mr. William Kent." Brettingham's engraved publication of Holkham credited Burlington specifically with ceilings for the portico and the north dressing-room.

Burlington's architectural drawings, inherited by his son-in-law the Duke of Devonshire are preserved at Chatsworth, and enable attributions that would not otherwise be possible.

1. Burlington House, Piccadilly, London: Burlington's own contribution is likely to have been restricted to the former colonnade. In London, Burlington offered designs for features at several aristocratic free-standing dwellings, none of which have survived: Queensbury House in Burlington Gardens; Warwick House, Warwick Street; Richmond House, Whitehall;

2. Tottenham Park, Wiltshire, for Charles, Lord Bruce: from 1721, executed by Burlington's protegé Henry Flitcroft. In the original house, the high corner pavilion blocks of Inigo Jones' Wilton were provided with the "Palladian window" motif to be seen at Burlington House. Burlington, with a good eye for garden effects, also designed ornamental buildings in the park.

3 Westminster School, the Dormitory: 1722 - 1730 the first public work by Burlington, for which Sir Christopher Wren had provided a design, which was rejected in favor of Burlington's, a triumph for the Palladians and a sign of changing English taste.

4. Old Burlington Street, London: houses, including one for General Wade: 1723. General Wade's house adapted the genuine Palladio facade in Burlington's collection of drawings.

5. Waldershare Park, Kent, the Belvedere Tower: 1725 – 27. A design for a garden eye-catcher that might have been attributed to Colen Campbell, were it not for a ground plan among Burlington's drawings at Chatsworth.
6. Chiswick House Villa, Middlesex: The "Casina" in the gardens, 1717, was Burlington's first essay. The house he designed for himself was demolished. The villa is one of the gems of European 18th-century architecture.
7. The Assembly Rooms, York: 1731 – 32. In the basilica-like space, Burlington attempted an archaeological reconstruction "with doctrinaire exactitude" of the "Egyptian Hall" described by Vitruvius, as it had been interpreted in Palladio's Quattro Libri. The result is one of the grandest Palladian public spaces.
8. Castle Hill, Devonshire
9. Northwick Park,
10. Kirby Hall, Yorkshire. An elevation

Richard married Lady Dorothy Saville on 21 March 1720. Dorothy was daughter of William Savile, 2nd Marquess of Halifax and Mary Finch.

Mary was daughter of Daniel Finch, 2nd Earl of Nottingham and Lady Essex Rich. Essex was daughter of Robert Rich, 3rd Earl of Warwick and Anne Cheeke. Anne was daughter of Sir Thomas Cheeke of Pirgo and a senior Essex Rich.

The elder Essex was daughter of Robert Rich, 1st Earl of Warwick and Penelope Devereux, Lady Rich. Essex was probably named after her maternal grandfather Walter Devereux, 1st Earl of Essex. Her maternal grandmother was Lettice Knollys.

Richard D'Oyly Carte

Without Richard D'Oyly Carte there would have not been any Gilbert and Sullivan Operas. Carte's unique combination of musical knowledge and business sense not only made a beginning possible but he formed a basis from which the whole combination could stand permanently.

Richard D'Oyly Carte was born in Soho on May 3rd, 1844. Sullivan was two and Gilbert was eight. Carte's father, also named Richard, was a partner in an instrument making firm, Rudall, Carte and Company. This company was responsible for bringing the recent invention of the saxophone to England for the first time. The elder Carte was a flute player, and had always been in the music business one way or another. Richard grew up in a family that was familiar with the arts and other cultures. Their house was always filled with musicians, poets, painters and other artists.

While Sullivan was singing in the Chapel Royal, Carte entered the University School of London. He, however, wanted to take a serious part in his father's business and so he left University before completing the course. All through his life he showed his mastery of the business of theater and culture in general. College education would not help him in this respect.

Carte was a bit of an amateur composer himself. At the age of twenty-four he wrote a score for a comic-opera, Doctor Ambrosias - His Secret. Other operettas followed over the next few years. Marie in 1871 and Happy Hampstead in 1877. Throughout his life his dream was to establish a vehicle for getting English Opera and Operetta onto the stage.

His career started by the establishment of an operatic and concert management agency near his father's shop. This little office grew large and important enough to handle some of the best performers who visited England. This clients included Adelina Patti, Oscar Wilde and Charles Gounod.

At an early stage in the business Carte hired a young girl to run the office. She was Helen Cowper-Black, or Helen Lenoir. She married Carte in 1888 and took over the running of the Opera company after his death in 1901.

In 1870 Carte suggested to Sullivan that he compose a comic-opera. The composer was far too involved in oratorio for any interest in that avenue. So Carte composed one himself but nothing came of it. Then he saw Thespis. John Hollingshead had brought Sullivan and Gilbert for their first production. It was a flop but Carte saw something in this combination and kept the thought at the back of his head for four years.

In 1875 Carte became the business manager of a little theatre in Soho, the Royalty. It was Carte's plan to build up a repertory of comic operas. He began with Offenbach's La Périchole, which would be the first performance in England. As it was too short a work for one evening he needed something else, preferably English.

Gilbert had a script which had originally been expanded from one of his Bab Ballads. It was called Trial by Jury. Carte immediately suggested that they approach Sullivan to compose the score. Gilbert agreed. Thus

the triumphant triple career of Gilbert, Sullivan and D'Oyly Carte began.

Trial by Jury was such a success that it embarrassed its partner, La Périchole, which Carte soon replaced with a less famous English work. The run could have gone on and on had not the leading man, Fred Sullivan, the composer's brother, taken sick. The production could not continue for he had a superb comic technique around which he had built the characterization of The Learned Judge.

With a success on his hands carte had no trouble interesting a few people to back a large company which would devoted to the production of english comic-operas. He formed the Comedy Opera Company, which leased the Opéra Comique. He commissioned new works. There were three teams: Burnard and Cellier, Albery and Clay and Gilbert and Sullivan. The first two produced nothing much of note, but the last brought out The Sorcerer late in 1877.

The cast for this first opera was chosen with an eye towards future productions, and the personalities of the people thus hired helped to determine the types of characters in later plays. Gilbert and Sullivan were allowed free reign, with no interference in matters of script, casting, rehearsal or production. carte managed the business of the theatre with an efficiency that rendered its mechanics invisible to the authors.

After The Sorcerer came H.M.S. Pinafore, which sailed along so merrily that a touring company was sent to the United States to produce an authorized version there under the personal supervision of Gilbert and Sullivan. There were several versions of Pinafore going on already in New York and Philadelphia, and there was no legal way to stop them. But when the real thing hit the Fifth Avenue Theatre, the

American's flocked to see the authorized production. Things went so well that the authors premiered their next work in New York. There was a single performance in England for copyright purposes.

The climax of the early period of Gilbert and Sullivan was Patience. This was Gilbert's satire on L'Art Nouveau, in which Oscar Wilde figured importantly. carte discussed the possibility of an American tour with Wilde, pointing out that the forthcoming opera would contribute to the artistic causes that Wilde toyed with and that it might increase the size of his own audience. Wilde did undertake the tour and he became a travelling advertisement for the opera that would follow.

Patience was an immediate success and Carte decided that a new theatre was necessary. It was not a Company matter; he would build it with his own money and lease it to the Company t a rate lower than it was actually worth. On the 10th of October the Savoy Theatre opened with a redressed production of Patience.

Carte's theatre seated 1292 people and was the first public building to be lit entirely by electricity. There were 1200 bulbs in the house powered by a steam generator in a separate building The savoy Theatre was a success. Carte later built a hotel next door.

During the period of Princess Ida, The Mikado and Ruddigore, the two authors began to have personal difficulties that tended to stretch their working relations to a dangerous point. Carte, although he sometimes sided with Sullivan, managed to keep himself pretty well out of it. Gilbert continually interfered with his part of the operation by demanding to be allowed to approve and disapprove of every business expense.

In 1888 carte married the girl who had been with him in the business from the beginning, Helen Lenoir. They lived ion a very large, very fashionable house. This included the first private lift.

At the time of The Yeomen of the Guard the relationship between the author and the composer began to deteriorate. Carte had to keep the peace and get the two to work together again.

What finally accomplished the reconciliation was Carte offering to stage the first English grand opera and to get Sullivan to compose the first work. Sullivan jumped at the chance and also allowed him to work on another comic opera with Gilbert. They decided on The Gondoliers and the rift was temporary healed.

When the expenses for The Gondoliers were tallied, Gilbert exploded. He objected to the costs of several items including £500 for a carpet in the front of the house! He could not see why the company should be responsible for the expeneses of the building Carte owned. Carte argued that was normal for a lesse to return a building to its owner in the condition in which he found it, and thta therefore the carpets that hd been worn down by the thousands who came to see Gilbert and Sullivan productions should be replaced by the Company that benefited from the sale of those thousands of tickets. Gilbert refused to accept the argument and demanded a full accounting from Carte. Carte pointed out that he had taken all the risks of putting up the building, had rented it at a figure below the normal rental to the Company, and had even included all the profits from concessions within the theatre as part of the receipts of the producing company. He was offended by Gilbert's outburst and told him so. The affair burst into court, where Gilbert proved the legal point and Carte proved the moral one. The result was no major chnge in the financial operations of the Company.

It was Helen Lenoir who stepped into the uproar. Both had spoken in anger and both had said things that neither would have said under normal circumstances.

Gilbert would have nothing to do with the new theatre Carte built for Sullivan's serious opera. Ivanhoe played a while and died. The home of English Grand Opera would fade into relative oblivion.

The Savoy was in a bad way also. There was no new opera to replace The Gondoliers. For the first time Carte permitted a different team of authors to write for it. They brought out The Nautch Girl with music by Edward Solomon. It closed after 199 performances. There followed The Vicar of Bray, also by solomon. It did a little better, but nothing compared to the works of Gilbert and Sullivan.

It 1893 the old team reunited with Utopia Ltd. Gilbert refused to work on the same contractual basis as before but preferred a definite percentage of the receipts as his share of the profits. Utopia Ltd did not last long enough to make a difference.

The last collaboration was the Grand Duke, also a failure.

The D'Oyly Carte Opera Company lived on. For a few years the money continued to flow in and Carte continued to distribute the profits as before. On the 7th of November, 1900, Carte wanted the three partners to take the stage for a bow together. He and Gilbert made it, each on canes, but Sullivan lay at home in bed in pain. He died near the end of the month.

Carte followed him, on the 3rd of April, 1901. He left his wife in charge of the Company, which she managed with continued success until her own death in 1913. His son, Rupert, then took over He rebuilt the Savoy Company. He died in 1949 and Bridget D'Oyly Carte took over, keeping the management within the family that has made the Company famous. Without Richard D'Oyly Carte, the successes of Gilbert and Sullivan would never have taken place

Robert Chambers

Robert Chambers was a prolific writer who is most famous for his enjoyable reference books. Along with his older brother William (1800-1883), he began in business as a bookseller in Edinburgh, and wrote in his spare time. In 1832 the brothers combined to form a publishing house. As authors and publishers they exercised great influence on both sides of the Atlantic.

Robert Chambers were born into a relatively prosperous, mill-owning family in the Scottish Borders, and much of their childhood was passed during time of war with the French. It was an indirect consequence of that war that so adversely affected the family fortunes.

His father extended many of the French prisoners-of-war garrisoned in Peebles credit to re-clothe themselves; the agreement being that the French prisoners would repay their debts as soon as they returned home. When the French let them down the Chambers family was ruined and in 1813 they left Peebles for Edinburgh. Robert remained in Peebles to finish his education.

Robert exhibited early evidence of unusual literary taste and ability. An avid reader, a small circulating library in the town, Elders Library in the High Street, and a copy of the Encyclopedia Britannica which Alex Elder had sold to his father, furnished him with stores of reading. Furthermore, a deformity in his feet had left him lame and unable to join in games at school so, it is claimed, he would swap his 'jeelie pieces' for books.

He later wrote of these early years:

"Books, not playthings, filled my hands in childhood. At twelve I was deep, not only in poetry and fiction, but in encyclopedias."

Straitened circumstances denying him his chance at university and a career in the church, in 1818, at just sixteen, Robert opened a bookstall in Leith Walk. The entire stock consisted of the remnants of his father's library and his own personal collection.

From such modest beginnings, they began to do well, helped in no small part by His brother William's undoubted business acumen and the habit of strict financial prudence acquired during his apprentice years when he would scrupulously account for every penny, maintaining a strict daily budget, and maximizing every potential economy. A keen reader, he would rise at 5 am to read by the early-morning light to save on candles. He then used this habit to supplement his meager diet with fresh baked bread earned by reading aloud to a baker and his son as they baked.

The brothers' new business received an unexpected, early, boost when, having helped unpack books for an Edinburgh book fair, William was offered £10 worth of stock; the money to be repaid when he had sold the books in his shop. This increased the shop's customer appeal, with concomitant increase in sales, and larger profits, some of which William applied to the purchase of an old, small hand press.

Untrained in either printing or binding, William and Robert, undaunted, shrewdly set about printing, binding and publishing 750 copies of The Songs of Robert Burns. An almost guaranteed best-seller in 19th-century Edinburgh, it further improved both profits and repute.

They also took work printing bills and notices and further success followed. Robert Chambers had shown an enthusiastic interest in the history and antiquities of Edinburgh and his first literary effort, Traditions of Edinburgh, published in-house in 1824, won him the approval and the personal friendship of Sir Walter Scott, and remains in print to this day. A History of the Rebellions in Scotland from 1638 to 1745, in 5 volumes, and numerous other works followed of which Robert was, in whole or in part, the author. Richly diverse, titles included The Biographical Dictionary of Eminent Scotsmen, The Cyclopedia of English Literature, The Life and Works of Robert Burns, Ancient Sea Margins, The Domestic Annals of Scotland and The Book of Days.

The Cyclopedia of English Literature presented a series of selected extracts from the best authors of every period, "set in a biographical and critical history of the literature itself whilst The Life of Burns was the product of diligent and laborious original investigations and the gathering of many previously unrecorded facts from the poet's sister, Mrs. Begg, to whose benefit Chambers generously devoted the whole profits of the work.

The Book of Days, Robert Chambers' last publication, and perhaps his most elaborate, was a miscellany of popular antiquities associated with the calendar, and many, especially his family, believed that his excessive labor in connection with this book hastened his death.

Robert Chambers died on the 17th of March 1871 at his house on the Scores, in his adopted home of St. Andrews. Its ancient University had conferred upon him the degree of doctor of laws two years before. He was further honored by being buried in St. Regulus Tower in the town.

Possibly as a result of their own curtailed formal schooling, education and making information available to as many people as possible were priorities for Robert.

In 1832 they launched Chambers's Edinburgh Journal, a weekly, 16-page journal containing articles - many of them written by Robert - on subjects such as history, religion, language and science. At first only a contributor, by the fifteenth number Robert had joined his brother as joint editor. It was an immediate success; within a few years the weekly circulation had risen to 84,000 copies Chambers's Instruction for the People - a series of sheets on subjects such as science, math, history, geography and literature, bound in sets followed in 1824. Eventually around 170,000 sets were sold, amounting to over 2 million individual sheets. This publication also saw some success abroad; a US edition was published, and it was translated into French and - perhaps more surprisingly - into Welsh.

In 1835, the brothers started work on Chambers's Educational Course, a series of short works and schoolbooks. There were eventually more than 100 titles in this series on almost every subject. 1859 brought the first part of Chambers's Encyclopedia, published in 520 parts between 1859 and 1868, and edited by Dr. Andrew Findlater. In 1867, they published their first dictionary, Chambers's Etymological Dictionary, by James Donald, with a larger version, Chambers's English Dictionary in 1872.

By the end of the 19th century, W & R Chambers' was one of the largest English-language publishers in the world. Success continued with Chambers's Biographical Dictionary in 1897, and a compact edition of the English dictionary, Chambers's Twentieth Century Dictionary, in 1901.

Constable took over the printing side in 1932, but the publishing side continues in Edinburgh to this day, producing dictionaries and other titles for a variety of users, including students and teachers of English as a foreign or second language. As well as the core business of publishing dictionaries and thesauruses, Chambers also publishes a range of titles on grammar and usage, single-volume reference titles on science, history, biography and quotations, as well as titles for Scrabble and crosswords.

Although educational publishing made William and Robert famous, Robert was a learned man in his own right. Acknowledged as the more literary and intellectual of the two, a genuine polymath and something of scientific geologist, despite having little formal scientific training, he toured both Scandinavia and Canada conducting geological exploration. His ensuing publications included Tracings of the North of Europe and Tracings in Iceland and the Faroe Islands.

However, what many are coming to regard as possibly his greatest achievement is a controversial book on evolution which predated Darwin's "On the Origin of Species" by 15 years and for which, until recently, he has certainly not had the credit he deserves.

Published in 1844, it took the form of a 400-page book with the grand title Vestiges of the Natural History of Creation, presenting a comprehensive account of the history of the Earth, from the formation of the Solar System through the development of plant and animal life, up to the origins of humankind.

Typically, it dealt with a dangerously taboo subject, rejecting as it did the testimony of Genesis, in an attractive and accessible style, clearly written to appeal to the widest possible readership – the general public rather than the social and academic elites. Vilified by certain sections as a result, applauded by others, containing many errors, and exhibiting a degree of naiveté and a certain lack of scientific circumspection, it still sold over 20,000 copies in a decade, making it one of the best-sellers of its time.

Incredibly, despite following it with a defense, including corrections and amendments based on collaborations with an extensive list of experts, its many subsequent editions, and its continued influence on Victorian science, art, and public opinion, Robert was able to maintain the anonymity throughout his lifetime. It was never acknowledged until the 12th edition forty years later!

Rightfully, and increasingly, Robert has begun to draw attention today. James A. Secord at Cambridge, Sondra Miles Cooney and Robert Scholnick in the USA, and Alistair McCleery here in Edinburgh, are just some of the notable academics currently involved in studies of the achievements of Robert Chambers.

Richard Arkwrightch

The man who started life as a lowly barber in Bolton became the world's first great industrialist, developing - if not inventing - the factory system that turned Britain into the workshop of the world, bringing riches to a few but misery to millions.

Arkwright was born in Preston in 1732, son of tailor Thomas Arkwright and his wife Ellen. He was the youngest of seven children, two boys and five girls, and his eldest brother reputedly joined Bonnie Prince Charlie on his march south in the 1745 Jacobite Rebellion.

Money was tight for the Arkwrights when Richard was a youngster and schooling was out of the question. He was taught to read and write by his cousin Ellen. Later he trained as a barber and in 1755 he opened his own business in Bolton.

At the age of 30, the ambitious Arkwright bought himself a tavern, the Black Boy, in Bolton, and he also started making perukes, or wigs, travelling all over the North West buying up human hair to use in his trade.

And it was during these travels that he heard about the race to perfect a practical spinning machine. Seven miles down the road from Bolton is Leigh, where reedmaker Thomas Highs lived, while a little further on is Warrington, home of clockmaker John Kay.

Highs originally produced a spinning-jenny that predated, and was probably the prototype for, James Hargreaves's effort. Then he and Kay got together to design a machine that utilised draw rollers, in the style of Lewis Paul. But their plans came to a halt because of a lack of funds.

This is where Arkwright came in. He seems to have got Kay drunk in a Warrington tavern and persuaded him to build him two models of Highs's brainchild. He used these to persuade a Preston acquaintance to invest.

Desperate to keep Kay away from Highs, who knew nothing of what was going on, Arkwright employed the clockmaker as his servant and took him with him, first to Manchester, then Liverpool and on to Preston. Kay, helped by two other local craftsmen, built a full-size version of what was to become the water frame, a machine that used three sets of rollers, spinning at increasingly faster speeds, to draw out the cotton roving before a twist was imparted.

Draw rollers were nothing new, as we have said. Paul patented a version in 1738 and, although it had deficiencies, he and his partner John Wyatt actually built a mill in Northampton in 1743 and operated it using the system for several years.

Arkwright moved back to Preston, taking Kay with him, and joined forces with John Smalley and David Thornley before decamping to Nottingham in April, 1768, to avoid the attentions ofmachine-breakers who were busy in Lancashire. There they set up a small mill in Woolpack Lane in the Hockley district of the city, close to Hargreaves's jenny mill.

It was powered by horses, but Arkwright was ambitious and the following year, he asked Nottingham banker Ichabod Wright to help him expand. Wright put him in touch with businessmen Jedediah Strutt and Samuel Need, and together they built the water-powered Cromford Mill in Derbyshire, with Strutt and Need taking Arkwright's entire initial output of thread for their stocking-knitting business.

This saw the start of a massive expansion of the cotton trade, and it was given a further boost in 1774 when Arkwright and his partners persuaded the Government to end the crippling import tariff on raw cotton, which had been imposed to protect the British woollen industry.

Arkwright was clearly the driving force and the visionary behind the consortium, even shrugging off the loss to fire-bombers of a brand-new mill in Chorley, Lancashire, in 1779.

When Need died in 1781, Strutt got cold feet and dissolved the partnership, nervous about Arkwright's ambitious plans to expand into Manchester and other areas, including Scotland, and possibly worried about the patent battles that were looming between Arkwright and men he claimed had pirated "his" inventions.

Arkwright was not an inventive genius and the inescapable evidence is that he stole the intellectual property of Thomas Highs and others to make his fortune.

His forte was being able to spot a good idea, and employing men with the talent to turn that idea into reality. Arkwright was more than happy to use the talents of other men as stepping stones for his ambition.

The Court of King's Bench said as much in 1785 when they rescinded his patents. The court heard evidence from Highs, Kay, Kay's wife, and James Hargreaves's widow, Elizabeth, among others. All testified that Arkwright had, in fact, stolen the inventions on which he had based his fortune.

Historians have pointed out that, although his machinery ideas were "borrowed," Arkwright did at least invent the factory system, the organisation and regimentation of labour in one specialised workplace giving the employer total control over the product and the means and cost of production.

But even this was not strictly true. Factories - particularly silk mills - had existed in England for more than 50 years before Arkwright opened his first big mill at Cromford in Derbyshire in 1771.

At least, say his supporters, he was a benign, humane employer, but this, too, was true only in relative terms. Unlike others, Arkwright did refuse to employ children under the age of seven or eight, but that did not stop him building Cromford like a fortress and using clever, physchological techniques to keep his work-force in fear.

Among these was a window - the Cromford window - he had built into an otherwise blank wall of his home, Rock House, which stood on an eminence overlooking Cromford Mill. The window provided an uninterrupted view of the yard and main mill buildings, giving workers the feeling that they were being watched at all times - even when Arkwright was away on business.

Despite that, however, his work-force were fiercely loyal, and hundreds of armed men were on instant call to defend the mill against the threat from machine breakers. Arkwright kept a cannon loaded with grapeshot just inside the main factory gate, to emphasise the point.

Arkwright's lasting achievement, perhaps, was in doing for cotton what others had done for silk - and with the potential market for cheap cotton products so much bigger, his efforts at Cromford, elsewhere in Derbyshire, and in Lancashire and Scotland inevitably triggered that quantum leap in national productivity that became known as the Industrial Revolution.

When Arkwright died at Rock House in 1792, he left a fortune estimated at £500,000. Maybe that doesn't sound much, but it's more than £200m in today's terms.

Sir Samuel Cunard

Cunard, Sir Samuel, merchant, shipowner, and entrepreneur; b. 21 Nov. 1787 at Halifax, second child of Abraham Cunard and Margaret Murphy; m. 4 Feb. 1815 at Halifax Susan Duffus, and they had two sons and seven daughters; d. 28 April 1865 in London, England.

Samuel Cunard's father was a descendant of German Quakers who had immigrated to Pennsylvania in the 17th century. His mother's family had immigrated from Ireland to South Carolina in 1773 and to Nova Scotia with the loyalists a decade later. In 1783 Abraham Cunard came with the British forces to Halifax where he was employed as a foreman carpenter in the army. On 7 Oct. 1799 Edward Augustus, Duke of Kent, commander-in-chief in British North America, appointed Abraham master carpenter to the Contingent Department of the Royal Engineers at the Halifax garrison; he continued to work for the army until his retirement on 22 Oct. 1822.

Abraham Cunard did not limit his career to his official duties. During the French revolution and the Napoleonic era the British army and navy greatly expanded their facilities at Halifax, creating a need for more houses, wharves, and commercial premises. Ignoring the stipulation of his appointment that he "give up every other occupation," from the 1780s to 1812 Abraham slowly acquired property in the north suburbs near the dockyard, some of which he rented. He was careful to obtain water rights for all lots fronting the harbour in order to build wharves.

The Cunards are remembered as a thrifty family, with Samuel knitting a sock as he drove the family cow to pasture, and the boys selling vegetables from their father's garden at the town market or to neighbours. Although he probably attended the Halifax Grammar School, Samuel was largely self-educated. He always emphasized the importance of a plain English education for a business career, but his own sons Edward and William received a classical education at King's Collegiate School and King's College, Windsor, N.S.

Samuel early proved to be a shrewd trader and at the wharves bought goods which he sold in town. Although he did not follow his father's trade, he had an extensive knowledge of timber. His father's acquaintance among the military enabled Samuel to train as a clerk for the Royal Engineers; from 1811 to about 1812 he was first clerk at the engineers' lumber-yard at a salary of 7s. 6d. daily and £20 lodging money annually.

About 1812 the firm of A. Cunard and Son was founded to enter the timber and West Indian trade. It had been granted considerable excellent timber land in Cumberland County, some of which was free and some purchased, and was selling timber abroad, chiefly in Britain, and to the Halifax Dockyard. The Cunards also profited from the War of 1812. They were licensed by Governor Sir John Coape

Sherbrooke to trade with the United States as early as 6 July 1812, and traded with New England. They imported goods from Britain valued at £6,272 in January 1814, and took part in the trade with Castine, Maine, after the British army captured that port.

The Cunard fortunes are reputedly based on the shrewd purchase at Halifax of an American prize with a valuable cargo. It is known, however, that the Cunards' schooner Margaret, on a voyage from Martinique to Halifax in 1814, was captured by an American privateer. Fortunately for her owners she was recaptured on 16 March and brought into Halifax, where Judge Alexander Croke of the Court of Vice-Admiralty returned the schooner to the Cunards upon payment of one-eighth appraised value for the ship and cargo of sugar, molasses, and rum.

The Cunard firm continued to be active in the West Indian trade. Customs returns in 1813 and 1814 show them importing spirits, molasses, brown sugar, and coffee from Martinique, St Lucia, Dominica, Jamaica, Guadeloupe, Trinidad, Demerara, and Surinam. A. Cunard and Son also acted as agents for various ships owned by others; these included in 1813 the White Oak, owned in Bermuda, and in 1814 the Liverpool schooner Harlequin.

Samuel Cunard was under middle height, with a well-knit frame, a mouth showing strength of character and decision, and brow and eyes indicating intelligence. As he was to write to his daughter Jane, government positions did not offer enough opportunities for an ambitious young man and "frequently lead to old age with a small pittance but little removed from poverty." A merchant, however, with patient industry generally succeeded. Throughout his life Samuel was to carry out his belief that no one succeeded without application and close attention to business, and he was long remembered for his brisk step, quick and ready movements, and his air of "push." He had the skill to choose for his staff men of high calibre who were hard and faithful workers and to inspire them to work as quickly as he did.

As an able-bodied young man during the War of 1812 Samuel volunteered for service in the 2nd battalion of the Halifax Regiment of militia and eventually became a captain. He was selected by the Halifax Court of Quarter Sessions as one of the citizens to organize a night watch to patrol the town after the disturbances in 1817. Samuel had become a member of the exclusive Sun Fire Company on 11 Feb. 1809 and was president in 1821. In this period Halifax was protected by volunteer fire companies which were as renowned for social activities such as balls and sleigh rides as for fighting fires. From 1821 to 1835 he was to serve as one of the firewards appointed by the Halifax Quarter Sessions to direct those fighting the flames and to decide on demolitions to stop the spread of fire.

By the end of hostilities between Britain and the United States in 1815, Samuel had become accustomed to conducting business in a wartime economy. Immediately after the war the Cunard firm continued to expand. That summer the Cunards purchased at a public sale for £1,325 two lots in the north suburbs of Halifax which were no longer needed by the military, in order to construct wharves and warehouses. Surveyor General Charles Morris supported their successful petition for water rights 500 ft out into the harbour in front of property they owned on Water Street because of "their well known character, for active exertion and enterprize in useful improvements and commercial pursuits."

With the withdrawal of most of the British naval and military forces, trade diminished and unemployment grew. This situation was aggravated by the arrival of large numbers of immigrants. Lieutenant Governor Dalhousie selected Samuel Cunard and Michael Tobin to assist penniless immigrants arriving from Europe and Newfoundland at Halifax, and in the autumn of 1817 gave them £100, which they used largely to transport newcomers to districts in the province where they could find work or obtain board on farms for the winter in return for their labour. To help Haligonians on the verge of starvation Tobin and Cunard opened a soup kitchen which distributed 100 gallons of soup daily. In the winter of 1820 Cunard, Tobin, and John Starr administered a soup house at an expense of 50s. daily, where 320 people received one meal each day, and in 1821 the provincial legislature granted £33 to continue its operation.

Although probably hampered by lack of capital Samuel decided to diversify and expand the Cunard business. From his position with the Royal Engineers he had become acquainted with army and navy officials and the company was soon known for prompt assistance to the admirals and generals and for obtaining needed supplies; it was paid generously with money or favours. The Cunard firm contracted to carry the mail by sailing packet between Halifax and Boston and Halifax and St John's, Nfld; it also sometimes carried the Bermuda mail after the British naval dockyard was moved there in 1819. A. Cunard and Son had also tendered in 1815 to supply a 100-ton vessel for government service to protect the trade and fisheries and prevent smuggling, to sail to New York for mail in winter, to transport the lieutenant governor on official tours, and to move men or supplies to military outposts. The firm purchased a vessel for £1,500, and after inspection by naval officers it was taken into service as the sloop Earl Bathurst. In the summer of 1817, however, Lord Dalhousie decided that a larger vessel was required. The Cunards sold the sloop for £375 and bought the Chebucto in England for £2,960. This brig was hired for government service at £2,400 sterling per annum. Although Samuel estimated annual expenses of £2,325, including depreciation, complaints were made from Halifax and London to Colonial Secretary Lord Bathurst that Cunard had boasted about profits of £1,930 on the vessel and an additional profit because British bills of exchange had a premium of 15 per cent at a time when foreign currency was scarce. In consequence the lieutenant governor was instructed to advertise for tenders in 1822; the lowest bid was for £1,500 annually from Cunard, who explained to Sir James Kempt that the firm had no other employment for the brig and was reluctant to dismantle her. An estimate made at the time for the Colonial Office of the annual operating costs for the services requested of this type of vessel was £1,400. The Cunards ran this service for the government until 30 June 1833.

By the early 1820s Samuel had become virtual head of the Cunard firm. His parents moved to a farm at Pleasant Valley in Hants County, and he became responsible for his younger brothers as well as his own wife and children; he also assisted his wife's family when the business of his father-in-law, William Duffus, failed. Abraham Cunard died at Rawdon on 10 Jan. 1824 and on 1 May S. Cunard and Company formally emerged. Abraham's will appointed his older sons Samuel, William, and Joseph as trustees of his property, and on 15 Dec. 1826 a settlement was made: for the sum of £1,550 Samuel and Joseph, the surviving trustees, transferred Halifax property to another brother, Edward, who had been taken into the business about 1825 to run the Halifax office after acting as master of various vessels owned by Samuel. Four days later Edward sold to Samuel one of the lots, which Samuel already occupied, and one-third of three water lots for £550, and to Joseph a one third share for £500. The younger brothers John, Thomas, and Henry did not share in the assets of the firm.

Apparently each of the Cunard brothers acted individually rather than as a company in buying and selling wooden sailing ships. The large number of Margarets and Susans and the frequent re-registrations make determining the exact numbers difficult, but Samuel had at least 76 sailing ships registered at Halifax between 1817 and 1850, and Edward registered five more vessels built by Alexander Lyle of Dartmouth in 1840–41 which are usually attributed to Samuel's ownership. Of the 76 it is estimated that 28 were sold abroad, 21 sold in Halifax, two in Pictou, one in Newfoundland, three in the West Indies and one in Saint John, 14 unknown, and six wrecked. Of the 28 sold abroad, ten were disposed of in London, ten in Liverpool, and one each in Hull, Bristol, Aberdeen, Dundee, Banff, Belfast, Limerick, and Galway.

Except for his mail boats Samuel Cunard kept his vessels for only a few years, to be sold when he needed replacements, or saw an opportunity for profit. At first he bought former prizes, but later purchased ships constructed in Nova Scotia and Prince Edward Island. Before 1827 Samuel sold some ships locally. Beginning in that year, however, he sold a few ships abroad from Halifax each year; three vessels registered in 1826 were sold in Britain in the summer of 1827.

Even during bad winter weather in the 1820s Cunard's vessels were sailing to and from the West Indies bringing in rum, molasses, sugar, and some coffee, and carrying out dry and pickled fish, hoops and staves, mackerel, alewives, codfish, lumber, tea, and oil. Mostly he used his own ships. Besides trade with the Miramichi area and with Newfoundland, Cunard imported cargoes from London and Liverpool of dry goods, anchors, cables, coal, and even a fire engine in 1827 ordered by the Halifax Fire Insurance Company; from Philadelphia flour, meal, and fruit; from Boston naval stores, flour, tobacco, and seeds; and from New York corn, wheat, apples, nuts, and books.

During the 1820s Cunard prospered. The adjustment to peace in Nova Scotia had been aggravated by crop failures, the readmission of the Americans to the fisheries the lowering of imperial duties on foreign timber, and the removal of the Royal Navy's dockyard facilities to Bermuda in 1819, but provincial trade expanded after 1824. The emergence of young entrepreneurs like Cunard and Enos Collins, alert to every opportunity for increasing their capital, was assisted by the death or retirement of an older generation of merchants, such as James Fraser, James Moody, William Forsyth, and John Black, most of whom had been financed from abroad, and by the return of others to Britain with their profits as soon as the war ended. Earlier businesses were branches of British merchant houses, but now native Nova Scotians began to dominate the business scene.

Both Cunard and Collins joined in petitions in 1820 from Halifax merchants to the assembly to ask for bounties on flour to allow Nova Scotians to compete with the Americans in the West Indian trade and for a duty on flour imported from the United States. Cunard's increasing importance in business circles is shown by his election to the Chamber of Commerce of the reorganized Nova Scotia Commercial Society in 1822; he was its president in 1834.

The Cunards' brig Prince of Waterloo engaged in the whale fishery off Brazil from 1819 to 1821, and in 1827 Samuel Cunard, Joseph Allison, and Lawrence Hartshorne were trustees for the Halifax Whaling Company, which employed the Pacific. In 1834 and 1836 the Cunards' ship Susan and Sarah went on whaling voyages, and their 421-ton Rose returned to Halifax in April 1839 after a two-year voyage with 2,400 barrels of black and sperm oil to learn that there were not enough funds left to pay her the full government bounty of £2 per ton.

Cunard subscribed £1,000 for stock in the Shubenacadie Canal Company and was chosen a vice-president in 1826. Along with Collins, Martin Gay BLACK, and five others, he was an original partner of the Halifax Banking Company formed on 1 Sept. 1825, subscribing £5,000 of its £50,000 capital. In 1831 the partners of this company held more than one-third of the provincial funded debt totalling £21,459, Cunard's holdings being £506 as compared to £2,559 for Henry Hezekiah Cogswell and £450 for Collins. There were objections in other parts of the province to the concentration of so much wealth in the capital. Cunard withdrew from the company in 1836, becoming a resident director of the Bank of British North America. Possibly this move was influenced by the fact that the Bank of Nova Scotia, formed in 1832 as a rival of the Halifax Banking Company, was the bank used by the General Mining Association.

Samuel Cunard was one of the small shareholders in the Annapolis Iron Mining Company, incorporated by the legislature of Nova Scotia in 1825 to smelt and manufacture iron in Annapolis County; the largest shareholder was Cyrus Alger of Boston. After some success the enterprise was abandoned because the American shareholders wished to concentrate on the sale of pig iron in the United States, and the Nova Scotians on manufacturing finished products, but the company may also have been influenced by a yield lower than anticipated.

Cunard was always looking for opportunities to expand his business. On 9 Jan. 1826 he made a proposal to Lieutenant Governor Kempt to lease the Cape Breton coal mines for 30 years at £6,000 per annum and a royalty of 2s. per chaldron on coal shipments over 60,000. He stipulated that Sydney be made a free port and emphasized the value of the American market and the necessity of investing capital in the equipment at the mines and of building wharves and breakwaters. A month later Kempt observed to Robert John Wilmot-Horton at the Colonial Office that if Sydney were made a free port, the demand for coal would increase so much that the Cunards' proposed lease and royalties would not be large enough, but he admitted that "The Messrs. Cunards are Persons of Considerable Capital quite equal to carry on this Establishment & perfectly acquainted with the Country." Later that year, however, the rights to exploitation of the province's minerals were granted to the General Mining Association, and Cunard's bid failed .

Cunard was more successful in obtaining the tea agency from the East India Company. When he learned in July 1824 of the proposal to ship cargoes of tea directly from Canton to Quebec in East India Company ships, he went to London to explain to the company the transportation problems of contrary winds and ice for ships sailing from Quebec to provide the Maritime provinces with their annual tea supply. On 11 Feb. 1825 Cunard and Zealmon Wheeler of Venner, Brown, and Wheeler, Saint John, N.B., applied jointly for the contract to import tea into Halifax and Saint John on the same terms as Forsyth, Richardson, and Company of Montreal , the agents for the Canadas. It was hoped that the lower prices offered by these firms would prevent smuggling of tea from the United States. Previously most of the tea exported from

London to Nova Scotia and New Brunswick had been shipped by Bainbridge and Brown, London commission merchants and ships' brokers, who purchased it at East India Company auctions in London. Bainbridge and Brown offered to sign bonds as security for Cunard and Wheeler. However, Cunard alone received the agency for the Atlantic provinces. John Bainbridge, an active member of a committee of London merchants trading in British North America which was particularly interested in the timber trade, was appointed provincial agent for the Nova Scotia legislature on 23 Feb. 1826, and remained Cunard's friend until his death.

After the first 6,517 chests of tea shipped directly to Halifax from China by the East India Company arrived, a public sale was held at Cunard's warehouse on 19 June 1826. Quarterly auctions at the stone warehouse by Cunard's wharf, with Cunard as auctioneer, became customary. He retained the agency until 1860.

In the 1830s Cunard was re-exporting equal amounts of tea to New Brunswick and Newfoundland, some packages to Jamaica, Bermuda, Demerara, and Barbados, some to Forsyth, Richardson, and Company at Montreal late in the season before navigation of the St Lawrence River was closed, and a few packages and chests each autumn to Prince Edward Island, without paying duty. In 1831 Enos Collins attempted to oust Cunard from the tea agency. Possibly Cunard was exaggerating his profits to his colleagues in the Halifax Banking Company. Between October 1825 and April 1831 he remitted approximately $95,362 in Spanish dollars and £85,754 sterling to the East India Company.

Cunard sold about two-thirds as much tea as Forsyth, Richardson and Company. Although Cunard's commission on East India funds was only 2 per cent, it was useful to have large sums of money available, even for a short period, to help finance his own operations. He may have used some of the capital for financing his part of the steamship line in 1839 by withholding payments to the East India Company, for he was prompt with his remittances until 1840. In that year and the following the company had to request Cunard to remit the balance due; he did so soon afterward.

Although in later life Samuel Cunard declared that "he kept his politics to himself," he was a strong supporter of the Tory party. In April 1826 he was persuaded by "merchants and other respectable inhabitants" of Halifax County to offer himself as a candidate for election to the provincial assembly and issued an election card. He withdrew early from the contest, however, because he objected to the candidates and voters having to waste three weeks on an election campaign at such a busy season of the year for farmers and fishermen, and thus allowed the other candidates to be elected by acclamation.

Cunard owed his appointment to the Council of Twelve in 1830 to his position in the mercantile community; by that time his fortune was estimated at £200,000. He took his seat in the Council on 6 Nov. 1830 after the Brandy Election and Joseph Howe expressed in the Novascotian the hope that "the same liberal and expansive views which have distinguished Mr. Cunard as a merchant, may be observable in his legislative character. He is wealthy and influential – he need fear no man, nor follow blindly any body of men; and we trust that he will not disappoint the hopes which many entertain of the benefit to be derived from his weight in the counsels of a branch, that, at the present moment, is really in no good odour throughout the Province." Alexander STEWART, a member of the assembly for Cumberland and a strong advocate for the Bank of Nova Scotia, objected to another appointment from the capital.

For the first three years Cunard faithfully attended both executive and legislative meetings of the Council, and was active on committees dealing with public accounts and revenue and the value of coinage. He was motivated by what he thought would be best for business. However, Cunard expected the same efficiency from public servants as from his own employees. In 1832 a committee of three councillors – Cunard, H. H. Cogswell, and Joseph Allison – investigated a complaint against William Cleveland, county treasurer, in his capacity as clerk of the licence, for allowing too many people to sell spirits without a licence, and reported that Cleveland "is an inattentive careless Officer, and has for a long time neglected to perform the duties of his office in a vigilant and effective manner. . . ." Cleveland was dismissed.

As the 1830s progressed the Council of Twelve came increasingly under attack by the Reformers, who objected particularly to the fact that five councillors, including Cunard, were directors of the Halifax Banking Company. Cunard also had increasing influence in British business and governmental circles. When Reformer William Young met Colonial Under-Secretary Henry Labouchere in London on 16 June 1839 he declared that "we were perfectly aware of all the influence at work against us, that of the Bishop, S. Cunard, Col.Yorke &c.

During most of 1834 and 1835 Cunard was absent from Council meetings. He was present for most of 1836 and 1837, but not active on committees. He remained an executive councillor when the Council was divided into executive and legislative branches in 1838, but attended only a few meetings between 1838 and 1840, when he had become involved in the beginnings of his transatlantic steamship line. Thus he probably did not mind being asked to resign on 1 Oct. 1840 at the request of Lord Falkland to make room for Reformers in the coalition. He was allowed to retain the title of "Honourable."

The Tory press was indignant that Cunard, "the greatest benefactor Nova Scotia ever had . . . is deemed unfit to have a seat in the councils of his country. . . ." The Reformers, however, said Cunard should not be in the Executive Council because he "is no statesman . . . nor does he aim at the amelioration of the political condition of his countrymen." In 1844 the editor of the Morning Chronicle wrote bitterly against the address of the Halifax Tories to Sir Charles Metcalfe which expressed concern about the "mischievous effects of party and intemperate Legislation." "This is a gross libel upon the people of Nova Scotia. Who utters it? Cunard, Collins & Co. The Old Bankers of the Old Council – who were dismissed by her Majesty from power, for their ultra-Toryism, and unfitness for office . . . who used the power with which they were clothed, for their own benefit and the benefit of their friends, regardless of the wishes or interests of the people. . . ."

After the breakdown of the coalition of Tories and Reformers in December 1843, the Tories formed a government under James William Johnston with a bare majority over the Reformers. By-elections became crucial, including one in the spring of 1845 in Pictou, where Cunard exerted his influence for the Tories and apparently arranged with local Reformers for a Tory victory by acclamation in return for a few minor offices for the Reformers. Howe was angry because there was no hope of defeating the Tories before the next election: "Such a treaty is worthy of such a negotiator, and will long be held in remembrance as a proof of the gentleman's talents for diplomacy, and the gullibility of the men with whom he had to deal." But in the 1847 elections for responsible government Cunard assured Howe of his neutrality.

The success of the Cunard firm in its early years had been based in large part on the timber trade with Britain, which was encouraged by the tariffs placed on Baltic timber during the Napoleonic wars. In 1821, when the British government announced its intention of reducing the Baltic duties, Cunard had been chosen by the Halifax Chamber of Commerce to deliver to the colonial secretary a petition to keep them. The expansion of the Cunard firm into the Miramichi area of New Brunswick was a natural outgrowth of its timber interests. The Cunards may have been at Chatham as early as 1820, and Samuel Cunard received a deed to Egg Island on 13 July 1821. After the Miramichi fire of 1825, Joseph and Henry Cunard used the capital of the family firm for the aggressive building of a timber empire over the south bank of the Miramichi in rivalry with Alexander Rankin. This rivalry became so important to Joseph that he ceased to worry about profits and when questioned about the prices Cunard brothers were selling at said: "We don't give a damn so long as we sell more deals than Gilmour, Rankin & Co." The business was conducted as Joseph Cunard and Company, the partners being Joseph, Samuel, Edward, and Henry. The Halifax-based firm of S. Cunard and Company provided most of the goods required by Joseph Cunard and Company, and shipped to Miramichi, Richibucto, and Bathurst most of the food products and manufactures needed by the lumbermen, the shipbuilders, and their families. It received in return shingles, staves, lumber, dry and pickled fish, salmon, and alewives, which they sold in the West Indies. S. Cunard and Company also sold tea and rum to Gilmour, Rankin, and Company and to Joseph Samuel at Miramichi.

The timber business necessitated large amounts of capital because two years elapsed between shipment of supplies to lumber camps and the receipt of cash from the sale of lumber. The situation was aggravated by the wildly fluctuating timber market in Britain. Bainbridge and Brown, writing from London to John Ward and Sons at Saint John on 20 Oct. 1826, reported poor prices for ships and timber in London and Liverpool and remarked: "We have two of Cunards Miramichi cargoes at the Clyde & two at Leith & cannot sell a stick . . . ." However, the demand for timber rallied in the 1830s and the Cunards expanded.

Samuel tried to control his headstrong younger brother Joseph. He wrote from Halifax on 28 Nov. 1838 to protest the additional capital sunk in a grist mill, pointing out the folly of discounting at 90 days and then having to pay four or five per cent for drawing funds in Saint John. Customarily merchants met their obligations by issuing notes or bills of exchange which were circulated like cheques; Joseph Cunard and Company in Miramichi issued large numbers for the convenience of the trade as there were no banks in the district. The notes were payable in Halifax at the office of S. Cunard and Company. In 1839 nearly every remittance received from the Miramichi by Halifax merchants consisted principally of

Cunard's notes; "Publicola" speculated in the Acadian Recorder on 2 Nov. 1839 that these notes in circulation amounted to £80,000. In Samuel's absence his son Edward Cunard denied that more than £10,000 had ever been in circulation, and insisted that the amount outstanding was £4,000. "Publicola" observed that this postponement of settling debts would allow the firm to pocket quietly £1,000 through interest saved, and also warned the merchants of Halifax that in a financial panic Samuel Cunard could refuse to honour the notes because they had been issued by Joseph.

In the 1830s the West Indian trade diminished in importance for Nova Scotia merchants because of increased American competition and a decline in sugar production. S. Cunard and Company was bringing in only enough rum, molasses, and sugar to supply lumbering operations in Miramichi and Prince Edward Island. The clear-sighted and enterprising head of the firm turned its warehouses into bonded warehouses for other firms, and attempted to expand its trade with Britain in such goods as flour, dry goods, cordage, and glass, as Halifax was still the leading wholesale centre of the Atlantic provinces.

By the spring of 1834 the depression in Nova Scotia had deepened. In Halifax there were 600 houses for rent, shops were glutted with produce, and cash was locked up in the banks. Cunard was astute in avoiding failure. He had already competed to secure the contract to provide wharf space in Halifax for the General Mining Association. The long-established firm of Belcher, Binney, and Company had expected to be agents for the English mining company, but, when the company's engineer, George Blackwell, had returned to England strongly recommending Cunard's wharf and warehouses, Cunard's offer was accepted in 1827. At first Richard Smith, a mining engineer from England, acted as general agent in Nova Scotia as well as superintendent of operations, but since the GMA monopoly was resented by local capitalists, in 1834 the association shrewdly appointed Cunard as their local business agent and a director of the corporation.

When Cunard became GMA agent, the company owed the Bank of Nova Scotia over £16,000. By 9 April 1835 the overdraft had risen to £25,480 and at the request of William Lawson, president of the bank, Cunard reduced it by £6,000. In the financial crisis of 1837 the board prevailed on Cunard to reduce it to £10,000. In 1839 Cunard's Halifax firm was awarded the contract to supply coal to the Halifax Dockyard, but his own ships seldom carried coal cargoes.

In December 1842 Cunard attempted to counter the popular supposition that the GMA was reaping large profits by stating that "no interest or return" had "yet been paid." Large capital expenditures had been made in expectation of almost unlimited demand for coal in the United States, but the company was meeting increasing competition from American anthracite coal. When the United States increased its tariff on foreign coal in 1842, Cunard asked the Nova Scotian government for a reduction in royalties and threatened that the GMA would lay off miners unless the government agreed; the royalties were reduced and the annual £3,000 rent was waived. Cunard's letters reveal his complete devotion to the interests of the corporation. As the GMA monopoly became steadily more unpopular over the years, Cunard became the buffer in conflicts between the British and Nova Scotian governments and in disputes between miners and owners. Yet it was acknowledged that under "his guidance and management the operations of the Company" were wisely and properly conducted. Cunard's connections with the GMA gave him a power base in Pictou County where he wielded political and business influence behind the scenes.

While in England in 1838, Cunard was approached about forming a Prince Edward Island land company by George Renny Young of Halifax, who was in London as legal counsel for a number of landowners in Prince Edward Island to present to Colonial Secretary Lord Glenelg their case against any escheat of their lands. Cunard was easily persuaded to join Andrew Colvile, Robert Bruce Stewart, and Thomas

Holdsworth Brooking, Young's father-in-law, in forming a joint stock company called the Prince Edward Island Land Company with a local board comprised of Young, Samuel Cunard, and Joseph Cunard. They purchased the 60,000-acre estate of John Hill for £10,000 and the mortgage on the 102,000-acre estate of John Cambridge for £12,000 sterling, £8,400 of which was paid immediately with the backing of London bankers Prescott, Grote, and Company and of the Liverpool Union Bank. Samuel and Joseph Cunard held six-tenths of the shares, Colvile two-tenths, and Brooking and Young one-tenth each.

In August 1838 Young and Cunard went to Prince Edward Island to visit their estates and to discuss the land tax with Lieutenant Governor Sir Charles Augustus FitzRoy. They assured him that they wanted "a common line of policy between the Proprietors and their tenants calculated to restore peace and to promote the prosperity of the Island." At a meeting in Charlottetown on 20 Oct. 1838 a disagreement over the appointment of a solicitor for the land company split the board when Young insisted upon his younger brother Charles, and Samuel upon his son-in-law James Horsfield Peters. This quarrel resulted in Samuel's buying out his partners on 26 March 1839, but it left ill feeling with the Youngs.

In the early years Cunard reserved the rights to all timber fit for shipping, shipbuilding, or exportation on leases which he granted; the timber taken off paid for the land. With his land purchases in Prince Edward Island, Samuel obtained the right to collect £2,535 in arrears of rent on the Cambridge estate. Many tenants paid but some cattle and land were seized for past rents by his agent, J. H. Peters, in 1842 and 1843, and new leases issued to new tenants. On Lot 45 in Kings County about 300 people assembled on 17 March to reinstate forcibly a man named Haney into possession of a house and farm from which he had been legally ejected; 50 soldiers had to be sent from Charlottetown to restore order on the Cunard estates.

As an alert shipowner Cunard was aware of the development in steam vessels and noticed increasing numbers of such vessels at Liverpool and on the Irish Sea. In 1825, in anticipation of the proposed steamship service by the American and Colonial Steam Navigation Company of Great Britain around the British Isles and once a fortnight to Halifax and New York, negotiations were begun for a steamboat between Quebec and Halifax to connect with the mail packets from Falmouth, England. With contrary winds sailing ships sometimes took 23 days to reach Quebec from Halifax. The Lower Canadian legislature offered £1,500 in three annual instalments and the Nova Scotian house offered £250, but no capitalists were attracted until subsidies were doubled in 1830. Samuel Cunard was only one of over 200 shareholders from Quebec and the Maritimes in the Quebec and Halifax Steam Navigation Company formed in 1830 and incorporated the next year. Among prominent businessmen and merchants of Lower Canada were John Forsyth, William PRICE, Sir John Caldwell, Noah Freer, George Black, and William Walker. Samuel was elected head of the Halifax committee of the shareholders.

The contract for building the steamship was given to John Saxton Campbell and Black. The SS Royal William, launched 27 April 1831 at Cape Cove, Quebec, sailed to Halifax on 24 August, calling at Miramichi and Pictou. J. G. Denter, second engineer on board, later recalled that Samuel Cunard repeatedly visited the Royal William and inquired into every particular regarding her speed, sea qualities, and consumption of coal. Unfortunately for the owners the outbreak of a cholera epidemic at Quebec in 1832 forced the ship into quarantine at Miramichi and Halifax; it sat idle a large part of the season and suffered heavy financial losses. In the spring of 1833 the steamship which had cost £16,000 to build was sold at Quebec to the mortgagees for only £5,000. In a letter of 7 May 1833 to Sir Rupert George, Nova Scotia's provincial secretary, Cunard bitterly blamed the Quebec committee for allowing the frost to burst the pipes and injure the machinery and he stated, "I do not think . . .

should be paid in consequence of the Boats only making one trip during the whole Season. . . . They have already received £3,975 from this Province the whole of which is lost by the Management of the Quebec Committee and the object in view frustrated."

Although rapid communication was imperative for colonial merchants, the mails for America were still carried by the Falmouth packets taking 30 to 70 days to cross the Atlantic. On 7 Nov. 1838 the British Admiralty advertised for tenders to carry mails by steam from England to New York via Halifax. Two tenders were received from Britain but neither was satisfactory. The closing date had passed before Cunard heard the news in Halifax. Believing "that steamers properly built and manned might start and arrive at their destination with the punctuality of railway trains on land," he sailed to England to submit his own plan for an "ocean railway," with a letter from Nova Scotia's lieutenant governor, Sir Colin Campbell, reminding the Colonial Office that Cunard was "one of the firmest supporters of the Government" with "a good deal of influence in this community . . . ."

Fortunately the comptroller of steam machinery and packet service and advisor to the Admiralty was Arctic explorer William Edward Parry, who remembered with pleasure his service as a young naval officer at Halifax during the War of 1812. On 11 Feb. 1839 Cunard offered to provide steamboats of not less than 300 h.p. to carry the mails from England to Halifax and back twice monthly, and also to provide a branch service in boats of not less than 150 h.p. to Boston, and one from Pictou to Quebec while the navigation was unobstructed by ice. For this he asked £55,000 sterling yearly for ten years, and he promised to have the steamers ready by 1 May 1840. The Admiralty accepted Cunard's offer.

In order to obtain steamships Cunard consulted James Cosmo Melvill, secretary of the East India Company. He recommended Robert Napier, a foundry owner and engineer in Glasgow who had provided steamships for the company.

On 25 Feb. 1839 Cunard wrote to William Kidston and Sons of Glasgow asking them to obtain estimates from Napier. The latter offered to build a vessel of 800 tons and 300 h.p. for £32,000 but agreed to lower his price to £30,000 when Cunard ordered three vessels. Napier, a leader in establishing Glasgow as a great steamship-building centre, decided before the contract was signed with Cunard on 18 March 1839 that these steamships would have to be larger for safe Atlantic voyages and offered to provide the extra work on the engines at no additional cost if Cunard would pay for the structural changes. The Nova Scotian agreed, indicating he wanted "to shew the Americans what can be done in Glasgow and that neither Bristol or London Boats can beat them."

When Cunard could not sell stock in his steamship company in Britain or America, Napier approached a fellow shareholder in the City of Glasgow Steam-Packet Company, James Donaldson, a wealthy cotton broker. Donaldson consulted George Burns of Glasgow, who controlled the Belfast trade and was interested in shipping as well as the commission business. Burns "entertained the proposal cordially," inviting Cunard to meet David MacIver, an ambitious young Scot, who was the agent for small firms in the coastal trade. After various negotiations Burns persuaded some friends to form a co-partnership on 14 May 1839 to take over Cunard's mail contract. In a few days 270,000 was subscribed for "The Glasgow Proprietors in the British and North American Royal Mail Steam Packet Company." At first Cunard subscribed £55,000 for his 110 original shares but that amount was only gradually paid up; in the final arrangements of 23 May 1840 Cunard subscribed £67,500, George Burns £5,000, his brother James £5,000, and David and Charles MacIver £4,000.

The Glasgow investors were businessmen - cotton brokers, West Indian merchants, insurance brokers, iron merchants, warehousemen, textile manufacturers, produce merchants, shipping agents, and so on. Some of them were now seeking outlets for capital because of the decline of the West Indian trade, but most were interested in steamship companies. There was no Nova Scotian capital except for Cunard's investment, the financial losses of the Royal William making it difficult to raise money locally.

Haligonians were delighted with Cunard's contract and immediately subscribed £8,000 to build a new hotel for the expected passengers. On 9 April 1839 the Halifax Times rejoiced that a "new era will commence in Provincial prosperity from the moment the first steam packet reaches Halifax – and . . . the time is not far distant when it will become the centre of steam navigation for the whole American continent." That spring, however, a meeting of Boston merchants requested larger steamships to run directly through to Boston, instead of a branch service from Halifax, and offered to provide a suitable pier and dock and facilities for a quick transfer to railways. Cunard agreed, and finally the Maritimes realized that Boston had become the western terminus instead of Halifax.

The first scheduled steamer, Britannia, arrived at Halifax at 2 a.m. on 17 July 1840 with Cunard and his daughter Ann on board, discharged passengers and mail as quickly as possible, and sailed on to dock at East Boston at 10 p.m. two days later. There Cunard received a warm welcome and 1,800 invitations to dinner. The Acadian Recorder commented: "We are quite sanguine that our Boston neighbours calculated right when they so nobly encouraged Mr Cunard's splendid project. His steamships will enable Boston to become more important than New York in a little time . . . ." It was the Bostonians who called the line the Cunard Steam Ship Company or the Cunard Line of Packet Steam Ships long before the company was legally incorporated as the Cunard Steamship Company in 1878. The regular service of the Cunarders increased foreign trade to Boston by 100 per cent in one year. Yet the expectations of both Halifax and Boston to become the centre of navigation for the whole North American continent failed because geography gave Montreal and New York access to richer hinterlands.

Although historians of Nova Scotia, Scotland, or England assume that the partner in the enterprise from their own country deserves sole credit for the success of the steamship line, available evidence indicates that all important actions were undertaken after consultation among the major partners, although Burns superintended shipbuilding activities and financing, Cunard had special responsibility for negotiations with the British government over contracts, and the MacIvers managed the operations of the fleet at Liverpool. A letter from David MacIver in Liverpool in 1841 chided Cunard for his low spirits over difficulties about the application to the British government for a second contract and the low profits. MacIver argued that this had been an experimental year and we "are now arrived at that point where we must turn this experience to profit."

Difficulties with his own financial affairs added to Cunard's concern over the lower-than-expected profits of the steamship contract. Although he blamed his brother Joseph's loose business methods for their financial crises, he himself was overextended because of his Prince Edward Island land purchases and his borrowing to pay Robert Napier, and because the sailing ships built by Joseph and Samuel were selling slowly. These problems coincided with a cyclical downturn in the British economy. When Cunard, Ingram, and Company in London failed to accept drafts, it precipitated the crisis of 1842.

On 25 Sept. 1841 Cunard had borrowed £15,000 sterling from the British and North American Royal Mail Steam Packet Company for two years and mortgaged his 110 original shares and all rights in the company and in five steam vessels registered in Glasgow. Profits and dividends on shares of stock and commissions due to Cunard or his son Edward as the company's agent in North America were to be used to pay interest on the loan and to pay up the stock subscription. Samuel was allowed five per cent on the gross earnings of the ships. This sum was to be placed to his credit until the steamship shares were fully paid up; then his creditors would receive any profits made.

Cunard was considered to be one of the wealthiest men in Nova Scotia when he suddenly departed London for Halifax by one of his steam-ships to escape a writ of attachment for £2,000 taken out against him by Leyland and Bullen, Liverpool bankers. Cunard's escape in March 1842 had been assisted by Duncan Gibb, a timber merchant and for many years Liverpool agent for Pollok, Gilmour, and Company, who had hidden him in a cottage and then provided a boat to row him out after the steamer had left her moorings. Cunard had arranged with most of his creditors for three years in which to discharge his obligations. His property was mortgaged for £47,000 and he owed about £130,000 sterling but claimed assets of £257,000.

Acting as his father's attorney in March 1842, Edward Cunard Jr was trying to collect as much money as possible, and even sold his father's farm in Rawdon. William Henry Pope later claimed that three lots purchased in Prince Edward Island in 1839 for £9,600 were resold in 1842 for £25,000. On 9 and 11 March 1842 Samuel Cunard and his brother Edward mortgaged their warehouses, wharves, and premises on the east side of Water Street in Halifax for £9,000 at 6 per cent interest to Samuel's good friend, Stephen Wastie DeBlois, a merchant and auctioneer at Halifax. John Duffus, Cunard's brother-in-law and a dry goods merchant, used his influence with the directors of the Bank of Nova Scotia and the Bank of British North America, of which Cunard was a director, to provide assistance in preventing his bankruptcy. A special meeting was held by the directors of the Bank of Nova Scotia on 5 April 1842, and four days later a directors' by-law was suspended to allow a £45,000 loan secured by Duffus. The president of the bank, Mather Byles Almon, along with Duffus, Alexander Murison, James Boyle Uniacke, and Joseph Starr, became trustees for the property of Samuel, Edward, and Joseph Cunard. In June and July 1842 the Bank of Nova Scotia reluctantly paid £4,000 sterling to enable the Cunards to liquidate the debt due to Leyland and Bullen to prevent a fiat of bankruptcy being issued against Samuel.

The trustees of Cunard's English creditors were Charles Walton, William George Prescott, and Robert Carter, all leading London businessmen. Among creditors were the Bank of Liverpool, North and South Wales Bank, and Prescott's bank in London, as well as others who had probably advanced shipbuilding supplies or were commission merchants.

Cunard was 55 years old in 1842 and might have been looking forward to some relaxation, perhaps retiring to a small estate as did many English merchants. He must have enjoyed being entertained in London, at parties given by such hostesses as Mrs Caroline Sheridan Norton, and his difficulties must have hurt his pride. He had to give up his directorship in the Bank of British North America. The English creditors allowed the Cunards living expenses but they could not leave their places of business in Nova Scotia and New Brunswick without permission from the trustees, and Edward Jr and Robert Morrow had to go to England for the firm. Ironically, in the midst of Samuel's financial crisis the citizens of Boston forwarded a large silver vase as a testimonial to the frequent, rapid, and safe steamship service between Liverpool, Halifax, and Boston.

Resolutely Samuel devoted his attention to the widespread interests of the Cunards. Shipbuilding activities were increased both in New Brunswick and at Alexander Lyle's shipyard in Dartmouth. In the fall of 1845 Cunard was one of the sponsors of a meeting to discuss the controversial proposal of an English company to construct a railway from Halifax to Quebec but the project collapsed amidst personal and political rivalries. Samuel and Edward Sr attempted to separate their business from Joseph's and the co-partnership was advertised to be dissolved on 31 Dec. 1845. But late in 1847 Joseph Cunard's enterprise on the Miramichi collapsed and during 1848 the timber trade in New Brunswick dropped to one-third of the 1847 value. As Joseph's ships and timber remained unsold in Liverpool, he admitted that the burden of his misfortunes in business had "in a great measure fallen" on his brother Samuel. Nevertheless, profits from the steamship company steadily paid off the loan borrowed from the Nova Scotia trustees and a formal deed was signed 1 April 1846 reconveying the steamship company stock to Samuel and his son. It is estimated that they received about £20,000 a year between 1841 and 1844 from commissions for the agency in Halifax and Boston and from dividends on the stock. The Bank of Nova Scotia loan was paid off on 11 Dec. 1850.

Cunard must have been delighted to resume his visits to Britain and to take a more active part in the steamship company. Even before his brother Edward died in 1851, Samuel evolved the pattern of travelling back and forth between England, Nova Scotia, Boston, and New York. With the help and experience of Henry Boggs, a longtime Halifax employee, he let his younger son William and his nephew James Bain Morrow run the Halifax firm, which was finding the GMA agency increasingly profitable. One or two of his daughters usually accompanied him on his visits to England.

In the negotiations of 1846 for the renewal of the mail contract of the steamship company, Cunard revealed great diplomacy and tenacity. Merchants and manufacturers in England objected to the renewal and the Great Western Steam-Ship Company of Bristol appealed for an open competition. The chancellor of the exchequer, Henry Goulburn, in defending the Cunard contract, differentiated the company from its competitors and stated that "this establishment owed its origin entirely to the activity of the colonists of Nova Scotia and its neighbourhood, and he for one would be sorry to do anything against the zeal and activity of the colonists." A ten-year contract with Cunard, George Burns, and Charles MacIver, with a yearly subsidy of £145,000, provided for weekly voyages from Liverpool alternating to Boston and New York after 1 Jan. 1848. By that date both the company and the British Post Office realized the necessity of New York sailings because of competition with the Oceanic Steam Navigation Company. Edward Cunard Jr was transferred to the New York office, and in 1849 married the daughter of a New York merchant. MacIver had become sole partner of D. and C. MacIver after his brother David's death in 1845, and in the next three decades became the leading figure among Liverpool shipowners. By 1867 the Burns, Cunard, and MacIver families owned all the shares in the company.

In the 1850s the English line had intense competition from the American Collins Line, which had faster, larger, and more luxurious ships and twice as large a subsidy from the American government, and from the Inman Line which by 1857 was carrying one third of the Atlantic passenger trade. The Cunard line met this increased competition with bigger ships, which recaptured the speed record from Collins and then lost it again. After two of Collins' steamers were shipwrecked, the Cunards stressed their reputation for safety. The competition ended when the Collins Line became bankrupt in 1858, but by the mid 1860s a score of companies were competing for passengers on the transatlantic route, and the Cunard firm had to turn to iron screwships which were more economical with coal consumption and which had more space, despite Cunard's preference for paddle-wheelers.

Cunard always seemed able to reach an understanding with the officials controlling post office contracts, for he wrote from London to his daughter Jane on 24 May 1850: "I have succeeded in making some very good arrangements about my contract have got it extended four years beyond the former period & some other advantages – they are always very good to me." The Canadian government wished arrangements to be made on the termination of the existing Cunard contract for the St Lawrence mail service to be transferred to the Allan Line, but while negotiations were still underway, the Cunard contract was renewed four years early. This 1858 contract required the Cunard line to provide at least eight vessels of 400 h.p., and weekly service from Liverpool to New York and a fortnightly service to Halifax and Boston for an annual subsidy of £173,340. The Cunard steamer stopped calling at Halifax after 1867.

The British government supported Cunard in part because of the strong recommendations from naval and military officers about the fitness of the Cunard vessels for war purposes and their more efficient convertibility into men-of-war as compared with any other vessels under contract for the packet service. With the outbreak of the Crimean War, Cunard immediately placed his ships at the service of the British government and advised the Admiralty about obtaining and adapting other steamships for war service. Eleven ships of the Cunard fleet were used to carry troops, horses, and supplies to the Crimea and two became hospital ships. On 9 March 1859 in recognition of the valuable services rendered by the steamship line, particularly during the Crimean War, Cunard was knighted.

Samuel had given his English residence as his permanent address for the first time on the 1858 contract, the year George Burns retired from active management in the company, but Cunard continued to maintain his home in Halifax also. Only his youngest daughter Elizabeth remained with her father; the others had married English army officers stationed at Halifax.

Cunard was still regarded by the Colonial Office as an expert on the Maritime provinces. By 1860 he had become the largest and most influential land proprietor in Prince Edward Island and was considered by the British government to be the landlords' spokesman. When the Island legislature requested a special land commission to settle disputes between landlords and tenants on the Island, the Duke of Newcastle consulted Cunard about appointments to the proposed commission. Not all the proprietors agreed to be bound by the commission's award but the most important did. The commission discovered that Cunard had 971 tenants in 16 townships on 999-year leases with terms of 1s. sterling per acre; the 64,889 acres leased should have paid £3,435 annually, but the average rent collected for the previous three years had been only £2,310. Some tenants had paid in cash and some in produce. By 1860 arrears of rent amounted to £17,073. In 1859 Cunard's agent, George W. Deblois, had remitted profits of about £2,000 in Island currency to Cunard in London.

The land commission proposed that the operation of the Land Purchase Act of 1853, brought in by George Coles' Liberal government, should be extended to the whole Island, the British Treasury guaranteeing the sum of £100,000, and that a system of compulsory sale by arbitration should be organized. Immediately upon publication of the commissioners' report in the Island newspapers, Cunard was writing to Newcastle on 2 Oct. 1861 as "one of the largest proprietors in the Island" to object to the proposal that the tenants be allowed to have their farms valued by arbitrators. He argued that although the maximum purchase price was to be the value of the rent for 20 years, the arbitrators might decide that a fair price was two or three years' rent. He feared that arbitration would subject the proprietor to enormous costs – perhaps half the value of the farm. Newcastle vetoed the Island assembly's attempt to implement the commissioners' proposals. Many Islanders blamed the influence of the London proprietors for the British government's refusal to provide funds to buy out the landlords and for not forcing them to compulsory sale by arbitration. Because Cunard and other landlords knew the Islanders would be disappointed by the failure of the commission, they made another offer after consultation among themselves, to be open for a five-year period from 1 May 1862, which would let tenants buy land at a price equivalent to 15 years' annual rent. The Executive Council of Prince Edward Island refused it.

All the proprietors found it difficult to collect their rents during the ensuing agitation sparked by the Tenant League. Cunard wrote to the Colonial Office on 24 Feb. 1863: "There is no tenant on the Island who cannot pay his rent, if he is industrious and sober," but pointed out that "while the agitation is kept up by designing people, rent will not be paid nor money laid up to purchase farms; time is wasted and money spent in attending political meetings." That year the Island government had appointed Edward Palmer and W. H. Pope to proceed to England to confer with the Colonial Office and the landlords. In October their request for implementation of the land commission's recommendations was forwarded by the Colonial Office to Cunard who objected to forgiving arrears of rent and to the proposed terms of sale to tenants. He pointed out that from 1841 to 1862 he had paid £8,641 for land taxes to the Island government on his own and his son's uncultivated lands, at a rate double that of cultivated land. Since the devaluation of Island currency reducing the pound sterling to 16s., Cunard claimed, the value of his rent and sales of land had been lowered by 25 per cent. He compared the 1863 rent paid by his tenants on the Island to that paid by a farm labourer in Britain "who cannot get shelter for his family for double that rate per week."

Pope declared that the Island was "Ireland on a small scale," vigorously disputed many of Cunard's contentions, and called upon the landlords to compromise. The Colonial office listened to Cunard's demand that neither the Island legislature nor the imperial government should interfere "with our property, in any manner different from that in which private estates in England could be dealt with." Despite these years of argument, the Cunard holdings of 212,885 acres were sold to the Island government in July 1866, a year after Cunard's death, for $257,933.30; the rents had become difficult to collect, and cash was needed to pay the legacies left to his daughters.

In his will Cunard left his real and personal estate to his sons Edward and William and £20,000 to each of his six daughters. In June 1865 Henry Boggs wrote from London to M. B. Almon: "I miss our old friend Sir Samuel C – I think he has left £600,000 – this is a good large sum for him to have accumulated since the date that you and I remember him to have had little or nothing – so much for Steam in 20 Years . . . ." Other sources estimated his fortune as £350,000.

Although early in life Cunard was imperious, he learned diplomacy and became a skilful and persuasive negotiator. His contemporaries admired him for the contribution to transatlantic communication by the line popularly called by his name. Without Cunard's prestige and diplomacy, the contract signed after his death in 1867 was far less favourable, paying only £80,000 annually for a weekly service from Liverpool to New York. Dividends which had been eight per cent under the old partners, dropped to two per cent or less.

In the early years of his career Cunard took a prominent part in community activities, St George's Anglican Church in Halifax, and various charitable organizations as well as mercantile affairs which extended throughout the Atlantic provinces. Although he supported the Halifax Mechanics' Institute with a handsome donation when it was organized in 1832, and was praised as "a gentleman whose purse is never closed when a good work needs encouragement," he did not take an active part in its meetings. He was one of the charter members of the Halifax Athenaeum established in December 1834. Most of his local activities were tapering off in the 1850s; he ceased to be lieutenant-colonel of the 2nd battalion of the Halifax militia in 1857, and after 19 years as president of the Halifax Steam Boat Company, he resigned in 1855. One of his first official appointments, on 9 April 1816, had been as commissioner of lighthouses on the Nova Scotia coasts. He retained his interest in lighthouses for the rest of his career, and in 1852, when he was consulted on the subject by Provincial Secretary Joseph Howe, he stated: "Altho I am occasionally absent from home I leave behind me those who are competent to do the duty and when I am here I do not spare myself and my experience may be considered worth something."

Cunard was gratefully remembered for employing his capital in shipbuilding activities in the hard times of the 1830s because this enterprise had circulated money "where there would otherwise be poverty and stagnation." He could be ruthless to a rival or an enemy, but, although legally he could have refused to assume Joseph's debts, the Halifax firm gradually made payments to the creditors year after year.

In the opinion of William James Stairs, Cunard was "the ablest man I have ever known as a merchant of Halifax" –

"he made both men and things bend to his will." His competitiveness and his obsession not to waste time were important characteristics of his personality. Peter Lynch, a prominent Halifax barrister, recalled Cunard as cool, calculating, a man of keen perception whose whole mind was devoted to carrying out any project he had in hand. Nevertheless Cunard was admired at home and abroad as a successful colonial and for his contributions to the steamship trade. He was one of the first native Nova Scotians to build a business empire, but, like the successful British businessmen and officials who made their fortunes in the colonies, he retired to England where his descendants settled. True to his family motto "By perseverance" he had overcome obstacles to become an English merchant prince.

Although many libraries and repositories and museums have items about the Cunard Steamship Company, no large collection of the letters and papers of Samuel Cunard himself has been located. The account books, ledgers, and letter books of the Halifax branch of S. Cunard and Company were destroyed when the firm's north pier and the Cunard office building and warehouse were demolished in 1911 and 1917. The attic of the old warehouse had been full of chests of old manuscripts and business papers and Dr Archibald MacMechan was told that it took three months to burn them on the wharf.

In 1919 Mr J. Noble Foster, managing director of S. Cunard and Company of Halifax, found 44 documents in the attic of Cunard Coal Company which were presented to the PANS. These documents are stock, dividend, and agency accounts of the British and North American Royal Mail Steam Packet Company from 1840 to 1847, some correspondence with Samuel Cunard's partners, George Burns and David MacIver, and with the British Post Office, and the Pictou mail contract.

The Cunard Steamship Company archives were deposited at Liverpool University in 1973, and cover the period from about 1840 to 1945. However, most of the manuscript material dates from the incorporation of the company in 1878, and there is little from the period when it was a private partnership and when Samuel Cunard was active. Professor Francis E. Hyde has been commissioned to write a history of the Cunard Steamship Company and an inventory is being prepared. There is material collected by the publicity department of the company and copies of Cunard material from other repositories.

Thomas Chippendale

Of all the names associated with antique furniture, Chippendale is the most well known. The Chippendale style dominated American furniture until the 1770s. Known by its exquisite and extensive carving, it takes its name from Thomas Chippendale, an 18th century cabinetmaker, whose furnishings reflected popular English tastes of the period incorporating English, Gothic, and Chinese motifs.

Chippendale's early career remains a mystery. Born in 1718 at Otley in West Yorkshire, England, son of carpenter John Chippendale, and served his apprenticeship there. He had a great head for business and as a social climber and self-publicist, he realized the importance of public relations and advertising. In spite of his membership of the Society of Arts and his fashionable wedding at St. George's Chapel, Society never accepted him, except in his trade and professional capacity.

But in 1754, Mr. Chippendale, as he was known in London, published his detailed collection, Gentleman and Cabinet-Maker's Director, a portfolio of fashionable English furniture design templates and one of the first furniture design books. In it Chippendale adapted existing design styles to the fashion of the mid-18th century. Both makers and sellers of furniture rushed to purchase it, making Chippendale a household name. And so pervasive was the influence of his book that the name of Chippendale is often indiscriminately applied to all mid-18th century furniture.

Chippendale created his Director as a catalogue from which his wealthy patrons could choose particular elements for their furniture, which would then be custom made for them in his workshop. It contained 161 plates, reflecting many elements of the Rococo, Chinese, Gothic and Neoclassical styles.

Publication of the Director clearly had a stimulating effect on Chippendale's career since all his known commissions date from after its publication. However, the Chippendale style didn't remain within the confines of the Chippendale workshops very long. So popular were the designs with the wealthy class that soon other furniture makers were using Gentleman and Cabinet-Maker's Director as a pattern book for their shops, too.

In 1754, the same year as the publication of his Director, Chippendale moved to spacious premises in the fashionable paved thoroughfare of St. Martin's Lane which his firm occupied for the next 60 years. He then formed a partnership with James Rannie, a Scottish merchant, who injected capital into the business. They employed between 40 and 50 artisans. And while the notes in his Director showed Chippendale possessed a sound practical knowledge of timbers and craftsmanship, he most likely, at this stage in his career, would have been responsible for design and management, instead of working at the bench.

A versatile man, he was willing to design and supply wallpapers, carpets, fire grates, decorative ormolu, chimney pieces, even complete room schemes, in addition to furniture. As well as equipping State Apartments with luxurious ensembles, his firm regularly supplied routine articles for the servants' rooms and domestic offices. He offered a complete house furnishing service, undertook repairs, removals, hired out furniture, compiled inventories and was even prepared to direct and furnish funerals for respected customers.

Chippendale style furniture was generally made of mahogany, imported from the West Indies. Though cabinetmakers occasionally used veneers, they're not typical of this style. Instead they preferred using solid wood to accommodate the elaborate carving found in this style. And they upholstered the newly introduced camel-back sofas in rich brocades, velvets, and damasks.

While cabinetmakers used Cuban, Dominican and Honduran mahogany during the latter part of the 18th Century, the finest was Cuban, a dense, heavy wood with a close grain. When they carved it, minute white flecks would appear in the wood. Honduran mahogany is lighter in weight and color. The mahoganies from the Dominican Republic and Jamaica fell somewhere between Cuban and Honduran in quality. Flame mahogany refers to the character of the grain, obtained by using the first branch or crotch of the tree. Another much sought-after grain was mottled, often referred to as "plum pudding" mahogany.

Nevertheless, in the Chippendale period in America, Connecticut cabinetmakers used cherry more often than mahogany. During the same period, furniture makers in Bermuda used local cedar which had an orangish hue. Throughout America, furniture makers used softwoods like white pine for the main carcase of furniture, but in England, they favored hardwood such as oak.

By mixing and melding the extravagant Rococo style with the Gothic and Chinese styles, Chippendale came up with a hybrid that displaced the more angular Queen Anne style. From the 1760's, the neoclassical work of architect Robert Adam, with whom he worked on several large projects, influenced him greatly.

He extensively employed the Queen Anne-style cabriole leg. While there are six different basic Chippendale style legs–the lion's paw, the ball and claw, the late Chippendale, the Marlborough, the club and the spade–he based three of them on the cabriole shape which is an elegant, serpentine style ending in a distinctive foot. These include the lion's paw, which ends with a lion paw shaped foot, the club, which is a simple round foot and the ball and claw, which looks like an eagle talon holding a ball. The remaining leg styles are straight–the Marlborough being a plain, square leg, the spade a tapered round leg often with a square or trapezoid foot, and the late Chippendale having a square leg with a square foot. Chippendale's Gothic and Chinese influenced designs had straight or tapering legs, tracery carving and fret and lattice work.

Block-front furniture–where the center front recedes in a shallow concave curve between slightly convex ends–seems to have been unique to North America. Chippendale never illustrated furniture of this type in his Director. Furniture connoisseurs believe that this style originated the area of Boston, Massachusetts, and assumed a Chippendale character.

Another characteristically American furniture form was the highboy. English cabinetmakers abandoned the chest-on-stand, of the late 17th and early 18th centuries, for the chest-on-chest where the lower section is supported on low bracket feet. Furniture makers supported the highboy, known back then as a high chest of drawers, on high cabriole legs, the top being surmounted by a swan-neck broken pediment sometimes known in America as a "bonnet." The center of the pediment was usually embellished with a cartouche showing the family's crest, except in American pieces this is smaller. It was customary to display these elaborately carved pieces in the drawing room, even though they were designed to hold personal belongings. The lowboy, or the lower part of the highboy, was usually elaborately embellished with carving and sometimes stood by itself.

Chippendale chairs often exhibit features of Queen Anne or early Georgian furniture. Often, American Chippendale chairs had Queen Anne back-splats or kidney-shaped seats. American cabinetmakers used doweled through tenon construction, even in sophisticated furniture, up to the late 18th century. In England this feature had died out in all but country furniture by the early 18th century. Of course, there are exceptions, so that identification is dependent upon more subtle points such as the less extreme line of the American back leg as compared with the English examples which are less vertical. However, in America, cabriole legs tended to be somewhat curlier than in England.

Another style of furnishing that's often associated with the name of Chippendale is the so-called "Chinese Chippendale" or Chinoiserie, which remained immensely popular, especially for bedrooms, despite the rise of Neoclassicism. Japanning, or painted decoration sometimes imitating lacquer, became the last word in chic.

While he based his work upon the general Queen Anne and Georgian characteristics of sober design and thoroughly fine construction, retaining many of the early 18th-century details, Chippendale introduced many other forms. Though collectors identify his name with the extensive variety of chair designs—from geometrical to Chinese, lattice, or sumptuously carved and interlaced forms, his workshop's output also included desks, mirror frames, hanging bookshelves, settees, china cabinets and bookcases–featuring fretted cornices and latticework glazed doors–and tables with delicately fretted galleries and distinctive cluster-column legs of Gothic inspiration.

Many fine pieces of furniture have been attributed to Thomas Chippendale, but verifiable pieces are rare. Chippendale never employed a maker's mark, so the only method of establishing his authorship is to find one of his original bills, usually preserved among estate papers, or equivalent documentation.

Even when a piece can be attributed with certainty to Chippendale's workshop, it's impossible to say for certain that he worked on the furniture himself. As the Chippendale firm became successful, his workmen, rather than Chippendale himself, carried out more of the work.

Another feature of 18th century Chippendale furniture was its irregularity. Cabinetmakers did all the work on this furniture by hand, thus it won't match the exact regularity of machine work. According to John Nye, director of the American furniture department at Sotheby's in New York, when examining a piece of Chippendale furniture to determine its age, collectors should look at the joinery closely. Hand crafted joints will be slightly irregular and may evidence tool marks, too.

Chair makers created detailed and deeply carved legs with precise joints, as well as stretchers, the horizontal rungs between chair legs for their Chippendale-style chairs. Seats were wood, upholstered or caned in either a rectangular or kidney shape.

Chair backs varied with the intended function of the chair. There were upholstered backs, rail backs, ladder backs, rung backs, splat backs, and carved backs. As with the legs, chair makers carved these deeply, with crisp details and often pierced them.

Records dating from before the American Revolution prove that there were many skilled craftsmen in the country. In Boston, for example, there were 150 known cabinetmakers, while Philadelphia had equally as many. In the South, craftsmen-slaves produced good work. It's not surprising, therefore, to discover that many of the cabinetmakers who produced American Chippendale furniture weren't of British descent. George Gostelowe who worked in Philadelphia was Swedish while Andrew Gautier was a Huguenot.

Some of the most remarkable makers of Chippendale furniture were Quakers, for example the Goddards and the

Townsends of Newport, Rhode Island Island, and William Savery of Philadelphia, Pennyslvania. In the history of American colonial furniture, the Townsends and the Goddards are truly remarkable for the quality of their work and for the number of them of different generations who made furniture–altogether some 20 individuals from three generations of the Townsends, including Christopher and his sons John and Job and his grandsons Job junior and Edmund were well known, while of the Goddards the best known was John.

It was the practice in the mid-18th Century to purchase a finely made piece of furniture or decorative object and then have copies made at a lower price to increase its number. These, as with modern reproductions, of the Chippendale style were often hand carved but don't have the depth and detail of carving that genuine Chippendale furniture has. Nye recommended that collectors look for evidence of craftsmanship–hand planing, hand sawing, handmade nails, as well as shrinkage in the wood. In addition, reproduction pieces will have been constructed of younger mahogany which isn't as dense and is grainier than the slow-growth wood used to make 18th-century pieces.

Thomas Chippendale, who's furniture designs today command stratospheric prices, had to, on more than one occasion, fight for payment on his commissions. Today, collectors should be wary of any piece of Chippendale furniture that doesn't have a four to six-figure price tag, especially for pieces made in Philadelphia, according to Nye. "If it's not appropriately priced, the dealer knows that it's not 18th century," said Nye. "A reputable dealer will give a written guarantee that the piece is authentic and the guarantee will include a detailed description of the piece and its provenance. Watch out for the 'too-good-to-be-true' price."

Nye also noted that while the market is strong for exceptional items, many Chippendale pieces are undocumented and unsigned, so collectors need to look at form and aesthetic attributes. "Many American cabinetmakers borrowed liberally from Chippendale's designs, so their pieces weren't as pure as English ones," he added.

The Chippendale Society, founded in England in 1963, owns an important collection of furniture and documents, usually on display at Temple Newsam House, Leeds, England.

Vijay Mallya

Dr. Vijay Mallya (born December 20, 1955) is a Bangalore-based billionaire businessman and Member of Parliament (Rajya Sabha since 2002) from India. He is the son of a famous industrialist Vittal Mallya and is the chairman of the United Beverages Group. Mallya has started a domestic airline in India called Kingfisher Airlines

He took over as chairman of the UB Group in 1983. Since then, the group has grown into a multi-national conglomerate of over sixty companies with an annual turnover which has increased by 439% to US$1.2 billion in 1998-1999 despite the frequent devaluation of currencies in many developing countries, including India, where the group largely operates. The focal business areas of the group encompass alcoholic beverages, life sciences, engineering, agriculture and chemicals, information technology and leisure.

Kingfisher Airlines is the first Indian company to purchase an Airbus A-380. It connects Mumbai, New Delhi and Bangalore. While initially, it was an airline with a single class, called Kingfisher, recently the airline has decided to introduce first class service as well. According to the airline website: "The Kingfisher Airlines family will consistently deliver a safe, value-based and enjoyable travel experience to all our guests."

Mallya has won trophies in professional car racing circuits and is a keen yachtsman and aviator. He is involved in a variety of sport by way of personal participation as well as promotion of sport and cultural activities by steering various sponsorships (particularly football and golf). He is a member of the East Bengal Club. He has also won numerous trophies in horse racing including several prestigious Derbies.

He entered politics in 2000 and became the president of Janata Party, a breakaway faction of the original Janata Dal party. His party contested for around twenty seats during the Karnataka State legislative election. He campaigned vigorously through the media, but his party failed to make any impact and couldn't win even a single seat. Following the party's failure in the elections, it has been largely ignored by the media. The Janata Party was originally headed by Subramaniam Swamy.

Achievements

* Establishment of Mallya Hospital in Bangalore, with a charity ward.

* Helped to establish the Mallya Aditi International School, a prestigious private school in Bangalore.

* Contributions to: the Victoria and Albert Museum, London; Prince's Youth trust; and the Duke of Edinburgh Awards Scheme.

* Buying back of Tipu Sultan's articles and belongings (the most prominent being his sword) in an auction in London.

* In March 2006, Forbes magazine described him as one of India's newest billionaires and one of the "World's Richest People."

Vijay Mallya is renowned for his lavish spending. His social gatherings have been attended by prominent politicians as well as other businessmen and have been much spoken of in the media.

The flamboyant businessman owns 26 homes around the world and is called the Richard Branson of India. Other expensive assets include a stud farm comprising over 250 race horses, 200 classic vintage cars, a castle in the United Kingdom and several yachts and private jets. Mallya owns a sprawling home on Bangalore's Vittal Mallya Road (named after his father); there is also a Vijay Mallya Road in Bangalore.

William Blass

William Ralph Blass, born in 1922 to a part-time dressmaker and a traveling hardware salesman, always knew his place was not in Fort Wayne, Indiana. Blass's father committed suicide when his only child was 5, and Bill quickly found refuge in movies and art.

A clothing designer revered as much for his drive to dress everyday men and women as for his flare in adorning the famous, Bill Blass was a rich amalgam of homespun charm and carefully built refinement.

The beauty of being able to draw, or paint, from an early age is that you never feel trapped, least of all by your immediate circumstances," Blass wrote in his 2002 autobiography, "Bare Blass." The young Blass filled the margins of his schoolbooks with drawings of Hollywood-inspired fashions. At 15, he began selling sketches of evening gowns for $25 each to a New York manufacturer. He saved the money and at 17 he left home to attend fashion school in New York. He settled at the YMCA, and later into a West 60s apartment he shared with some friends. Blass excelled at his studies and at 18 became the first man to win *Mademoiselle*'s Design for Living award. Once ensconced in New York, Blass wasted no time shedding his Midwestern persona. He took up smoking and adopted a faintly British accent. And when he found work as a sketch artist with the sportswear house of David Crystal, Blass spent most of his $30-per-week income on clothing, shoes and as many elegant meals out as he could afford.

Blass, who in time became known for intense privacy and an aversion to romantic attachment, nonetheless formed strong and lasting friendships. In 1942, after good friend Ed Guild was killed in a military accident, Blass enlisted in the Army.

Blass was assigned to the 603rd Camouflage Battalion with a group of 1,000 artists, writers, sound engineers, theater technicians and other creative professionals. The battalion was classified: its mission was to fool the German army, through the use of recordings, dummy tanks and other false materiel, into believing the Allies were positioned other than where they actually were. Blass's troops drew fire, leaving other Allied troops to advance on the enemy by surprise. Blass's outfit fought in more campaigns than any other unit in the European Theatre, quietly saving the lives of countless American soldiers. Despite privation and ever-present danger, Blass was content. "I was truly on my own for the first time in my life," he reports in his autobiography. "So, naturally, in that exuberant state of mind, I didn't always notice how bad things were."

His mind was never far from fashion. In idle hours, Blass filled his notebooks with sketches and drawings, incorporating into them the interlinking B logo that decades later would become world-renowned. Blass left the Army in 1945 and came back to New York, where he went to work for Anne Klein and started hitting the social circuit and getting his name into society columns. Klein fired Blass less than a year later, calling him mannered but talentless. Undaunted, Blass eventually dug himself in as an assistant designer at Anna Miller and Company, and later at renowned fashion house Maurice Rentner, and began establishing himself in women's fashion.

The hallmark of Blass designs was that they were always wearable. In the days when high fashion more resembled unreachable artwork than anything anyone would be seen in on the street, the term "wearable" was an industry epithet. But Blass didn't care. He wanted to make clothing that women could adorn themselves with day into night. He may have designed for high-society New York debutantes and grande dames; he may have dressed movie stars and presidents' wives, but the rest of the country's women knew his look would flatter them, too—and they flocked to buy his pieces.

Blass is credited not only with producing stunning evening attire, but also with pioneering the American casual style of fashion. His high-quality, expensive pieces were offhandedly sophisticated, as if the wearers, though lounging on a manor porch, could at any moment be off for a spontaneous cross-country road trip.

"He took American sportswear to its highest level...giving it new, clean, modern, impeccable style," former Saks Fifth Avenue fashion director Ellin Saltzman told a New York Times reporter. "He, probably better than any other designer, knew his customer and understood her."

Throughout the 1950s and '60s, Blass designed wildly popular sportswear, evening wear and accessories. But it was his menswear lines of the 1960s that placed him solidly in the limelight.

"The success of the first collections was immediate," he wrote. "Men were going into Bonwit's and buying shoes without even trying them on. There was no place to sit down anyway. They would hold up the shoes to the bottom of their feet, and say, 'That's a fit. I'll take them.'"

In 1970, Blass established Bill Blass Limited and over the next 29 years expanded his award-winning offerings to include everything from swimwear to furs, bed linens to perfumes, luggage to chocolates, sunglasses, automobiles and more. Blass traveled to Europe for work, and in between collections he traveled for fun—around the globe and to various U.S. resort destinations, nearly always with friends in tow. As his fame and his income grew, so did his charitable contributions. His $10 million gift to the New York Public Library is one of the most high-profile of his public acts of generosity; numerous other gifts he bestowed anonymously. But as worldly, social and charitable as Blass could be, he was, at heart, a fiercely private homebody. He invited small groups of friends to his home for cozy dinners, but left easy chairs and sofas out of the impeccably designed rooms so his guests would not be tempted to stay long. Especially later in his life, Blass simply preferred the company of his dogs and his books to the whirl and drama of parties.

In December 1998, Blass suffered a minor stroke while at a department store event in Houston. His company had grown to a $700-million-a-year concern. But after he presented his final collection to a standing ovation in September of 1999, the designer sold Bill Blass Limited for $50 million and retired to his home in New Preston, Connecticut. The stroke was just the beginning of Blass's health troubles. A review of photographs from Blass's long life reveals a man seldom without a cigarette. In 2000, he was diagnosed with oral/tongue cancer, which later became throat cancer. He and his doctors fought the disease into remission, and Blass began writing his autobiography.

"All my experiences, all my yearnings, have been those of a typical American boy becoming a typical American man, except that my focus was on clothes rather than on oil drilling or banking or some other great commodity," he wrote in summation. "It was a typical American success story after all."

He finished "Bare Blass" in 2002, but never lived to see it published. The oral cancer had returned, as is often this case with this particular disease, and Bill Blass died June 12 of that year in New Preston.

William Butlin

William Heygate Colbourne Butlin was born in Cape Town, South Africa on 29th September 1899. His father, who was the son of a clergyman, had been sent to this hot and humid climate as he was what was then known as a "remittance man" which is now more commonly known as a "black sheep". Butlin had the good fortune to have a choice of two paths from which he could choose for his future. One path was to follow his grandfather into the church and the other was to take to the road as a traveling showman just like his mothers side of the family, thankfully for everyone Bill chose the fairground. Bill's father, also called William Butlin, was a well educated man and a typical country gentleman of his time. He was not trained for anything and had never expected to work for a living. His mother, Bertha Hill, was the daughter of a small town baker who had become a traveling showman.

The Butlin family has always been well connected although this did not help Bill in his early struggles. In the eighteenth century the family owned a bank in the town of Rugby. Butlin's Bank was established in 1791 but was absorbed by Lloyds Bank in 1868. Bill Butlin was not the first Butlin to have been knighted as his great uncle, who lived from 1845 to 1912 was the eminent surgeon Sir Henry Trentham Butlin. He held several senior posts at St. Bartholomew's Hospital in London, he was also President of the Royal College of Surgeons and President of the British Medical Association and his crowning glory was the invention of a new type of surgical scissors.

Bill's grandfather was a vicar for twenty seven years at the beautiful Priory Church of St. Swithun in Leonard Stanley, Gloucester. It is here the story of Billy Butlin really starts for it was here that the traveling fair came to visit and William Butlin and Bertha Hill met for the very first time and by all accounts, it was love at first sight. They eventually got engaged and married but in the social climate of the time neither family was happy about a marriage of such contrasts and so, with the quiet encouragement of both families they emigrated to South Africa. There they settled in Mowbray, a small suburb of Cape Town. Their house was a small timber built affair and from this they started a bicycle business in a shed at the rear of the house selling and hiring out the new safety cycle, the successor to the Pennyfarthing. As was mentioned earlier William never expected to work and spent most of his time playing tennis, so it was left to his wife to run the business of importing, assembling and hiring out the new bicycles as well as raising their two young children born while they were out there. The cycle business was unfortunately like their marriage doomed to failure.

Bertha returned home with the young Bill and his brother Binkie to her family in Bristol England her marriage to William was unfortunately "on the rocks". Leaving the two boys with her sister Jessie, she traveled around the summer fairs in her caravan running a gingerbread stall for her brother Marshall. A year passed and Bertha decided to return to Africa to try to patch up her marriage. Sadly her attempts failed and so once again she returned to England. Travelling the fairs again, Bill and Binkie had to once more stay with Aunt Jessie. They had not been in England long when Binkie sadly died of infantile paralysis and so Bill then joined his mother on her travels. With all this traveling Bill's education was very haphazard, and his greatest lesson in life was earning about people. It was a hard life with many times during the winter months when they could not afford coal for heating or cooking. Fortunately Bill's uncle Jack Watts a miner used to bring them coal which he had scrounged from the slag heaps.

In 1911 Bertha met Charles Rowbotham, who worked for the Bristol gasworks, they were soon married and emigrated to Canada. Both thought it too big a risk to take young Bill and so they boarded him out with a widow in Bedminster, Bristol. Being stuck in one place meant that education now played a big part in Bills life and for two years he attended the St. Mary Redcliffe school at Bristol. Although he could read very well he was very slow in other practical subjects, he did however discover that he had an aptitude for drawing and painting which he then concentrated on. Bill's life was soon in upheaval again when Bertha and Charles sent for him to go to Toronto. The journey took him thirteen days, ten at sea and three by train, but Bill soon settled into his new life very well. The family lived on the outskirts of Toronto, in a modest house in Young Street. Charles worked for the Toronto Gas Company as a salesman, and even though he was not earning a fortune they were by no means a poor family. Although education once again played an important part in Bill's life he only stuck with it until he was twelve years old. He was very unhappy at school and was always being mocked because of his English accent which he did not speak correctly as he kept dropping his aitches. With this and coupled with the fact that his family needed money he found himself a job with a firm that collected waste paper, for this he was paid two dollars a week. Always on the lookout for something better he eventually got a job as a messenger boy at Eaton's, Toronto's largest department store. Ever ambitious to move on Bill attended art school in an evening to try to develop his gift for drawing and painting. He eventually found himself transferred to the art department at Eaton's. Being the youngest and least experienced member of the department he found himself being restricted to drawing the easiest of objects. One of the best aspects of working for the company was that he was able to visit their summer camp, which gave him his first taste of a real holiday, indeed a taste of what was to become a very big part of his life.

On February 17th 1921 Bill arrived in England with just £5 in his pocket and headed straight for Dorney's Yard, Bristol and the winter quarters of the fairground folk in the hope of finding the Hill family, Bertha's family. Not wishing to waste his 5 he decided to hitchhike but in those days there was very little traffic on the roads and so the journey took 5 days. Upon arrival at the yard and after settling in he was given the job of painting and refitting rides owned by the Hill family. Eventually with assistance from his uncles he set up a small hoopla stall at a cost of 30 shillings with prizes loaned to him by his kinsfolk. His first fair was at Axebridge, where business was very good Billy made 10 pounds clear profit, a good deal more than the other experienced stall holders. How did he do this?, simple, whereas the other stall holders aim was to make money and not give away the prizes, Bill decided that it would be better if the public were to win more often thereby making them come back more to try their luck. On a normal hoopla stall the blocks under the prizes are too wide thereby making it very difficult to get the hoop over, Bill made his blocks smaller so that the hoops went over more easily. He therefore got rid of all his prizes and made a very nice profit.

Ever on the look-out to go bigger and better he had the idea of adding a goldfish stall, by throwing a ping-pong ball into a bowl you won not only the bowl but a goldfish. To look more the part he kited himself and his workers out with a uniform which was made by Wildmans, a local Skegness outfitter, adding the now familiar "B" to his pocket. By wearing these outfits his workers became the first amusement park employees to wear uniforms. Another familiar trademark which appeared in those early days were Bill's painted stalls in blue and yellow. This colour scheme would appear at his first camp, Skegness, some fifteen years later.

During his travels Bill heard that Bertram Mills had started an annual Christmas circus at Olympia London which ran for six weeks. The stalls and side shows were rented out and were pitched along the outside of the big top. As Christmas approached Bill traveled down to Olympia to view the site, on arrival he noticed a certain part of the Olympia where the crowd gathered whilst waiting to enter the big top. Bill decided that this was the best spot from which to run a stall. At the end of the next season Bill traveled to London again this time to see Miss Agnes Moore, secretary to Bertram Mills. She informed him that it would cost 40 per week to have a site eighteen feet in diameter. There were many sites available to him but Bill knew exactly where he wanted his eighteen feet to be and in true Butlin tradition he got it. Realising that his customers would now be more up-market he decided that he must offer better prizes. He remembered a shop that he used to pass in Tottenham Court Road London that sold budgerigars, and bought almost the entire stock. By the end of the season Bill had been so successful that he could now afford to bring his mother over from Canada.

With the arrival of the charabanc people's leisure habits changed, instead of staying in their own towns where the traveling fairs came to them. They were instead traveling out to the coast, a place which many people had only ever seen in picture books. Whole villages and factories would save together for the year so that they could hire a charabanc to take a trip to the coast. Only the women and children could go as the men were unable to take the time off work, as this was in the days when there was no such thing as a "paid holiday". Bill being the shrewd businessman he was noticed the move towards the coast. So, not being one for sitting on his laurels he decided after having lengthy conversations with two fellow showmen to go and see for himself. Scouting along the seafront on a cold day in 1927 for a suitable site, Butlin found a piece of land which he leased from the Earl of Scarborough. The site he had chosen left much to be desired, consisting mainly of sand dunes. These needed to be levelled before any form of amusement site could be built, this was a huge job and although Bill was doing rather well he could not afford to pay to have them removed. Once again this proved no problem for Bill as he soon realised that sand was an expensive commodity for certain businesses and so he placed an advert in a local paper selling the sand for five shillings a lorry load with the provision that the buyer must move it himself. It didn't take long before the site was cleared and once this task was accomplished he set up four hoopla stalls, a tower slide, a haunted house ride that he built himself and the following year in 1928, he added a scenic railway.

To oversee the running of his new venture he sent for his mother. During the winter months when the amusements at the seaside would be normally closed, Bill would rent old factories and put in stalls and side shows. He also rented disused bus garages at Whitechapel, Brixton, Tooting, Putney, Hammersmith and Marble Arch in London and turned them into successful funfairs.

Within a few years Bill had moved to a bigger and better site continuing to expand with bigger, better and sometimes unusual attractions. One such attraction was Dare-Devil Peggy, a one-legged woman diver who would plunge from a height of sixty feet into a tank of water no more than ten feet deep!. Another attraction was "Alf", who would be buried alive in a coffin with no food. The only contact with the outside world was a pipe which ran from the coffin to the surface to allow Alf to breath. When the amusement park closed for the evening fellow amusement park workers would pour food down the pipe, he lived on anything that was runny and managed to stay underground for up to two weeks at a time.

A brand new ride that Bill brought to Britain was the Dodgem cars, he had first seen them in Toronto and had wrote to a friend requesting more information. After many months negotiation with the manufacturers the first Dodgem cars weaved their way about Skegness seafront in 1928. They were an immediate success and with an eye for further profit Bill obtained the sole agency rights throughout Europe. After conquering Skegness with the dodgems he placed them at Bognor, Clacton, Rhyl and Felixstowe. Bill continued to expand his empire with new fairs and rides opening up all over the country and in 1930 he really moved up in the world when for the first time since leaving Toronto he lived in a house of his own. Although, he actually spent very little time in it as he was constantly traveling around the country checking on his fairs. Bertha continued to help and support him in every way she could. But in 1933 she caught a chill whilst traveling, this was nothing serious in itself but it turned into a severe mastoid condition and Bertha was rushed to a London hospital. Unfortunately she never recovered and sadly she died before seeing Bill's greatest achievement, the building and opening of his first holiday camp. The idea of a holiday camp had been running through his mind for quite some time, his amusement parks had caught on because he had anticipated the holiday makers need. The idea developed from his observation of the seaside landladies who used to literally throw their guests out between mealtimes whatever the weather. He remembered seeing the hoards of holiday makers wandering around in the rain with nowhere to go. His mind wandered back to the lakeside holiday centres he had seen in Canada, which combined the adventure of camping with all-weather enjoyment.

William Henry Ashley

William Henry Ashley was born a poor man in Powhatan County,Virginia in 1778. He later moved to St. Genevieve, Mo., in 1803. This area had been controlled by the Spanish until late 1800 when it was ceded by Spain to France. On Easter, 1803, Napoleon announced his decision to sell the Louisiana Territory to the United States. Ashley was in this new territorty the year that it became part of the U.S. He arrived in this new territory with "a knowledge of surveying and a slight familiarity with geology". Lewis & Clark began their historic expedition from near St. Louis May 21, 1804 and returned to St. Loius on Sept. 23, 1806. They used the Missouri and Yellowstone Rivers much the same way that Ashley and his men would in later years.

Ashley moved to St. Louis around 1808 and became a Brigadier General in the Missouri Militia during the War of 1812. Before the war, he operated a gunpowder factory after discovering a cave in Texas County, Missouri that was a source of saltpeter, a vital ingredient of gunpowder. His future partner, Andrew Henry owned a factory that produced bullets. This is how the two earned their first fortunes.

After the war, Ashley became a merchant and performed some surveying. Ashley was then elected as Missouri's first Lieutenant Governor in 1820 and served until 1824.

I call Ashley 'the reluctant adventurer'. According to Don Berry, in his book, A Majority of Scoundrels, he states that

Ashley's first love and focus was politics and he wanted to become the governor of the state. But, then as now, politics requires money, so Ashley turned to the fur business as a source of revenue to support his run for the governorship.

In 1822, William Ashley & Andrew Henry began posting the now famous ads seeking the 100 enterprising young men to ascend the Missouri River to its source. Ashley was the businessman behind the operations while Henry was the field commander. Henry had knowledge-of the fur business and had been to the Snake River area in 1811.

Berry describes Ashley as being a cautious and an ambitious man. He was in his mid forties at this time, and becoming known as a great adventurer would probably be considered ludicrous by Ashley. He picked good men to do the job, but when those he had hired were unable to do the job or when, as Henry did, retired from the business, he went into the field and personally led the expeditions. As a result of these explorations, he made his place in history and helped open the lands west of the Rockies to the new country of the United States. In 1822, the new company of Ashley and Henry attempted to send three keelboats up the Missouri River. Henry led the first of the three all the way to the mouth of the Yellowstone and built a post that later became known as Fort Henry. This expedition consisted of 150 men, 60 horses and one keelboat. The second keelboat met disaster and sunk with all the provisions onboard for a loss of $10,000. Ashley then made the decision to lead the expedition with the third boat to meet Henry.

After reaching the Yellowstone and delivering his supplies and men, Ashley immediately returned to St. Louis to start building the supply expedition for the men now stationed at Fort Henry. Jedediah Smith and a small group of men accompanied Ashley downriver.

In 1823, Ashley made another expedition up the Missouri. At the Arikara Villages near today's Pierre, South Dakota, the expedition ran into trouble.

In our research, it appears that Ashley generally had good relations with the Indians, with the exception of the Arikaras. The evidence points to the fact that he tried to trade with the Indians, if given a chance, and relied upon them for information, horses and food. In fact, Ashley and his men in the other expeditions often camped with or near Indian villages. Ashley seemed most impressed with the Shoshone. He did have trouble with the Crows, though, when they stole some of his horses. In 1824, Andrew Henry retired and Ashley was left without his field commander. Once again, William Ashley was forced by the circumstances to unexpectedly lead an expedition into the mountains. The goal was the reach the Three Forks area in the Rocky Mountains. After his experience the year before with the Arikaras up the Missouri and since they were surely sore after Pilcher's men burned their villages, Ashley decided to go overland this time. This expedition, which lasted from Nov. 3, 1824 through Oct. 4, 1825 is the one where Ashley made his place in history.

Ashley went up alongside the Missouri River, then up the Platte River and finally the South Platte River until it reached the Front Range of the Rockies. At this point, he headed in a northwesterly direction until he reached the wide and sandy pass that is now known as South Pass in southwestern Wyoming. This pass at 7,000 ft. remained snow free longer than the mountains on either side.

The Rocky Moutains presented a major detriment to western settlement. Much of Ashley's route from St. Louis and through South Pass later became the Oregon Trail which led to the California Trail. The tracks left by the wagon that Ashley had on the expedition were later used by the first wagon trains as they made their way across the country in a migration that saw hundreds of thousands of settlers move west. The Pony Express came through South Pass in 1860 as well as the Mormons that settled Utah earlier in 1847.

All of this trailblazing was being accomplished by the ambitous, but reluctant adventurer, William Ashley. Lewis and Clark had crossed the Rockies, but they made their crossing farther north near where Yellowstone is located and much too far north to be considered a viable route for the settlers. Once Ashley crossed the continental divide, he split his expedition into four parties and sent them in different directions. Ashley led one party and they built a bullboat and covered it with buffalo skins which they used to float down the Green River. Before they split and went in their different directions for trapping and exploring, Ashley gave each team detailed instructions and gave each group information about where and how they would later rendezvous. It was these instructions for this first rendezvous which was the event that revolutionized the fur trade: The British tried moving their entire operations in and out of the mountains in expensive and time-consuming ventures. Ashley was developing a new method by leaving the men in the mountains year round and supplying them in a predetermined spot in an annual rendezvous.

Before they rendezvoused, Ashley and his party had a memorable adventure as they became the first men in recorded history to go down the Green River... a ferocious river with rapids and waterfalls, all while flowing through narrow canyons with steep cliffs bounding the river on each side. The river flows through what is now known as Flaming Gorge and Dinosaur National Monuments. It was in the middle of Red Canyon near the falls that named Ashley Falls before the reservoir covered them. It was near here that Ashley painted his name and date on an overhanging cliff.

William Maxwell Aitken

William Maxwell "Max" Aitken, 1st Baron Beaverbrook, PC was a Canadian - British business tycoon and politician.

He was born in Maple, Ontario, Canada and at an early age his family moved to Newcastle, New Brunswick, the place he would always call home and where, at the age of 13, he published his first newspaper. Although he wrote the entrance examinations for Dalhousie University and registered at the Saint John Law School, he did not attend either institution. His only formal higher education came when he briefly attended the University of New Brunswick. Aitken worked briefly as an office boy in the law office of Richard Bedford Bennett, in the Town of Chatham, New Brunswick. Bennett later became Prime Minister of Canada and a business associate.

As a young man, he made his way to Halifax, Nova Scotia where John F Stairs, part of the city's dominant business family, employed him at his newly formed Royal Securities Corporation. Under the tutelage of Stairs, who would be his mentor and lifelong friend, Aitken engineered a number of large business deals and mega-mergers. On January 29, 1906 in Halifax, he married Gladys Henderson Drury, daughter of Major General Charles Drury. They had three children before her untimely passing in 1927.

Soon, Aitken moved to England, where he bought and later sold control of the Rolls-Royce automobile company and began to build a London newspaper empire. He often worked closely with Andrew Bonar Law, another native of New Brunswick, who became the only Canadian to be Prime Minister of the United Kingdom. In 1911, he was knighted by King George V. During World War I, the Canadian government put him in charge of creating the Canadian War Record's Office in London and Aitken then made certain that news of Canada's contribution to the War was printed in Canadian and British newspapers. Aitken also established the Canadian War Memorials Fund that evolved into a collection of war art by the premier artists and sculptors in Britain and Canada. His visits to the Western Front during World War I resulted in his 1916 book Canada in Flanders, a three-volume collection that chronicled the achievements of Canadian soldiers on the battlefields. After the War, he wrote several books including Politicians and the Press in 1925 and Politicians and the War in 1928.

Adding to his chain of newspapers, which included the London Evening Standard he bought a controlling interest in the failing Daily Express from Lawson Johnson on 14 November 1916 for £17,500; he had been lending money to the paper and its proprietors since January 1911. He always obscured this transaction because it was at the same time as the Parliamentary crisis which replaced Asquith with Lloyd George, in which Beaverbrook's ally and protegé Bonar Law played a great part; A. J. P. Taylor, Beaverbrook's friend and biographer, assures us that this was a mere coincidence, brought on by Johnson's eagerness to be quit of the paper.

Over time, he turned the dull newspaper into a glittering and witty journal, filled with an array of dramatic photo layouts and in 1918, he founded the Sunday Express. By 1934, daily circulation reached 1,708,000, generating huge profits for Aitken whose wealth was already such that he never took a salary. Following World War II, the Daily Express became the largest selling newspaper in the world, by far, with a circulation of 3,706,000. He would become known by some historians as the first baron of "Fleet Street" and as one of the most powerful men in Britain whose newspapers could make or break almost anyone. In the 1930s, while personally attempting to dissuade King Edward VIII from continuing his potentially ruinous affair with American divorcee, Wallis Simpson, Lord Beaverbrook's newspapers published every tidbit of the affair, especially the heir apparent's cosiness with Adolf Hitler.

During World War II, from his home Cherkley Court, Leatherhead in Surrey he joined the British cabinet as minister of information and in 1940, Winston Churchill, the new British Prime Minister, would appoint him as Minister of Aircraft Production and later Minister of Supply. Under Aitken, fighter and bomber production increased so much so that Churchill declared: "His personal force and genius made this Aitken's finest hour".

After the war, Lord Beaverbrook served as chancellor of the University of New Brunswick and became the university's, the city of Fredericton's and the Province's greatest benefactor. He would provide additions to the University, scholarship funds, the Beaverbrook Art Gallery, the Beaverbrook Skating Rink, the Lord Beaverbrook Hotel, The Playhouse, and numerous other projects.

In 1957, a bronze statue of Lord Beaverbrook was erected at the centre of Officers' Square in Fredericton, New

Brunswick, paid for by money raised by children throughout the province. A bust of him by Oscar Nemon stands in the park in the town square of Newcastle, New Brunswick not far from where he sold newspapers as a young boy. His ashes are in a plinth of the bust.

Beaverbrook was both admired and despised in England, sometimes at the same time: in his 1956 autobiography, David Low quotes H.G. Wells as saying of Beaverbrook: "If ever Max ever gets to Heaven, he won't last long. He will be chucked out for trying to pull off a merger between Heaven and Hell after having secured a controlling interest in key subsidiary companies in both places, of course."

In England he lived at Cherkley Court, near Leatherhead, Surrey. Beaverbrook remained a widower for many years until 1963 when he married Marcia Anastasia Christoforides, the widow of his friend Sir James Dunn. Lord Beaverbrook died in Surrey in 1964. The Beaverbrook Foundation continues his philanthropic interests.

Lord Beaverbrook and his wife Lady Beaverbrook have left a considerable legacy to his adopted province of New Brunswick and the United Kingdom, among others. His legacy includes the following buildings:

- University of New Brunswick
    - Aitken House
    - Aitken University Centre
    - Lady Beaverbrook Gymnasium
    - Lady Beaverbrook Residence
    - Beaverbrook House
- City of Fredericton, New Brunswick
    - Lady Beaverbrook Arena
    - The Beaverbrook Art Gallery, including world-renowned art collection

    - The Fredericton Playhouse
    - Lord Beaverbrook Hotel
- City of Miramichi, New Brunswick
    - Lord Beaverbrook Arena
- City of Campbellton, New Brunswick
    - Lord Beaverbrook School
- City of Saint John, New Brunswick
    - Lord Beaverbrook Rink
- City of Calgary, Alberta
    - Lord Beaverbrook High School